DARLINGTON - LEAMSIDE - NEWCASTLE

Roger R Darsley

Series Editor Vic Mitchell

MP Middleton Press

Front cover: The driver of class V3 2-6-2T no.67691 waits for the signal at Washington station with a Miners' Gala Special to Durham via Leamside on 19th July 1958. The attention of the children is divided between the train and the signalman. (I.S.Carr)

Rear Cover: What might have been – a regional Express Service between Tyne, Wear and Teesside using the Leamside line. In fact no.158745 and its sister unit are the diverted 17.02 Newcastle to Liverpool passing the site of Leamside station on 14th April 1991. (N.E.Stead)

Readers of this book may be interested in the following societies:

Darlington Railway Centre and Museum,
North Road Station, Hopetown, Darlington DL3 6ST
www.drrcm.org.uk/menu
(This is the home of the Ken Hoole Study Centre)

Darlington Railway Preservation Society
The Old Goods Shed, Station Road, Hopetown, Darlington DL3 6ST
www.angelfire.com/mt2/drps

A1 Locomotive Trust
The Locomotive Works, Darlington DL3 6RQ
www.a1steam.com

North Eastern Railway Association
c/o Mr T.Morell, 8 Prunus Avenue, Kingston Road, Willerby, Hull HU10 6PH
www.communigate.co.uk/ne/nera

North Eastern Locomotive Preservation Group, Hopetown Carriage Works
c/o 32 Woodlea, Houghton-le-Spring, Tyne & Wear, DH6 8HT
www.nelpg.org.uk

Railway Correspondence and Travel Society, N.E. Branch
c/o Mr J.Sedgwick, Brick House Farm, Danby Wiske Road, Northallerton. DL6 2NT
www.rcts.org.uk

Published May 2008

ISBN 978 1 906008 28 4

Design Deborah Esher

Printed & bound by Biddles Ltd, Kings Lynn

Published by
Middleton Press
Easebourne Lane
Midhurst
West Sussex
GU29 9AZ
Tel: 01730 813169
Fax: 01730 812601
Email: info@middletonpress.co.uk
www.middletonpress.co.uk

INDEX

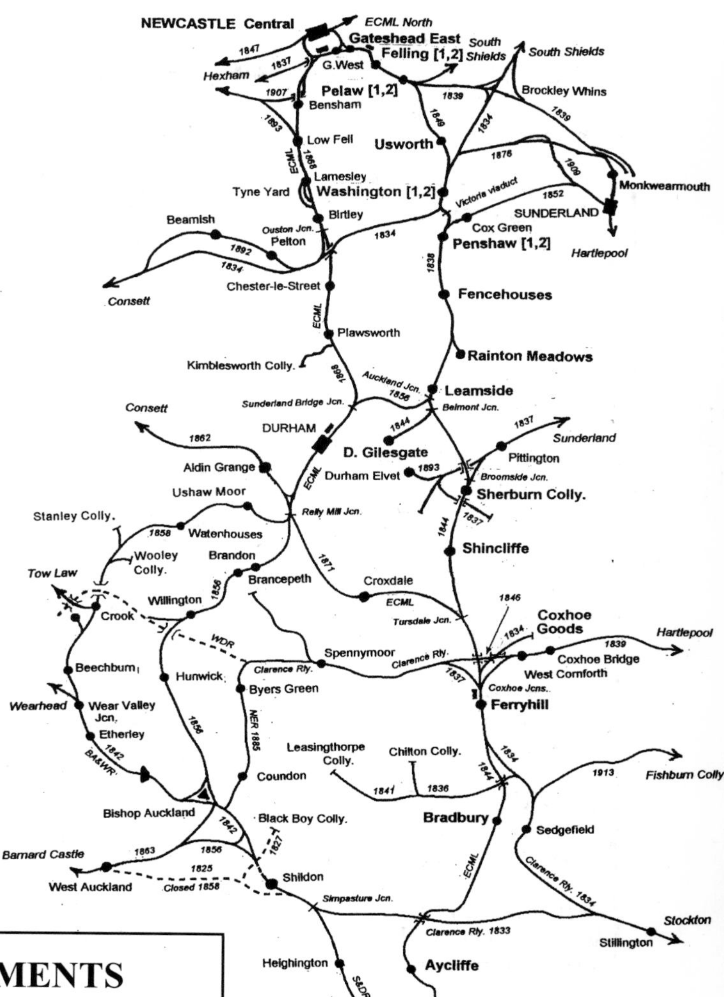

I. Railways of the area in 1921 with closed and subsequent stations added.

ACKNOWLEDGEMENTS

It can be fun to research and write a book like this, but it cannot be worthwhile without the help of local experts, archivists and other enthusiasts. My thanks go to those who are acknowledged in the photographic credits and to A.C.Carder, D.G.Charlton, G.Croughton, R.Kell, N.Langridge, S.Lockwood, C.E.Mountford, P.J.Robinson, A.Thompson, D.Tyreman, C.Woolstenholmes, as well as to M.Grout at the Ken Hoole Study Centre, J.L.Harrop at Beamish Museum, K.Williamson at Darlington Borough Library, J.Boothroyd at Gateshead Central Library, J.Gill at the Durham Record Office, J.Clayson at Tyne & Wear Museums and staff at Newcastle City Libraries. My special thanks go to my wife, Norma, for secretarial assistance – and for indulging her favourite 'anorak' once more.

GEOGRAPHICAL SETTING

County Durham has three major rivers. The Tyne borders the north and the Tees the south. Our line crosses the basin of the River Wear, as it drains down from the Northern Pennines. Both the Tyne and the Wear flow to the sea through narrow gorges.

Underlying the county is the Great Northern Coalfield which was laid down as a continuous sheet of carboniferous sediment. The bituminous coal seams were from 1½ft. to 10ft. thick. In the west of the county these seams came to the surface and were mined first but it was expensive to get this coal to the sea, where it could be shipped to London. The early waggonways were devised to do this economically; some of the earliest reaching the River Wear at Fatfield near Penshaw. The Stockton and Darlington Railway of 1825 was the first coal exporting railway from the west to the coast in the east.

The strategic railways were built between centres of population and in County Durham this meant south to north. A major barrier was the thick layer of Permian limestone that came to the surface in the form of a ridge at Ferryhill. East of a line from Ferryhill to Boldon, the coal measures were deeper and it needed an advance in mining methods to sink shafts through this limestone cap. But the limestone, coal, iron ore and the resulting manufacturing made Durham a county of urban villages and industrial towns. At nationalisation in 1947 there were 127 collieries with a network of private railways as well as national ones. Yet by 1993 all the collieries had gone as well as most of the heavy industry.

Our line is the original main line from Darlington to Newcastle, cobbled together at speed in 1841 by George Hudson. It was a circuitous route of some 39 miles breaching the limestone ridge at Ferryhill, crossing the Wear by the Victoria Viaduct and travelling west through South Tyneside to reach Gateshead. The High Level Bridge was built across the Tyne to reach Newcastle in 1850.

The maps in this volume are scaled at 25 inches to 1 mile and are dated 1896 unless otherwise stated. North is at the top unless indicated differently.

Gradient Profiles.

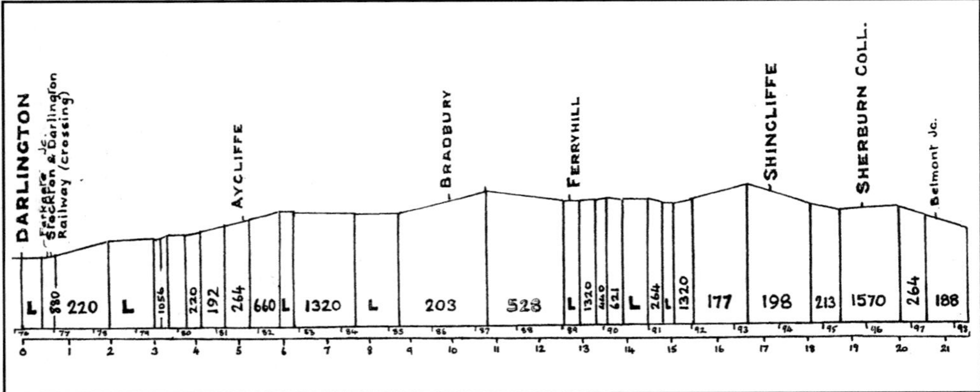

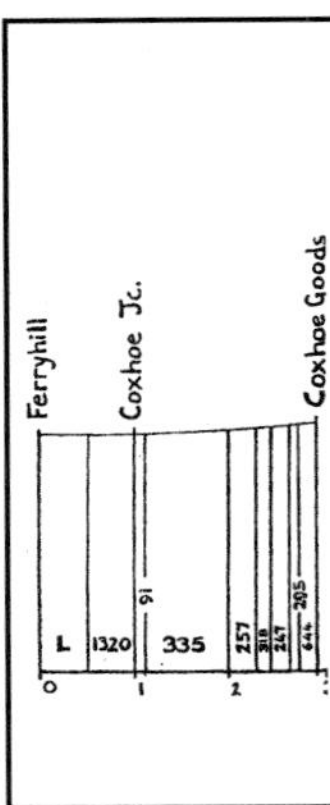

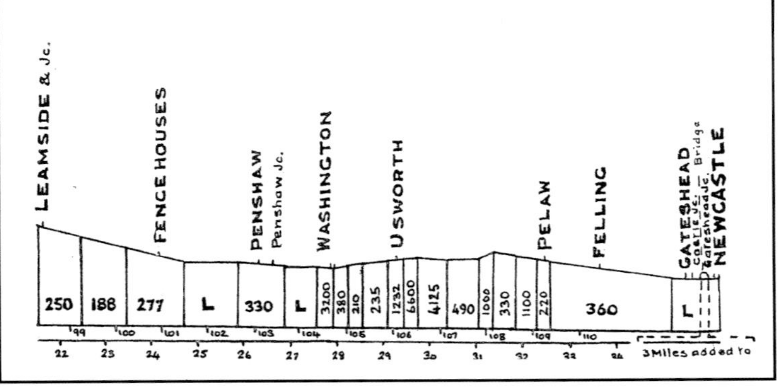

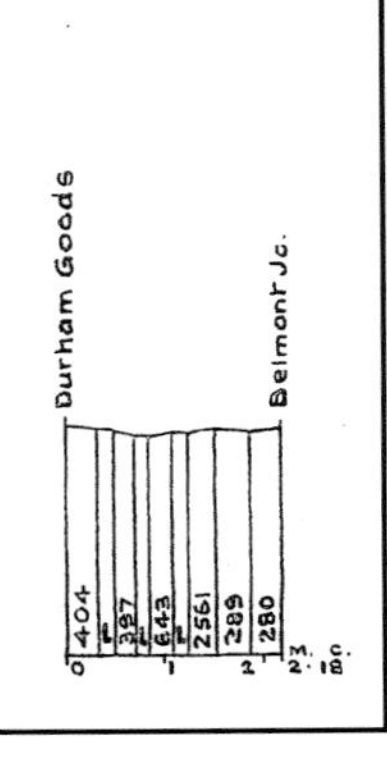

HISTORICAL BACKGROUND

The coal from mines in south west Durham had 30 miles to travel to reach the navigable Tees. This was the incentive for the Stockton & Darlington Railway (S&DR) of 1825, which passed north of Darlington's centre with North Road station at Hope Town. A competitor running to the north and roughly parallel to the S&DR, was opened in 1833. It was named the Clarence Railway after the popular Duke of Clarence (later William IV). The Clarence planned a branch to the city of Durham and reached Ferryhill where they cut an important cutting through the limestone ridge in 1835. The railways were bitter rivals. However, the Clarence was never prosperous like the S&DR and after this effort was effectively bankrupt.

The S&DR looked south to provide an interchange for Yorkshire trade and built a branch to Croft via Bank Top, Darlington, which opened on 27th October 1829. In the Railway Mania of the 1840s there was a race to get the first line from London to Edinburgh. The Great North of England Railway (GNofER) built a line from York to Darlington which opened on 30th March 1841. It entered Darlington Bank Top using part of the S&DR Croft branch but then also ran out of money and could go no further north.

The York entrepreneur, George Hudson, came to the rescue. He organised the Newcastle & Darlington Junction Railway (NDJR) in 1842 and with characteristic briskness, had it opened by 18th June 1844. To do this, he got control of every available bit of existing railway that might get him there quickly, even if it was circuitous. Up till then northern bound travellers had found it quicker, cheaper and more comfortable to go by S&DR from Darlington to Stockton, cross the Tees and take the coastal trains to Sunderland, cross the Wear to Monkwearmouth and take the Brandling Junction Railway to Gateshead. 56 miles by rail with two river crossings was still better than 34 miles of the Darlington to Newcastle road! His route was from Darlington Bank Top north to Ferryhill. There he made use of the Clarence Railway cutting to head north as far as Rainton Crossing. With advice from Robert Stephenson, he obtained control of the Durham Junction Railway (DJR), the Pontop & South Shields Railway (P&SSR) and the Brandling Junction Railway (BJR). The DJR was to run from the Stanhope & Tyne Railway (S&TR) at Washington station across the River Wear at Fatfield by the Victoria Viaduct and on to Durham. The construction of this viaduct had run the DJR out of money. The S&TR had also massive financial problems and the P&SSR was formed from its eastern section. The BJR also connected with the S&TR. Hudson sorted out the finances and combined them into a larger NDJR. This made it possible to get to Gateshead via Leamside, Boldon and Pelaw. He built an elegant station at Greenesfield in Gateshead, and then set up a separate company to bridge the River Tyne. North of the Tyne he took control of the Newcastle & Berwick Railway (N&BR).

Hudson formed the York & Newcastle Railway (Y&NR) on 3rd August 1846 by merging the NDJR with the GNofER. The N&BR was amalgamated with the Y&NR on 9th July 1847 to form the York, Newcastle & Berwick Railway (YN&BR). But in the Spring of 1849 Hudson's financial dealings came under severe scrutiny and he was forced to resign. Newcastle Central station and the High Level Bridge across the Tyne were under construction by then. Queen Victoria opened the bridge on 28th September 1849 and with Prince Albert, opened the Central Station on 29th August 1850.

On 31st July 1854, the YN&BR joined with the York & North Midland Railway, the Leeds Northern Railway and the Malton & Driffield Junction Railway to form the North Eastern Railway (NER) on 31st July 1854. The NER began to consolidate its position in County Durham and began to construct the more rapid route from Darlington to Newcastle that forms the current ECML. (See *Darlington to Newcastle via Durham* in this series)

The Team Valley route was from Durham (Newton Hall Junction) to Gateshead and was opened for goods on 2nd March 1868 and for passengers on 1st December 1868. A new nine mile link between Durham and Ferryhill was authorised in 1865 and opened on 1st October 1871 for freight and on 15th January 1872 for passengers.

Prior to this development, Durham had been served first by Shincliffe Town which was two miles from the city, and then by the Durham Gilesgate branch which opened to goods on 15th April 1844 and to passengers on 19th June 1844. The present Durham station was built on the Sunderland to Bishop Auckland line in 1857 but the new direct route meant that Durham Gilesgate became the Durham Goods station and that the Leamside line lost its major express services except in times of diversion.

The Leamside line then became a major channel for freight traffic, especially coal, with almost every station serving at least one colliery. The short branch from Ferryhill to Coxhoe Goods is included in this. The development of the coal trade in Durham in the 19th century was so great that the landowners and colliery owners built their own railways, often based on the early waggonway routes to the sea. Around Ferryhill, the Rosedale and Ferry Hill Iron Co. and later Dorman Long and Co. Ltd had influence. From Durham to Fence Houses, the Londonderry Railway of the Marquis of Londonderry carried coal to Seaham Harbour. North of Fence Houses to Washington was the Earl of Durham's domain. His Lambton Railway had running rights over the NER line between Fence Houses, Washington and the coal staiths on the River Wear at Sunderland.

In 1923 the NER became a major player in the London & North Eastern Railway (LNER). At Nationalisation on 1st January 1948 the line was first part of British Railways, North Eastern Region and then became part of a larger Eastern Region on 1st January 1967. In 1968 British Railways became British Rail (BR). The exhaustion of the Durham coal reserves and the local nature of the passenger services had a marked effect on the line's viability. Shincliffe, the first station to close, did so in 1941. The village and suburban stations followed in the 1950s, as did some of the feeder services such as the Ferryhill to Spennymoor and Hartlepool services. Local freight survived until the 1960s, when there was a wholesale closure of goods facilities and branch lines. Heavy freight continued with the Tyne Dock to Consett ore trains. These were diverted via the Team Valley line in 1966 allowing the P&SSR to be closed from Brockley Whins Junction to Washington. The line was upgraded between Tursdale Junction and Washington in March 1974 to take the Redcar to Consett ore trains using 100 ton wagons and hauled by two Class37 locomotives. These ran until March 1984.

A belated modernisation of freight handling led to the building of Tyneside Central Freight Depot (TCFD) at Borough Gardens in 1963, but parcels freight continued to move to road transport and it closed in 1991. While freight traffic had grown, the Freightliner terminal at Follingsby, opened in 1967, was seen as unprofitable and closed in 1987 when Freightliner decided to concentrate on journey distances of 200+ miles. In the 1980s, BR was divided into sectors. In 1987 Trainload Freight from all sectors: aggregates, coal, metals and petroleum were seen on the line.

At privatisation in 1994 all Trainload Freight in the area became Load Haul which was bought by EWS in 1996. The Nissan car factory was using rail from Tyne Dock to Italy via the Channel Tunnel and it was hoped that a rail facility could be put directly to the factory from Usworth. However Nissan has found it more economic to send its cars to mainland Europe by sea, even though they have to be double-handled by road from the factory to the car pound at Tyne Dock. A modern coal concentration and store was built at Wardley, near Follingsby Lane, but was on a care and maintenance basis in recent years. By 1992 the line from Follingsby Lane to Tursdale Junction had been mothballed.

In 1996 responsibility for the track passed to Railtrack. They were replaced on 3rd October 2004 by Network Rail, who in December 2006 announced that they were going to recover the track from this central section, though they would leave the bridges and embankments intact. They had been rather embarrassed in 2004 by an enterprising gang who cut up one and a half miles of track without anyone realising. The last open section of this line, from Pelaw Junction to Follingsby Lane, was closed in July 2007.

The line between Darlington and Ferryhill remains part of the East Coast Main Line (ECML) with franchised passenger services run by Great North East Railway (GNER), Virgin Cross Country, and a consortium of Serco and Ned Railways who run local services under the 'Northern Rail' brand. TransPennine Services were run by First Group. In 2007, the Virgin franchise was re-tendered with different geographical boundaries and won by Arriva Cross Country from 11th November. The GNER franchise was also re-tendered and won by National Express East Coast (NXEC) operating from 19th December 2007

The section of our journey between Pelaw and Newcastle developed a suburban passenger service within the triangle; Sunderland – South Shields – Newcastle. The Sunderland and South Shields lines joined with the Leamside line at Pelaw. The line to South Shields was electrified by the LNER with 3rd rail 600 v DC in 1938. BR converted the line to diesel multiple units (DMU) in 1963 but it became part of the Tyne Wear Metro and was re-electrified with 1500v overhead in 1981. The Sunderland line followed in 2002. The Sunderland line is shared from Pelaw to Sunderland by the Tyne Wear Metro, Northern Rail and freight companies and was the first such venture on the national network. From Pelaw to Newcastle, the Tyne Wear Metro has its own tracks and will not be covered in this book.

PASSENGER SERVICES

In 1841 as the GNofER reached Darlington, train working was still in its infancy so when Mr Joseph Pease arrived at York too late to join the first train to Darlington, which made the journey at a sedate 15mph, he hired a special to follow which did so at an average of 26mph. The passenger workings on the DJR from 1840 to 1850 also added a spice to life as the down passenger trains were fly-shunted across the Brockley Whins Junction to speed up the train reversal. The opening train between Darlington and Newcastle left from

Euston at 5.03am on 18th June 1844, the anniversary of the Battle of Waterloo. It travelled by Birmingham, Derby, Sheffield and York to arrive at Gateshead Greenesfield at 2.24pm; 303 miles at an average of 32mph. On the Leamside line the special was drawn by *Cleveland.* Three trains of six carriages left Gateshead at 9.05am with Edinburgh as pilot and *Nathaniel Ogle, Brandling* and *Mountain* as train engines. Finally the processional train of 39 1st class carriages hauled by *Wear, Glasgow* and *Edinburgh* left Darlington for Gateshead. The earliest timetables show that on average there were three trains each way each day between Darlington and Newcastle.

Things had speeded up by 1854, the first year of the NER, when there were eight up trains and seven down trains between York and Newcastle on weekdays and these trains travelled by the Leamside line. Two trains, each way, had accommodation for 3rd class passengers. The average speed was 39mph for express and mail trains and 22mph for slow or stopping trains. Comparison between the timetables of 1854 and 1866 showed little improvement. From 15th January 1872, the East Coast expresses went via Durham and the Team Valley route and the 'Race to the North' speeded up all the timetables. From Darlington to Ferryhill the passenger service has always had the full panoply of the ECML expresses and, while many of the famous named trains – the "Silver Jubilee", "The Coronation", "The Capitals Limited", the "Tees Tyne Pullman", "The Elizabethan" have come and gone, the line will always be remembered as part of the route of the immortal "Flying Scotsman". On this section the all stations stopping trains to Newcastle were withdrawn in stages between 4th June 1945 and 5th December 1955, with the really rural stations closing first. It was a surprise, however, when Ferryhill was closed on 6th March 1967, as it was a local transport hub and still had six long distance trains stopping each day connecting with Leeds, Liverpool and Bristol. More details of the ECML trains can be found in *Darlington to Newcastle via Durham.*

The central portion of our route between Ferryhill and Pelaw reverted to local passenger services though it continued to be used for express diversions. There were six trains from Bishop Auckland to Sunderland via Leamside and two from Durham to Sunderland on weekdays. On Sunday there were two from Bishop Auckland and one from Durham. There was a similar pattern in the up direction. Two were Government trains and one was a Mail train. The Ferryhill to Coxhoe Goods or Coxhoe (W.H.) had a service of two trains a day each way until 1902, when it closed to passengers.

By late NER days the service ran from Newcastle to Ferryhill via Leamside and then on to Stockton and Middlesbrough. Excluding Durham to Sunderland trains there were seven through trains plus three Newcastle to Leamside only. Sundays saw two trains to Ferryhill with down services similar. One unusual working was the York to Edinburgh and Glasgow sleeping car train which in 1920 became an all stations via Leamside to Newcastle in the early morning.

The LNER timetable was effectively a morning and evening work time train in each direction with the evening working becoming a midday working on Saturdays to reflect Saturday half-day working. There was also a very early up train leaving Newcastle at 4.35am and eventually terminating at Middleton-in-Teesdale! The Sunday service was one train each way, Newcastle to Durham, but not at convenient times for a day out.

In 1947 the service was the workman's service from Newcastle to Washington and back, with the Durham to Sunderland service calling at Fence Houses and Penshaw. With the ending of the Durham Miners' Gala trains, the closure of Washington and Usworth in 1963, and the Durham to Sunderland service in 1964, the only passenger trains traversing the line were non-stop diversions of which the last occurred in the week ending 17th May 1991 and was due to alterations to Durham Viaduct.

Northern Rail removed all but three of its services from the ECML, concentrating on the coastal route from Newcastle through Sunderland to Teesside. While most of the slots released were taken by Virgin Trains, it did remove the apparent pressure for passenger slots. On the ECML, oil and coal freight has increased, but so has the size of the trains allowed.

Between Pelaw and Newcastle, Northern Rail maintained an hourly service stopping only at Heworth on their way to Sunderland and Teesside. A half hourly service was run until 2006, when Nexus, which subsidises these trains as well as the Metro, reduced the frequency to invest the money saved in improvements at Sunderland station. In 2008 the Metro frequency between Pelaw and Newcastle was every six minutes (eight minutes on evenings and Sundays).

II. This map, at a scale of 6 inches to 1 mile, shows Darlington, now a railway town, in 1898. The first station at Bank Top was built in 1841. The present station was built in 1887 and is shown here with its pronounced curve at the north end. Darlington North Road station is at Hope Town, which since 1825 had merged into central Darlington. At North Road is the NER locomotive works. Albert Hill had become a major industrial area with the Alliance Works. East of the River Skerne is Darlington Forge and the main line north.

For further maps and photographs of Darlington Bank Top see *Darlington to Newcastle via Durham* **nos 1-22**

1. Darlington will always be known for the Stockton & Darlington Railway. George Stephenson's 0-4-0 no.1 *Locomotion* was placed on a plinth outside the NER Hopetown carriage works. It was removed for the 1925 Centenary celebrations and then placed in Darlington Bank Top station with S&DR 0-6-0 no. 25 *Derwent*. The carriage works became the locomotive scrap yard but is now the site where the construction of A1 class 4-6-2 no. 60163 *Tornado* was completed in 2008, and the repairs of North Eastern Locomotive Preservation Group engines are done. (G.Nairn coll.)

2. The 1841 GNofER station was known as Darlington NE and was to be called Darlington Central. An artist's impression shows a rectangular shed with a single clerestory roof to vent the smoke. It had one through platform with a bay at each end. It was enlarged in 1863 by Thomas Prosser. The station was called Darlington Bank Top from 1870 to 1934, after then it was simply Darlington. The present 1887 station, designed by William Bell, is altogether grander, as is shown by this view of the down platform, No.4, facing north. It is a quiet afternoon in 1899. (K.Hoole coll.)

3. Class 9F 2-10-0 no.92168 was photographed from the station footbridge on 25th July 1958. Today modernisation of this bridge keeps the passengers dry but denies the photographer a viewpoint. Behind this up freight class A3 4-6-2 no.60045 *Lemberg* and a large tank engine are on the shed road. The coaling plant can be seen behind the prefab houses. An up passenger train is entering platform 1 and below Darlington North signal box are the retaining walls of Parkgate under-bridges. (R.Leslie)

4. At the north end of the station were platforms 5 and 6, now converted into car parking spaces. Type 4 1-Co-Co1 no. D282 is leaving for Newcastle with the Leeds to Glasgow "North Briton", while Metro Cammell diesel multiple unit no.E50242 waits for passengers for Penrith via Barnard Castle, the Stainmore summit and Kirkby Stephen. The date is 17th December 1960. (Stephenson Locomotive Society coll.)

5. The 150 lever signal box and the semaphore signals have gone in this scene of 3rd April 1980, but the retaining walls of the entrance from Parkgate can be more clearly seen as the High Speed Train 254002 arrives on a Newcastle to Kings Cross express. Diesel multiple units have taken over the local services and class 08 0-6-0DE the pilot duties. (T.Heavyside)

6. The clock and the north end of the station are highlighted again in this 2006 photograph. The main lines were electrified with 25kv AC catenary in 1989. On 1st August, Virgin's no.220.028 *Black Country Voyager* is at platform 4. The rail-bus link is a service to Durham Tees Valley airport and, while the official entrance is from Victoria Road, the bus link and most passengers use the road entrance from Parkgate that lies between the main platforms. (R.R.Darsley)

NORTH OF DARLINGTON

Darlington Shed

III. The carriage and freight sidings began just north of Bank Top station on the other side of Parkgate. Darlington locomotive shed (51A) opened on 19th February 1885 on the original wagon works site. The wagon works moved to Shildon and the S&DR engine shed at North Road was closed. The NER added a roundhouse, but in 1939 the shed was rebuilt as a long straight shed with a mechanised coal loading tower. This is the 1898 map.

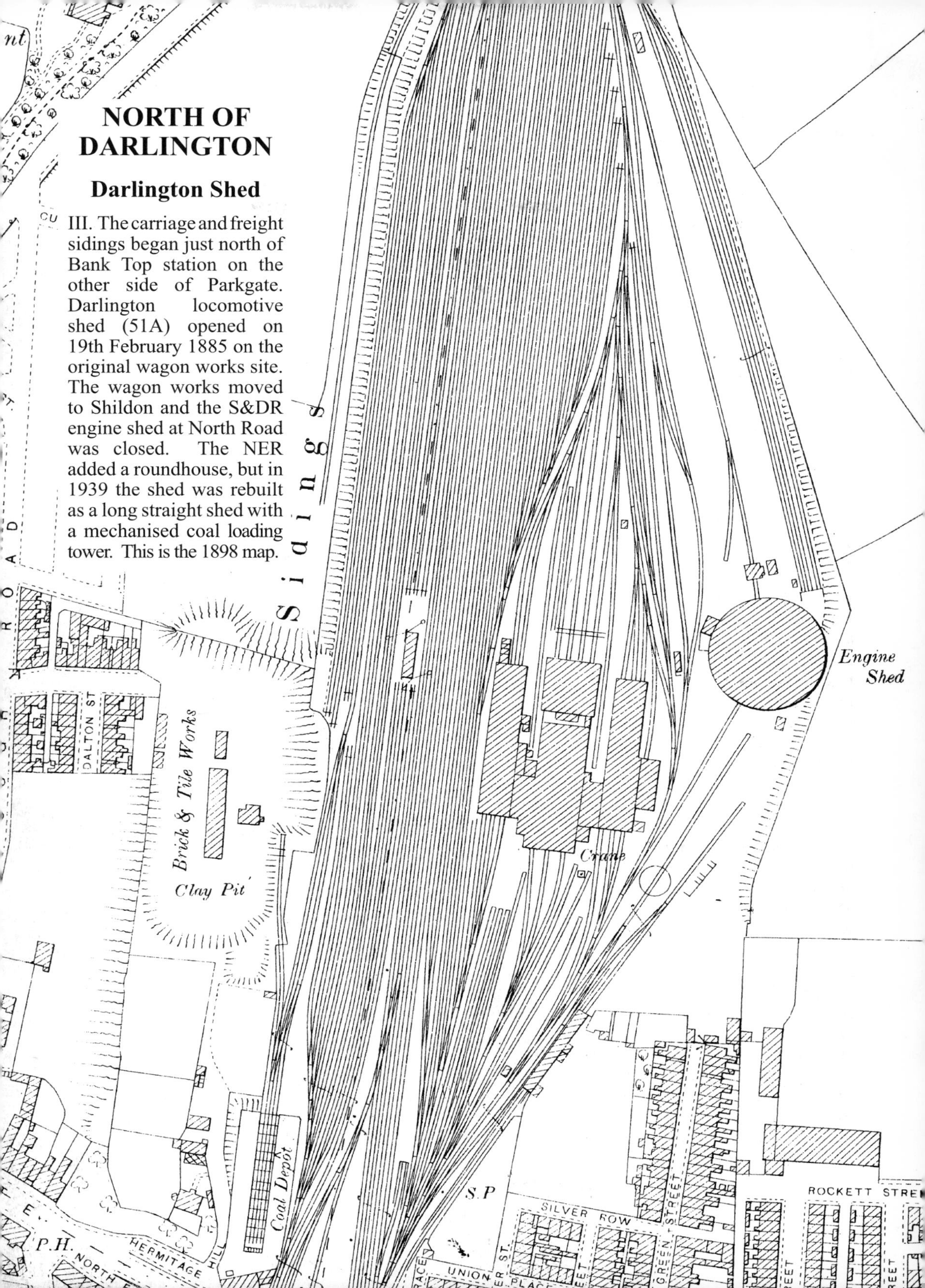

7. When the LNER modernised the shed in 1939, the roundhouse survived as a place for stabling pilot and shunting locomotives. Here class F8 2-4-2T 279 and class J71 0-6-0T 1163 pose outside. No. 279 was withdrawn in September 1931 and 1163 in October 1933, though the last of its class survived to February 1961. Both 279 and unusually 1163 were fitted with a Westinghouse brake. No. 1163 in ex-works condition dates the photograph to 1925. (K.Hoole coll.)

8. During the summer of 1953 the roundhouse held class J25 0-6-0 no.65702, withdrawn class G5 0-4-4T no.67272, 0-6-0Ts class J77 no.68432, class J72 no.68679, and class J21 0-6-0 no.65098. The 45ft. turntable was open to the elements. The G5, from West Hartlepool, went into store when the West Hartlepool to Ferryhill passenger service closed on 7th June 1952. Darlington steam shed closed on 27th March 1966. (N.E.Stead coll.)

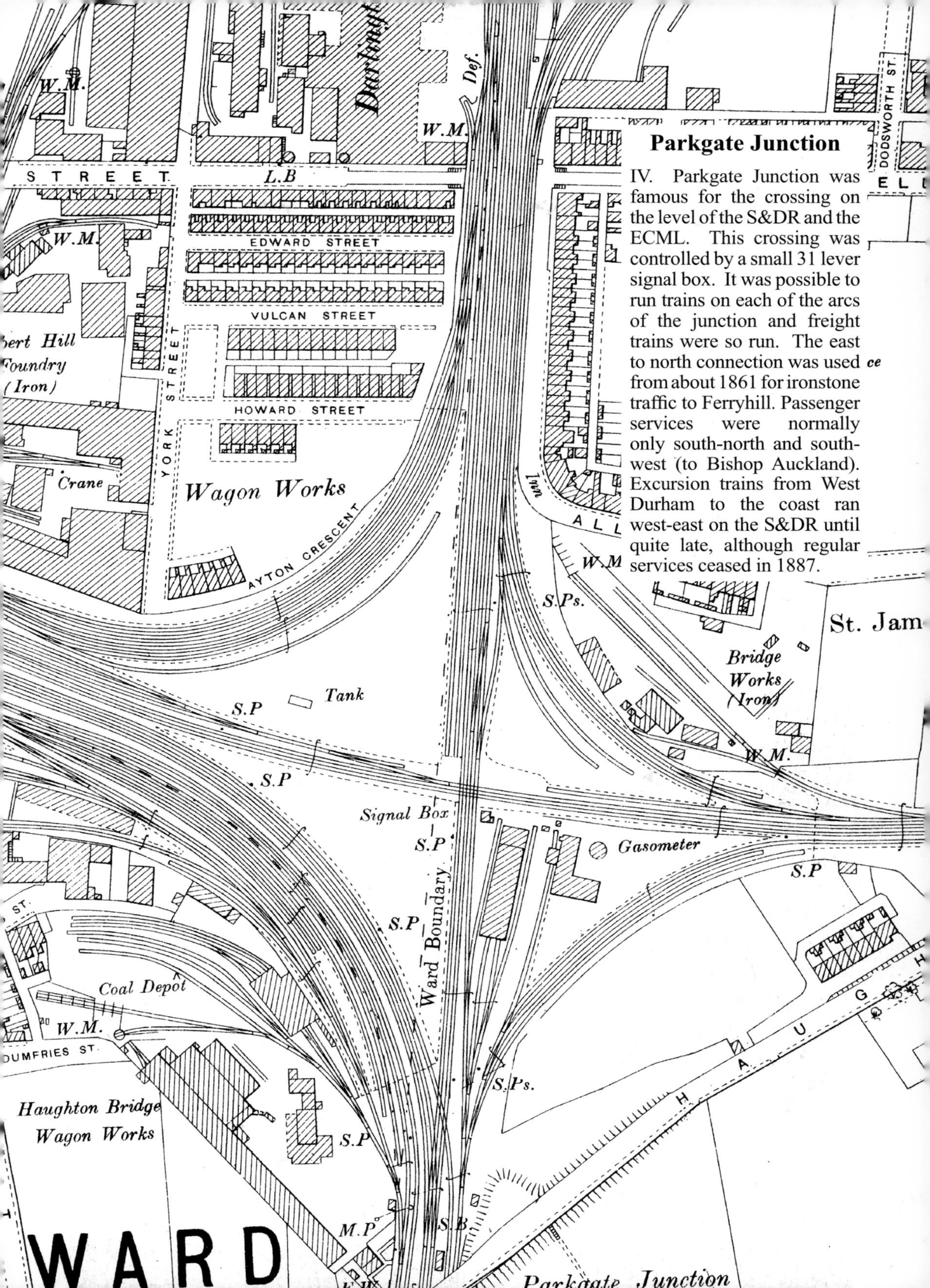

Parkgate Junction

IV. Parkgate Junction was famous for the crossing on the level of the S&DR and the ECML. This crossing was controlled by a small 31 lever signal box. It was possible to run trains on each of the arcs of the junction and freight trains were so run. The east to north connection was used from about 1861 for ironstone traffic to Ferryhill. Passenger services were normally only south-north and south-west (to Bishop Auckland). Excursion trains from West Durham to the coast ran west-east on the S&DR until quite late, although regular services ceased in 1887.

9. Class A8 4-6-2T no.69891 is viewed from Haughton Road bridge bringing a train from the east to the south of Parkgate crossing. The Saltburn train has been diverted round by Fighting Cocks on the S&DR due to engineering works between Oak Tree Junction and Darlington South. The flagman is by the signal, with his bike propped against the shed. Behind the 90 lever Parkgate signal box is the 1841 GNofER engine shed and the S&DR crossing with its own signal box. (J.W.Armstrong Trust)

10. By 24th July 1980 the S&DR crossing had long gone, though the sign marking its position can be seen by the third carriage of the train which is the 8.15am Newcastle to Liverpool hauled by Co-CoDE no.47519. The GNofER shed remains, though in 2008, it was without any use. The lines curving to the west are to North Road and Bishop Auckland. The large buildings are on Cleveland Street and mark the site of Darlington Forge. The remains of Albert Hill foundry are being demolished. Three rows of houses and the wagon works have already gone. (T.Heavyside)

11. Springfield signal box marked the outer limits of Darlington and was a favoured spot for photographers. No.4772 was the second class V2 2-6-2 to be constructed, emerging from Doncaster in August 1936 and allocated to York. It was withdrawn in October 1962. These mixed class locomotives were equally at home on fast freights or passenger trains. No.4772 (later 60801) has lamp codes for an up through freight, although hauling a very long rake of mainly clerestory coaches. The photograph is 1936 so the locomotive could well be on test. (J.W.Armstrong Trust)

12. This is Springfield signal box interior in the same year. The box controlled the entry to Robert Stephenson & Co. Ltd works at Springfield built in 1901. In 1937 the firm became Robert Stephenson & Hawthorns Ltd. Springfield signal box had 32 levers. It closed on 31st October 1954. (J.W.Armstrong Trust)

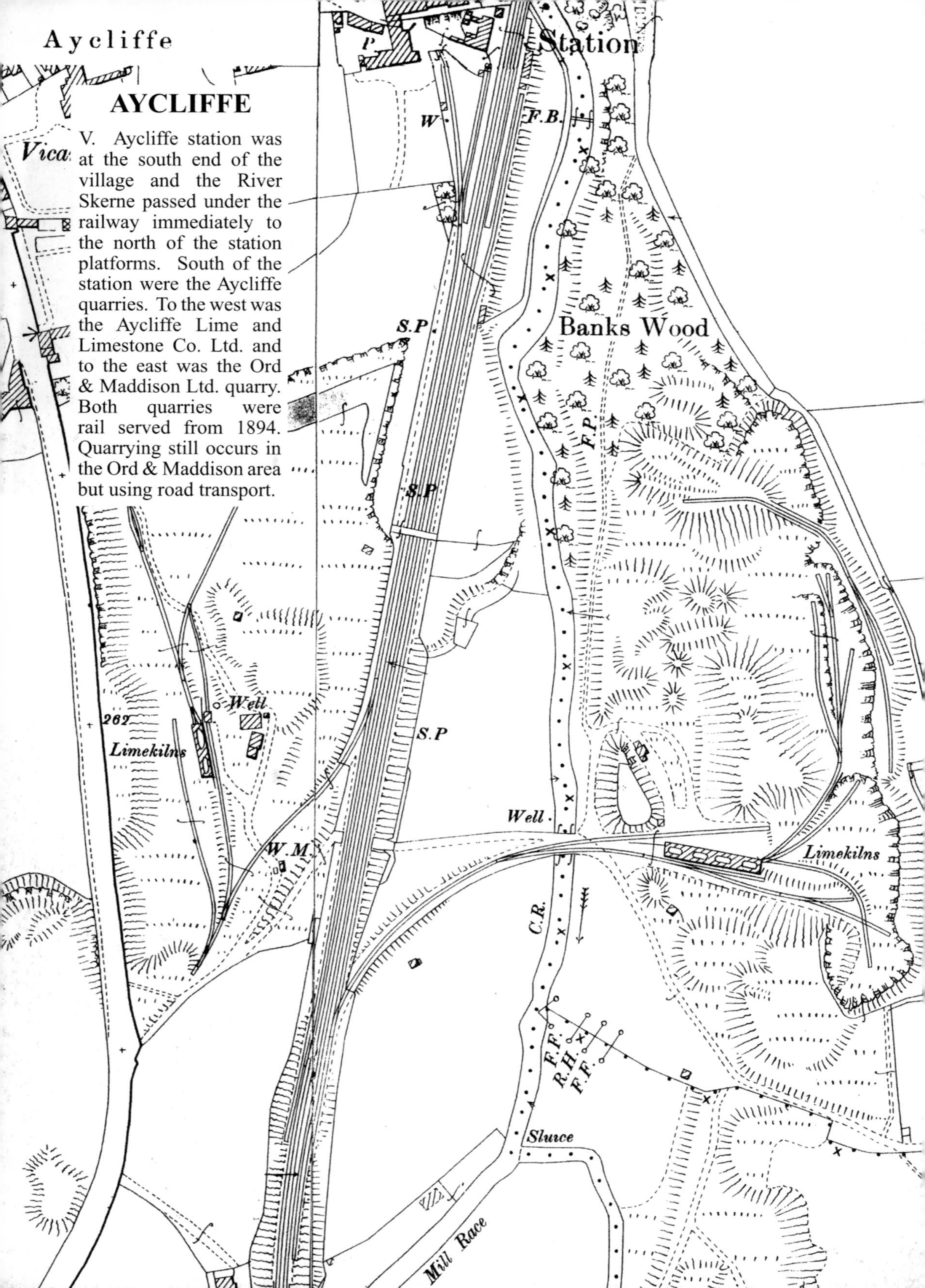

AYCLIFFE

V. Aycliffe station was at the south end of the village and the River Skerne passed under the railway immediately to the north of the station platforms. South of the station were the Aycliffe quarries. To the west was the Aycliffe Lime and Limestone Co. Ltd. and to the east was the Ord & Maddison Ltd. quarry. Both quarries were rail served from 1894. Quarrying still occurs in the Ord & Maddison area but using road transport.

13. Beyond the bottom of Map V is Holme Mill. The railway crosses the access road and the River Skerne by a low eight-arch viaduct. It is so low that it has provided the owner of the farmhouse with five useful storage sheds! Bo-BoWE no.91115 *Holyrood* heads north with a GNER express on 19th October 2006. (R.R.Darsley)

14. This is the Ord & Maddison Ltd quarry with its lime kilns about 1894. The horse drawn narrow gauge railway brings the limestone from the quarry. The main line runs on an embankment across the middle distance and the smoke and chimney of the Aycliffe Lime & Limestone Co. Ltd. can be seen in the distance underneath the church. Ord & Maddison quarries were shunted by the LNER until at least 1937. (Beamish Museum)

15. The western quarry was started in the 1880s by George Chapman, a local farmer. Hanson, Brown & Co. Ltd. worked it until 1920, when Aycliffe Lime & Limestone Co. Ltd. took over. The firm became a subsidiary of Gjers, Mills & Co., Middlesbrough. This was their *Hazels*, the only standard gauge well tank built by Chapman and Furneaux of Gateshead. It was photographed on 27th August 1948 and was scrapped in 1951. Rail traffic was shunted by road tractor from 1961 and the quarry itself was closed shortly afterwards. (D.G.Charlton)

16. This is the station looking north in about 1912. The main buildings, rather pleasant with gables and bay windows, are on the down platform. A staff and family group are posed on the up platform in front of a standard wooden waiting room. The line crosses the River Skerne again just past the signal box. (Lens of Sutton coll.)

17. 28th February 1953 was the final day of passenger services to the station which formally closed on 2nd March. Class V3 2-6-2T no.67653 is hauling a stopping train to Newcastle. After closure the station was demolished and a single storey office now occupies the site. (J.W.Armstrong Trust)

NORTH OF AYCLIFFE

18. The ECML passed underneath the Clarence Railway north of Aycliffe. The section of the Clarence Railway from Shildon to Newport, Middlesbrough, was electrified by the NER from 1915 until 1937. In 1957 class 4MT 2-6-0 no.76050 with a guards van in tow crosses the ECML. (K.Hoole coll.)

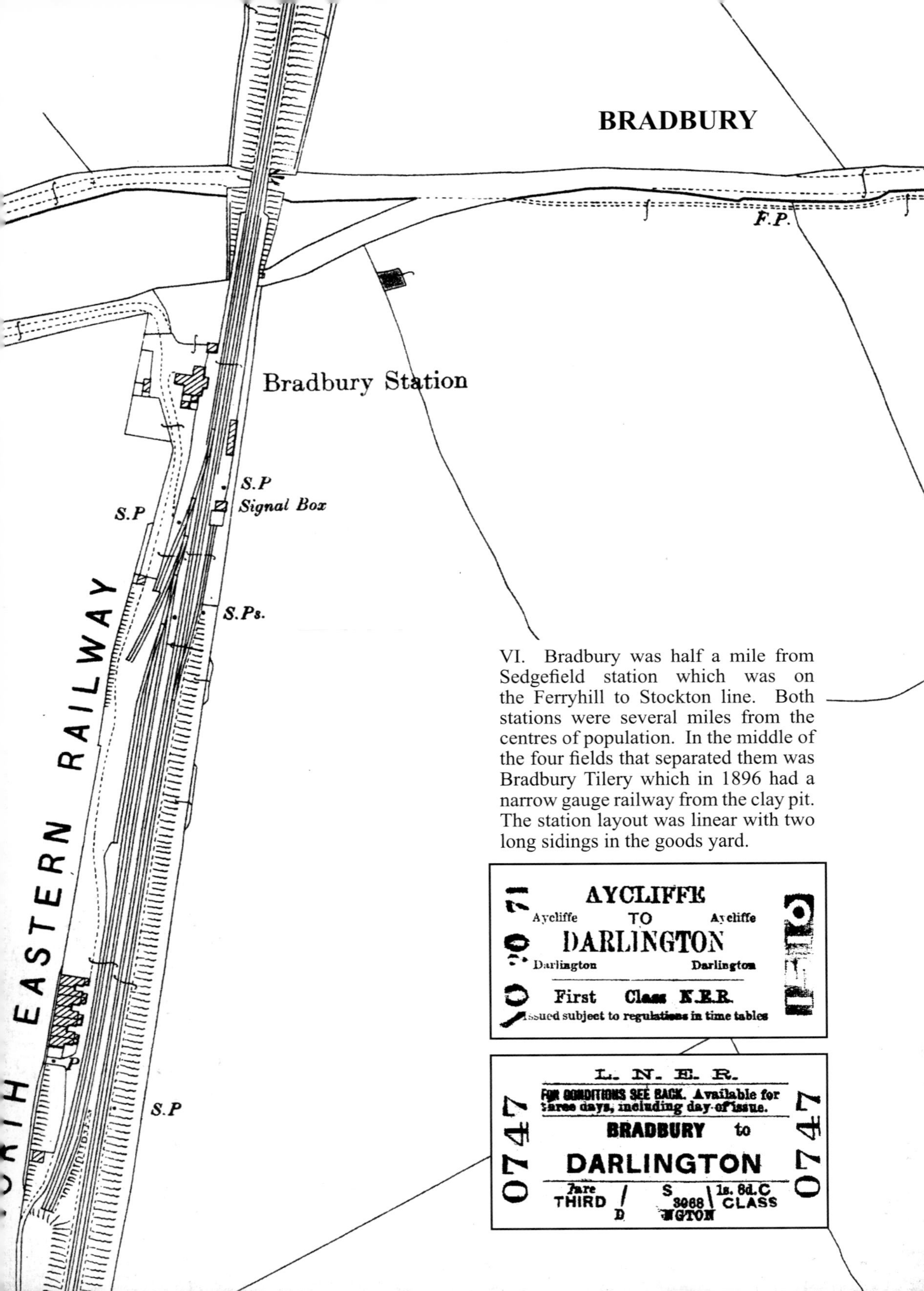

VI. Bradbury was half a mile from Sedgefield station which was on the Ferryhill to Stockton line. Both stations were several miles from the centres of population. In the middle of the four fields that separated them was Bradbury Tilery which in 1896 had a narrow gauge railway from the clay pit. The station layout was linear with two long sidings in the goods yard.

Compliments of the Season

19. The main buildings were again on the down line and to the same style as Aycliffe, though with a different arrangement. This photograph of 1905 has been used to make an early form of Christmas postcard. Maybe the barrels are full of festive cheer? (G.Nairn coll.)

20. The stationmaster was very keen on the station garden. There are clumps of sunflowers along the fence and the station name is spelt out in something like a box hedge at the entrance to the goods yard. This postcard is dated between 1902 and 1910. (G.Nairn coll.)

21. The photographer is standing near the station garden as the down Scotch express goes through Bradbury. The locomotive is a NER 4-4-0 class Q (later a LNER class D17/2). These were the NER top express locomotives when they appeared in 1896, but were displaced by the class R (D20) in 1900 and disappeared from the ECML after 1910. The buildings on the right are the row of railwaymen's cottages. (F.Cooper/G.Nairn coll.)

22. The station was closed to passenger and goods traffic on 2nd January 1950. In 1955, the workmen were unaffected by the passage of a very grubby class A1 4-6-2 on a fitted freight. Today nothing of the station remains; the ECML is a clear, fast track. (Stations UK)

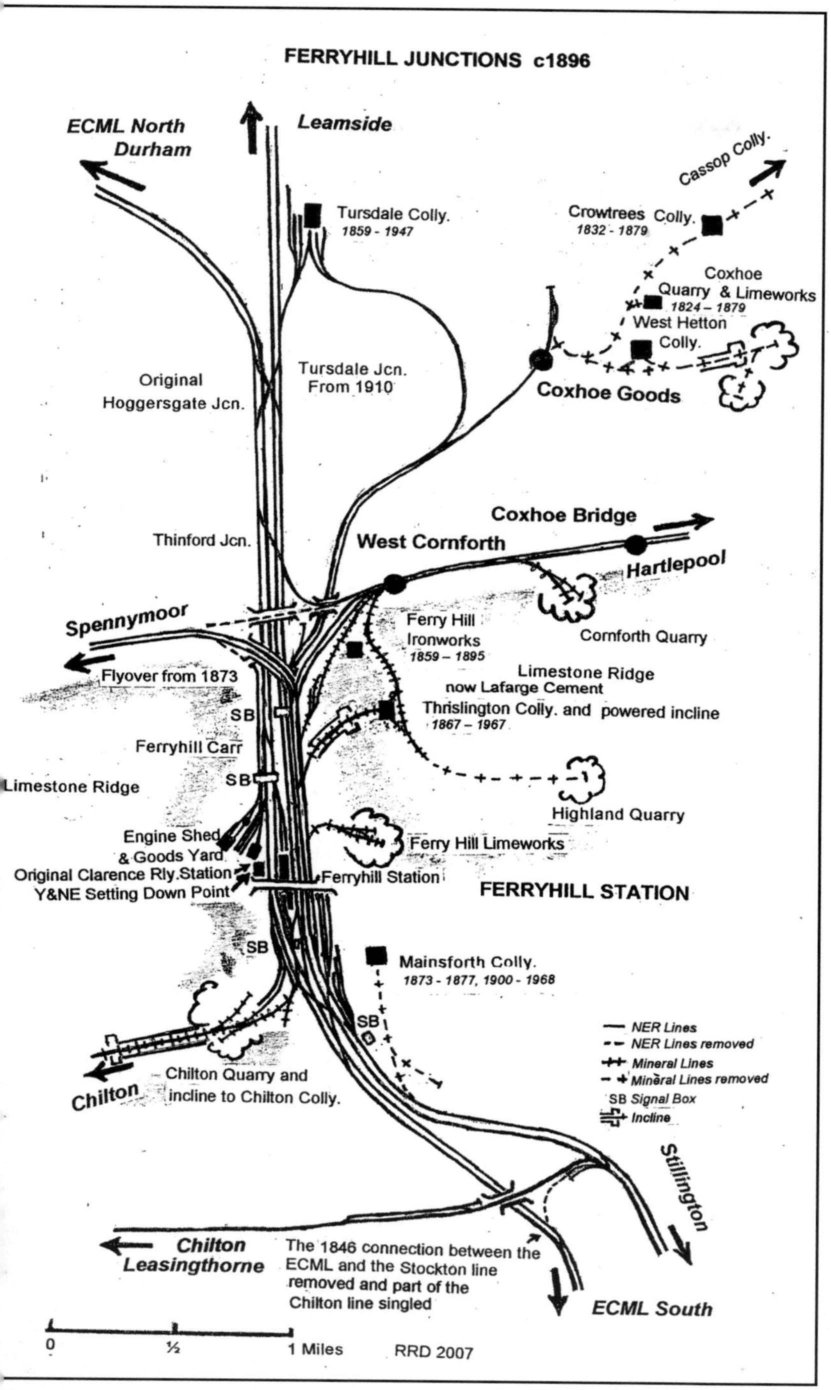

FERRYHILL

FERRYHILL JUNCTIONS c1896

ECML North Durham
Leamside
Cassop Colly.
Tursdale Colly. 1859 - 1947
Crowtrees Colly. 1832 - 1879
Coxhoe Quarry & Limeworks 1824 – 1879
West Hetton Colly.
Original Hoggersgate Jcn.
Tursdale Jcn. From 1910
Coxhoe Goods
Coxhoe Bridge
Thinford Jcn.
West Cornforth
Hartlepool
Spennymoor
Ferry Hill Ironworks 1859 – 1895
Cornforth Quarry
Flyover from 1873
Limestone Ridge now Lafarge Cement
SB
Thrislington Colly. and powered incline 1867 – 1967
Ferryhill Carr
SB
Limestone Ridge
Highland Quarry
Engine Shed & Goods Yard
Ferry Hill Limeworks
Original Clarence Rly.Station
Y&NE Setting Down Point
Ferryhill Station
FERRYHILL STATION
SB
Mainsforth Colly. 1873 - 1877, 1900 - 1968
SB
NER Lines
NER Lines removed
Mineral Lines
Mineral Lines removed
SB Signal Box
Incline
Chilton
Chilton Quarry and incline to Chilton Colly.
Stillington
Chilton Leasingthorne
The 1846 connection between the ECML and the Stockton line removed and part of the Chilton line singled
ECML South
0 ½ 1 Miles
RRD 2007

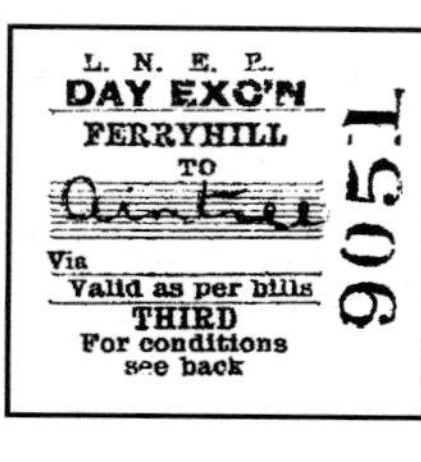
L. N. E. R.
DAY EXC'N
FERRYHILL
TO
Aintree
Via
Valid as per bills
THIRD
For conditions see back
9051

VII. The area of market gardens for the Bishops of Durham, known as Ferjenc or Ferye-on-the-Hill, may not have had a Ferry but it certainly had a hill and the Clarence Railway, in 1835, hewed a cutting 67ft deep and 75 yards wide through the ridge, using men and black powder to remove 100,000 cubic yards of limestone. This cutting was the key to the route north. Early Coxhoe mines and quarries came under the control of the Rosedale and Ferry Hill Iron Co., which went bankrupt in 1879. So the 1896 map shows quarries and mines closed. The ironworks was demolished in 1895.

23. This view of the station and engine shed is looking south. Entrance to the station was from the road bridge. The hipped glass roof to the north covered both mainline platforms and the bays. A five coach stopping train is at the up platform. A class J27 0-6-0 is on shed and eight locomotives are stabled in the yard, including class J21 0-6-0 and one class F8 2-4-2T. The date is between 1894 and 1902. (G.Nairn coll.)

24. The station looking north shows the approach bridge and the smaller hipped glass platform roof on the south side. A NER coach is visible in the south bay. A northbound train is at the main platform while a NER class 398 0-6-0 with clerestory guards van is on the freight lines. Several of these locomotives were shedded at Ferryhill. (Beamish Museum)

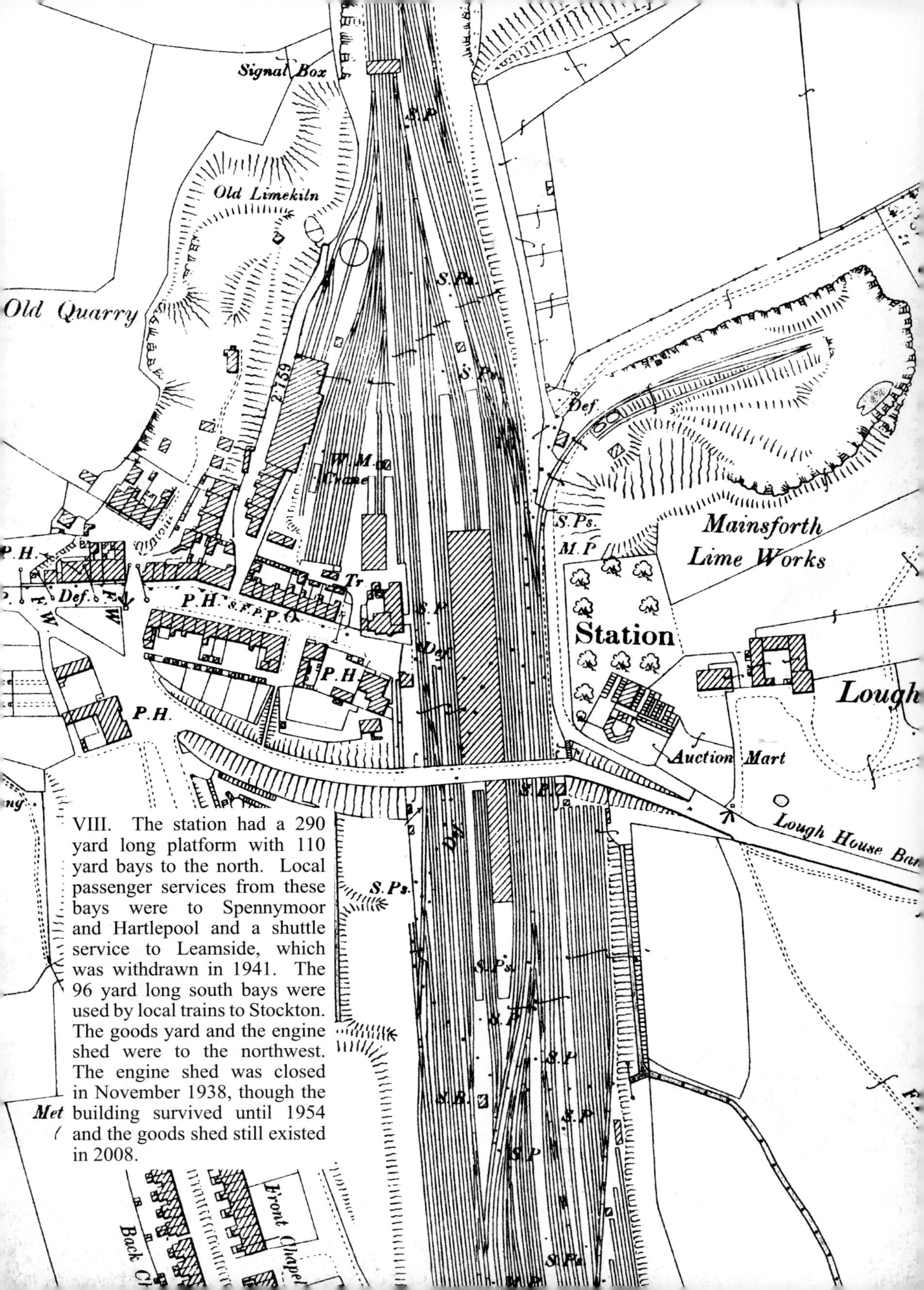

VIII. The station had a 290 yard long platform with 110 yard bays to the north. Local passenger services from these bays were to Spennymoor and Hartlepool and a shuttle service to Leamside, which was withdrawn in 1941. The 96 yard long south bays were used by local trains to Stockton. The goods yard and the engine shed were to the northwest. The engine shed was closed in November 1938, though the building survived until 1954 and the goods shed still existed in 2008.

25. Mainsforth Colliery began in 1873 but closed down in 1877, The Carlton Iron Co. Ltd recommenced work in 1900 and production began in November 1905. It was taken over in May 1923 by Dorman, Long & Co. Ltd. It became part of the NCB in 1947. Production ceased due to flooding on 3rd December 1968. The fine NER van highlights that the NER provided most of its own stock. There is only one private wagon visible, that of Bolckow Vaughan & Co. of Middlesbrough. Vaughan discovered the Cleveland Ironstone deposits. (G.Nairn coll.)

26. A northbound passenger train hauled by V2 class 2-6-2 no.60835 *The Green Howard, Alexandra, Princess of Wales's Own Yorkshire Regiment* is at Ferryhill with a class G5 0-4-4T on the Spennymoor local at the bay platform in the early BR days. Spennymoor and West Hartlepool trains ceased in 1952 and Ferryhill itself closed to passengers on 6th March 1967, although the Ferryhill population had risen to over 10,500. (K.Hoole coll.)

27. Ferryhill had several signal boxes. No.3 box was at South Junction. The Sidings box, south of the station road bridge, closed in 1954. No.1 and Coxhoe Junction boxes were elevated NER boxes straddling the fast and slow main lines respectively. No.2 and Tursdale were more conventional lineside buildings. No.2 was rebuilt and reopened on 13th December 1953. It was still open in 2008 to deal with the Tursdale Junction to Stockton line, but lost its ECML responsibilities with the opening on 12th April 1991 of the Tyneside Integrated Electronic Control Centre (IECC) at Chaytor's Bank, Gateshead. An up GNER express is passing it on the ECML on 21st September 2006 propelled by Bo-BoWE no.91105 *County Durham*. (R.R.Darsley)

28. Looking north from the station, we can see the wooded cliff that is the Clarence Railway cutting. Transrail liveried Co-CoDE no.37413 *Loch Eil Outward Bound* hauls 4-6-0 no.75014 and its support coach which are on the slow line prior to taking the Stockton route on 28th September 1996. Behind the train is the goods shed, now in private use, and the site of the engine shed. (T.Heavyside)

29. On the eastern ridge of the Ferryhill Gap is the very large LaFarge cement works at Thrislington. Below it in the trees are the silos of the rail loading terminal. This is the remaining source of freight traffic from Ferryhill and Co-CoDE no.60041 is collecting a rake of lime containers for Margam (South Wales). The date is 21st September 2006. (R.R.Darsley)

30. Coxhoe Junction gantry signal box controlled both the slow main lines and the higher level junctions on the Spennymoor and Hartlepool branches. It lost its mainline functions in January 1965. From 20th August 1967 the remains of the Hartlepool line were operated as a single line to Kelloe Bankfoot by Ferryhill No.1 box. Coxhoe Junction box still survived, opening daily for a very short time to work the freight train to Coxhoe Goods. It was finally demolished in February 1971. The Coxhoe Goods branch is the line under the bridge furthest on the right. Class G5 0-4-4T no.67305 is propelling the Spennymoor push-pull train from the flyover towards Ferryhill on 15th March 1952. (J.W.Armstrong Trust)

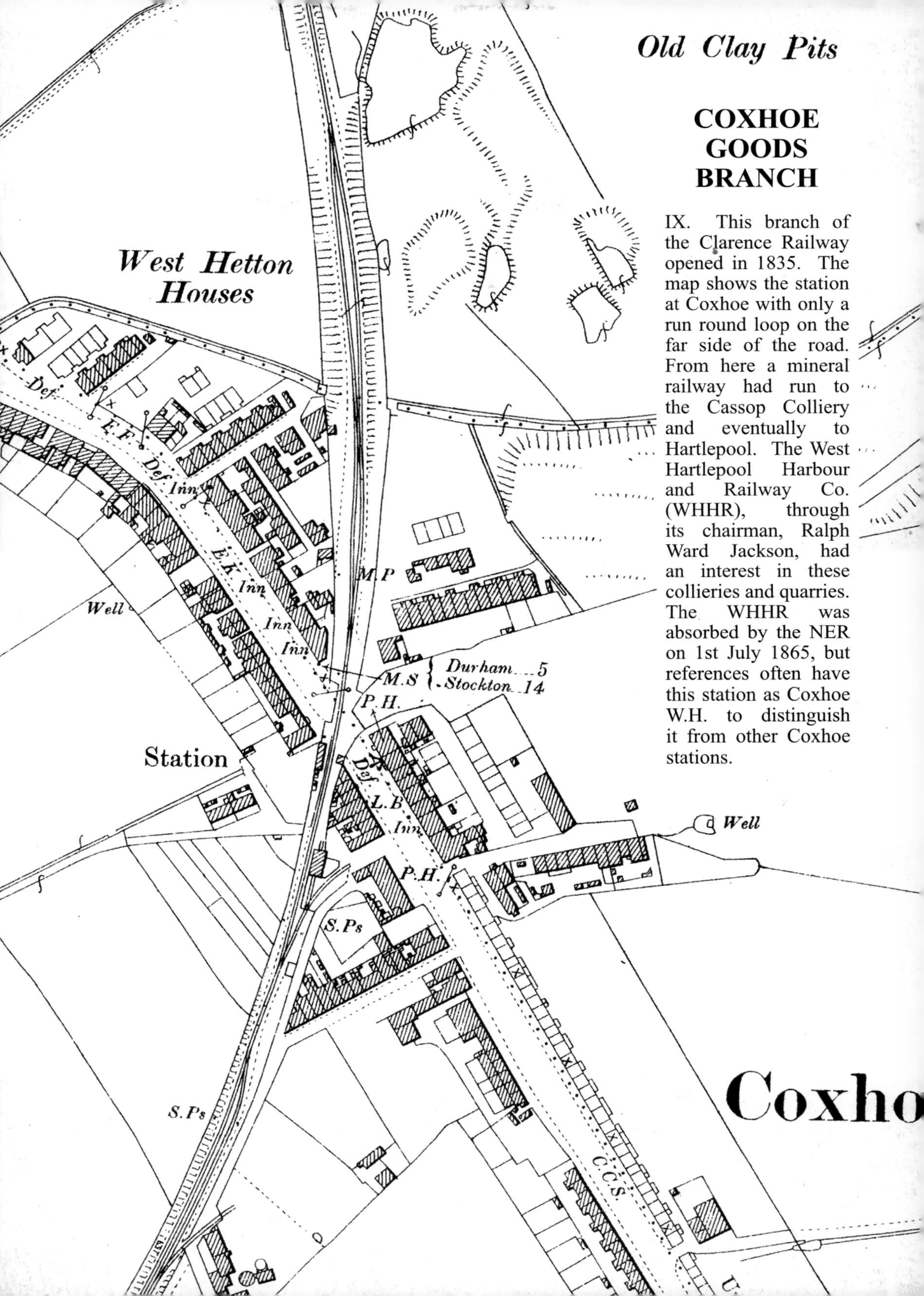

COXHOE GOODS BRANCH

IX. This branch of the Clarence Railway opened in 1835. The map shows the station at Coxhoe with only a run round loop on the far side of the road. From here a mineral railway had run to the Cassop Colliery and eventually to Hartlepool. The West Hartlepool Harbour and Railway Co. (WHHR), through its chairman, Ralph Ward Jackson, had an interest in these collieries and quarries. The WHHR was absorbed by the NER on 1st July 1865, but references often have this station as Coxhoe W.H. to distinguish it from other Coxhoe stations.

31. With the closure of West Hetton colliery and the Coxhoe limestone quarries in 1879, the branch settled down to a local existence. It had a passenger service until March 1902, 0-6-0WT no.124 running twice daily from Ferryhill (see 75). The station was photographed on 25th October 1958. The line lasted until 1984. The goods shed still exists as a double-glazing workshop. Inside is the platform with NER weigh scales, and double shed doors! All else including the one ton crane, has gone and the trackbed is a designated footpath. (N.E.Stead coll.)

NEWCASTLE, LEAMSIDE, FERRYHILL, STOCKTON, and MIDDLESBROUGH.—North Eastern.

Miles	Down.	Week Days. mrn	mrn	mrn	mrn	mrn	aft	aft	aft	aft	aft	aft	aft	aft (Wednesdays only.)	aft (Saturdays only.)	Sundays. mrn	aft
	Newcastle (Cen.) ..dep.	4 55	6 56	8 52	...	1027	1225	1 35	...	...	5 12	7 5	8 5	1033	...	6 18	5 12
½	Gateshead East	4 58	6 59	8 55	...	1030	1228	1 39	...	...	5 15	7 8	8 8	1036	...	6 23	5 16
2¼	Felling	5 3	7 4	9 0	...	1035	1233	1 43	...	...	...	7 13	8 13	1041	...	6 28	5 21
3½	Pelaw	5 9	7 9	9 5	...	1040	1238	1 47	...	...	5 21	7 17	8 18	1045	...	6 37	5 26
7	Usworth	5 17	7 19	9 13	...	1048	1246	1 56	...	...	5 30	7 25	8 26	1053	...	6 46	5 34
8¾	Washington	5 21	7A32	9 17	...	1052	1250	2 1	...	...	5 35	7 30	8 30	1057	...	6 51	5 39
10	Penshaw 545	5 26	7 38	9 22	...	1057	1256	2 6	...	...	5 41	7 36	8 35	11 2	...	6 56	5 44
12	Fencehouses	5 32	7 44	9 28	...	11 3	1 2	2 12	...	...	5 46	7 42	8 41	11 8	...	7 3	5 52
14½	Leamside 545 arr.	5 38	7 50	9 34	...	11 9	1 8	2 18	...	...	5 52	7 48	8 47	...	...	7 9	5 58
	Leamside 545 dep.	5 55	7 56	...	...	1113	...	2 22	...	...	5 53	...	8 53	...	...	7 15	6 9
17	Sherburn Colliery	...	8 3	...	...	1120	...	2 29	...	...	5 59	...	9 0	...	...	7 22	6 16
19½	Shincliffe	...	8 9	...	...	1126	...	2 35	...	...	6 5	...	9 6	...	...	7 28	6 23
23¼	**Ferryhill 535, 545** arr.	6 13	8 22	...	...	1137	...	2 46	...	...	6 13	...	9 16	...	...	7 37	6 33
36½	536 Darlington * arr.	...	9 6	...	...	1221	...	3 25	...	...	6 40	...	...	...	...	8 10	7 7
80¼	536 York "	...	1148	...	...	2 27	...	4 48	...	...	8 30	...	...	...	...	10 6	9 5
—	536 Newcastle ....dep.	...	7 5	...	...	1033	...	...	2 10	3 47	5 15	...	...	...	7 30	...	...
—	**Ferryhill** dep.	6 35	8 36	...	9 47	1155	...	...	3 26	4 38	6 53	...	...	...	9 25	...	...
26¼	Sedgefield	6 42	8 44	...	9 54	12 2	...	...	3 35	4 45	7 2	...	...	...	9 33	...	...
31¼	Stillington	6 50	8 52	...	10 2	1210	...	...	3 43	4 53	7 10	...	...	...	9 42	...	...
33	Carlton [561b	...	8 56	...	10 5	1214	...	...	3 47	4 57	7 14	...	...	...	9 47	...	...
37	**Stockton 551, 553,** arr.	7 4	9 7	...	1016	1226	...	...	3 58	5 8	7 28	...	...	...	10 0	...	...
42	**Middlesbrough 554** "	7 22	9 22	...	1032	1247	...	...	4 23	5 51	7 43	...	...	...	...	...	...

Miles	Up.	Week Days. mrn	mrn	mrn	mrn	aft	aft	aft	aft (Leaves Durham at 5 27 aft., see page 545.)	aft	aft	aft (Saturdays only.)	aft (Saturdays only.)	Sundays. mrn	aft
—	**Middlesbrough** ....dep.	...	7 10	8 45	9 20	...	1230	3 8	...	5 51	7 45	...	8 23	...	...
5	**Stockton** "	...	7 28	9 1	9 43	...	1 43	3 28	...	6 26	8 25	...	1020	...	...
9	Carlton	...	7 38	...	9 54	...	1 53	3 38	...	6 36	...	...	1030	...	...
10¾	Stillington	...	7 44	...	9 59	...	1 58	3 43	...	6 41	8 40	...	1035	...	...
15¾	Sedgefield	...	7 54	...	10 9	...	2 8	3 53	...	6 51	8 50	...	1045	...	...
18¾	**Ferryhill 534, 545** arr.	...	8 3	9 25	1017	...	2 18	4 2	...	7 0	8 59	...	1054	...	...
41¾	534 Newcastle ....arr.	...	9 16	1023	1137	...	3 22	5 26	...	8 31	1030	...	...	...	...
—	534 York ....dep.	3 50	...	...	7 5	...	1256	...	...	4 50	...	...	...	6 30	6 43
—	534 Darlington * "	4 54	7 49	...	9 3	...	2 5	...	...	6 35	...	...	...	8 25	8 6
—	**Ferryhill** ....dep.	7 34	8 29	...	1023	...	2 37	...	...	7 12	...	9 5	...	8 56	8 34
22¼	Shincliffe	7 45	8 39	...	1034	...	2 48	...	...	7 23	...	9 16	...	9 6	8 44
25	Sherburn Colliery	7 51	8 45	...	1040	...	2 54	...	...	7 29	...	9 22	...	9 12	8 50
27½	Leamside 545 arr.	7 57	8 52	...	1046	...	3 0	...	5 34	7 35	...	9 28	...	9 19	8 56
	Leamside 545 dep.	7 59	8 59	...	1050	1 50	3 1	...	5 36	7 46	...	9 29	...	9 24	9 3
30	Fencehouses	8 5	9 5	...	1056	1 56	3 7	...	5 42	7 52	...	9 35	...	9 30	9 9
32	Penshaw 545	8 10	9 10	...	11 1	2 1	3 12	...	5 47	7 57	...	9 40	...	9 35	9 14
33¾	Washington	8 15	9 15	...	11 6	2 6	3 17	...	5 53	8 3	...	9 45	...	9 41	9 20
35	Usworth	8 20	9 20	...	1111	2 10	3 22	...	5 57	8 8	...	9 50	...	9 46	9 26
38½	Pelaw 541, 543	8 28	9 28	...	1118	2 18	3 29	...	6 4	8 16	...	9 58	...	9 55	9 36
39¾	Felling	8 32	9 32	...	1122	2 22	3 33	...	6 8	8 20	...	10 2	...	9 59	9 41
41½	Gateshead East [to 549	8 38	9 40	...	1128	2 30	3 39	...	6 14	8 26	...	1010	...	10 7	9 49
42	**Newcastle** (Cen) 538 arr.	8 43	9 43	...	1131	2 33	3 43	...	6 17	8 29	...	1013	...	1010	9 52

A Arrives Washington at 7 23 mrn. * Bank Top Station.

June 192

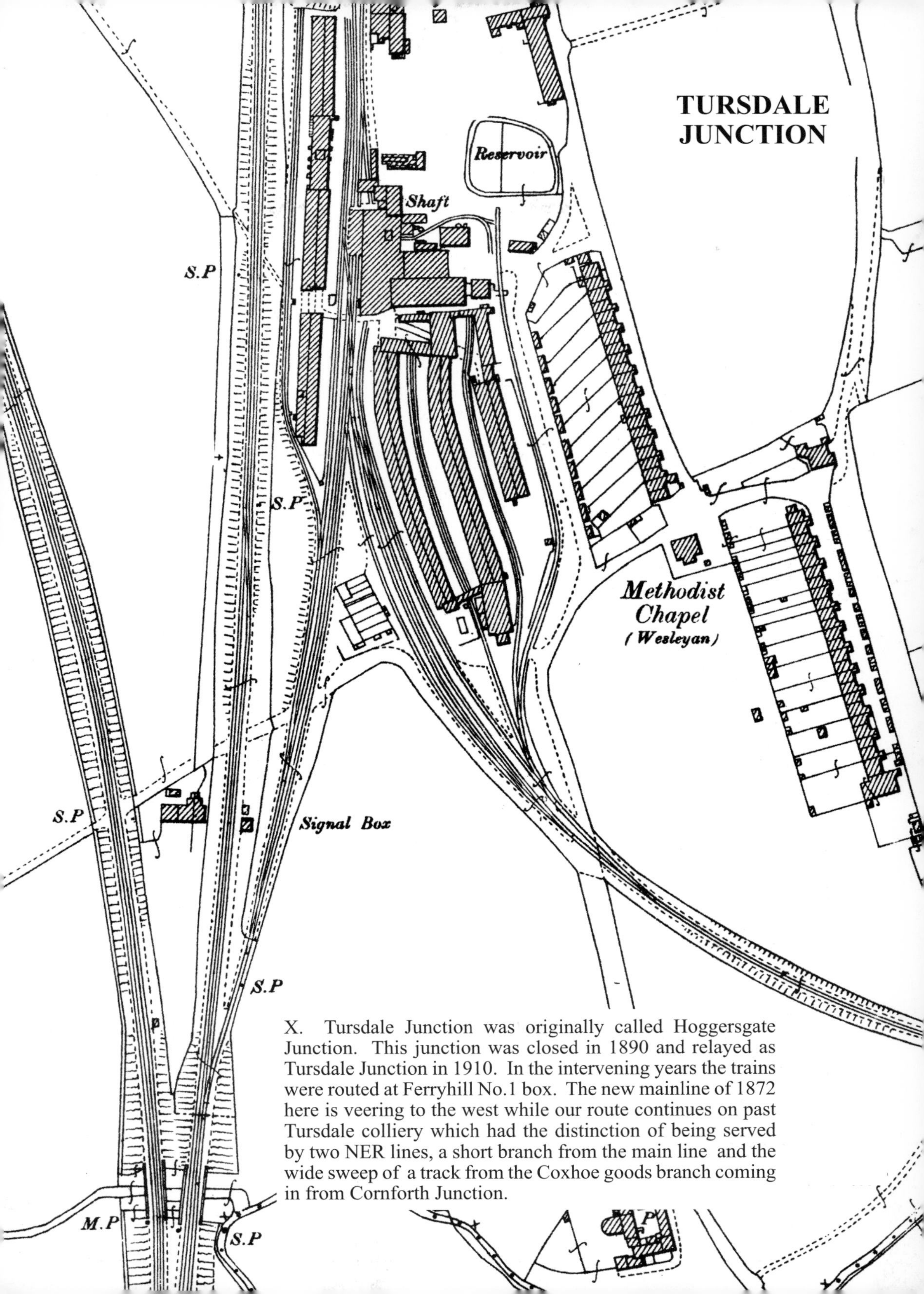

X. Tursdale Junction was originally called Hoggersgate Junction. This junction was closed in 1890 and relayed as Tursdale Junction in 1910. In the intervening years the trains were routed at Ferryhill No.1 box. The new mainline of 1872 here is veering to the west while our route continues on past Tursdale colliery which had the distinction of being served by two NER lines, a short branch from the main line and the wide sweep of a track from the Coxhoe goods branch coming in from Cornforth Junction.

32. Co-CoDE no.47490 *Bristol Bath Road* brings a diverted south bound train off the line at the junction on 29th January 1989. The electrification posts are being erected on the 1872 diversion line, now the present mainline. Behind the train is the site of NCB Durham No.4 Area workshops built on the site of Tursdale colliery which closed in 1931. This is now an industrial estate. (I.S.Carr)

33. The grass was encroaching on the remaining single track of the Leamside line on the 21st September 2006. A GNER High Speed Train on the ECML passes towards Ferryhill with Bo-BoDE no.43106 *Fountains Abbey* as the rear locomotive. (R.R.Darsley)

BOWBURN

34. The first Bowburn colliery was at the end of the Coxhoe Goods line. It was sunk in the 1840s and abandoned in 1857. North of Tursdale Junction was a short branch to the second Bowburn colliery which opened in 1908. It was linked underground with Tursdale colliery. Between then and 1916 it was shunted by a steam crane which is seen here by the winding gear in about 1911. (G.Nairn coll.)

SHINCLIFFE

XI. Shincliffe station is in rolling country with only a substantial sawmill in the station yard to give any semblance of industry. The station opened in 1844 and is not to be confused with the 1839 terminus of the line from Sunderland. The first Shincliffe had Town added to its name in 1861 and was closed in 1893. This station closed to passengers on 28th July 1941.

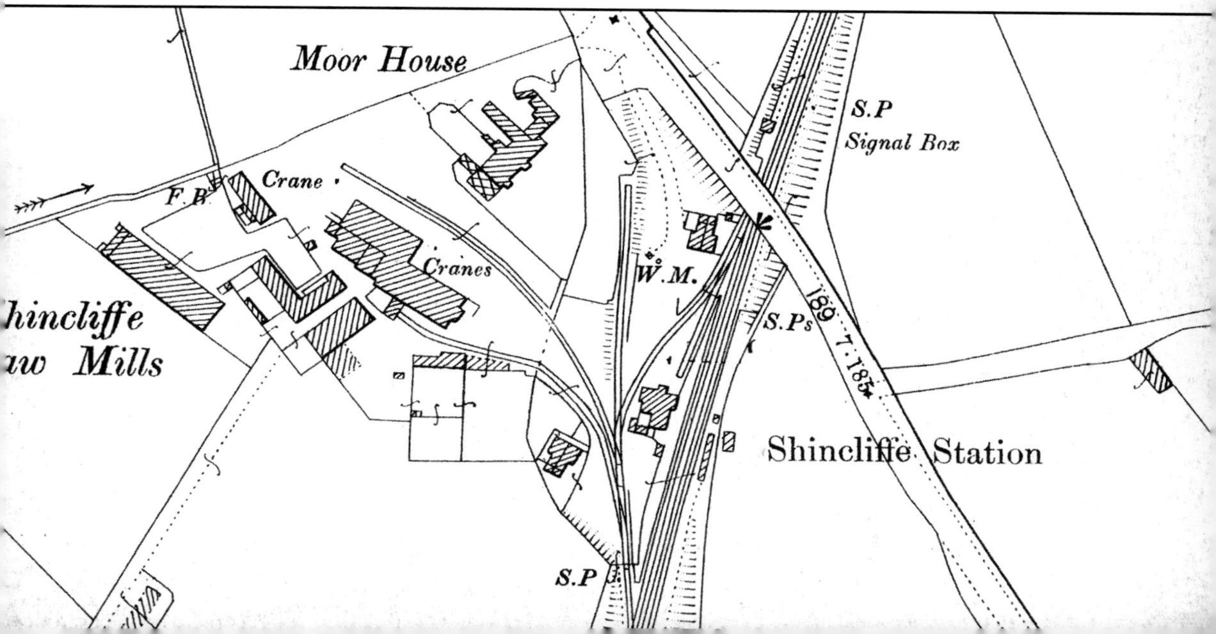

35. The station master's house was built at right angles to the station platform. A line of vans occupies the siding nearest the station. The main sidings were to the right, passing in front of the house and were served by a one and one half ton crane. There was no footbridge but the photograph was taken from the convenient road bridge. (Stations UK)

36. This was the view north on 20th October 1951. The convenient bridge is on the right. This photograph shows the signal box and the waiting rooms. It is evident from the concentration of the buildings on the down platform that most passenger traffic was to the north. The population of the village was around 750 for the period 1901 to 1961. (N.E.Stead coll.)

37. Co-CoDE no.37320 *Shapfell* passes Shincliffe with a northbound train on 16th March 1989. The signal box and platforms have gone but the station clock remains on the wall of the station buildings. The station house has an imposing double door entrance. It was a B&B hotel but has reverted to a private house. Some of the railway cottages and the sawmill buildings remain as houses, though greatly modified. (I.S.Carr).

SHERBURN COLLIERY

38. Sherburn colliery, also known as the Lady Durham pit, began production in August 1854. This 1891 photograph shows the winding house and head stock and the sorting shed. In the foreground is a rake of chauldron waggons, the bottom emptying wooden waggons distinctive of the North East Coalfield and used well into the 1960s. (Tyne & Wear Museums/A.Lynn coll.)

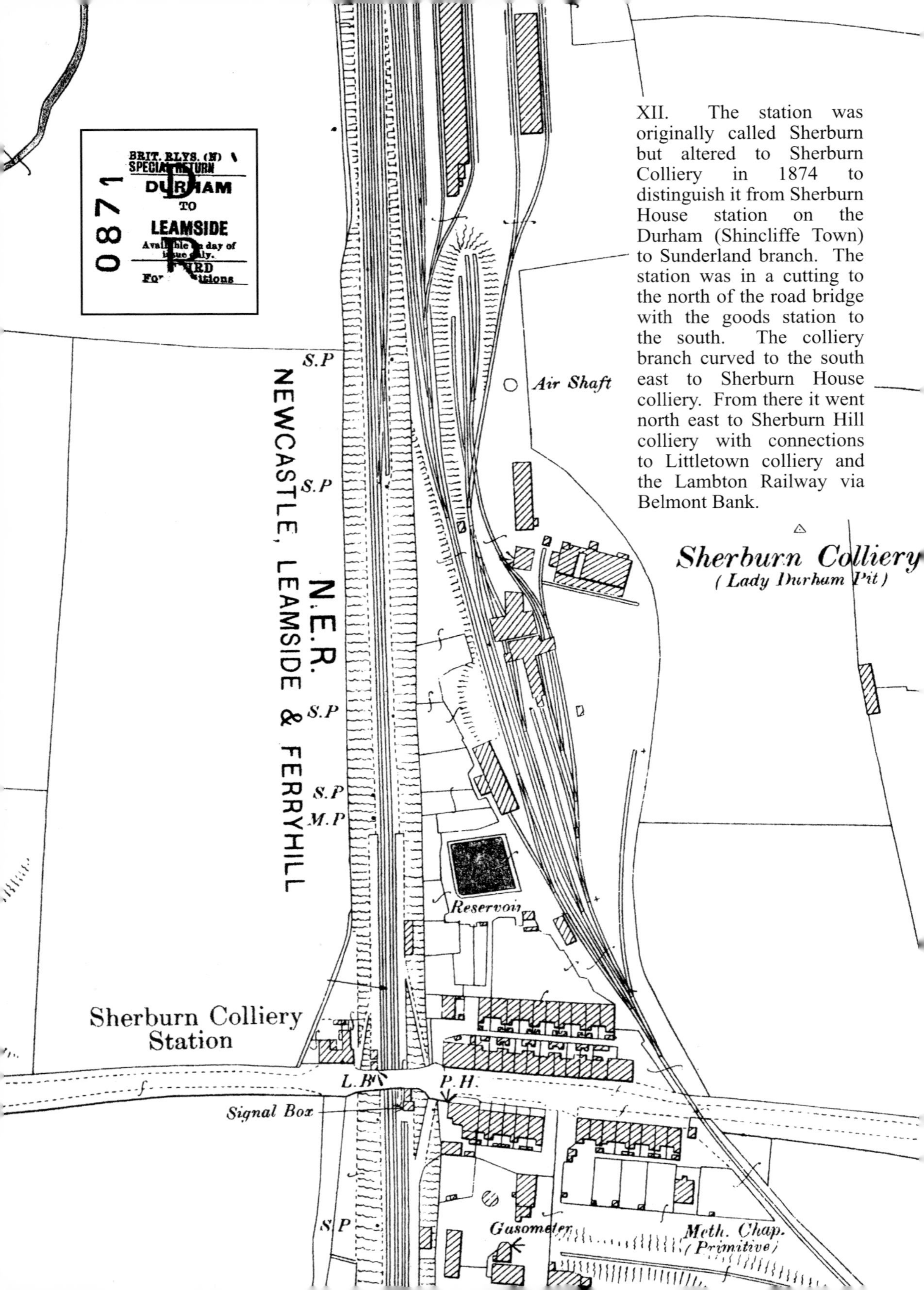

XII. The station was originally called Sherburn but altered to Sherburn Colliery in 1874 to distinguish it from Sherburn House station on the Durham (Shincliffe Town) to Sunderland branch. The station was in a cutting to the north of the road bridge with the goods station to the south. The colliery branch curved to the south east to Sherburn House colliery. From there it went north east to Sherburn Hill colliery with connections to Littletown colliery and the Lambton Railway via Belmont Bank.

39. A northbound Q6 class 0-8-0 no.63445 hauling mineral wagons approaches Sherburn Colliery South signal box. A lone wagon is at the goods platform. The station is under the bridge and the down platform is visible. It closed to passengers on 28th July 1941. (W.Longstaff/K.Hoole coll.)

40. Class K1 2-6-0 no.62059 is passing through the station with train of empty rail carriers. Neat piles of cable troughs are on the up platform suggest some signalling maintenance work on the line. There was no evidence of the station in 2008 but remains of the goods dock and the 2-ton goods crane can be found. (Stations UK)

41. Sherburn colliery winding gear is visible in the background as class A1 4-6-2 no.60145, *Saint Mungo* speeds through the station. Its sidings connected to the NER north of the station and while most coal went via the Lambton Railway after 1904, Lambton locomotives travelled to and from their works at Philadelphia, near Fence Houses, via the NER. (N.E.Stead coll.)

June 1869

SUNDERLAND, LEAMSIDE, DURHAM, and BISHOP AUCKLAND.—North Eastern.

	Week Days.									Sundays.		
	mrn	mrn	mrn	mrn	aft		aft	aft	aft	mrn	mrn	aft
180 Newcastle dep	5 20	7 15	8 30	1115	1 50		4 30	7 8	9 0	6 15	8 20	5 20
180 Sth. Shields ..	5 10	7 0	8 0	11 0	1230		4 5	6 15	8 35	6 0	8 0	5 0
From Seaham, see page 189.	1&2 gov	1&2 gov	1&2 mrn	1&2 c	1&2 aft	1,2,3 e	1&2 gov	1&2 mail	1,2,3 aft	1&2 gov	1,2,3 mrn	1&2 gov
Sunderland .. dep	1, Station for W. Auckland.	7 20	8 30	1115	1 30	3 35	4 35	6 50	9 0	6 20	8 35	5 25
Millfield		7 25	8 35	1120	1 35	3 40	4 40	6 55	9 5	6 25	8 40	5 30
Pallion		7 29	8 39	1124	1 39	3 47	4 44	6 59	9 10	6 29	8 44	5 34
Hylton		7 33	8 43	1128	1 43	3 54	4 49	7 3	9 15	6 33	8 49	5 38
Coxgreen ....(shaw		7 37	8 47	1133	1 48	4 2	4 54	7 8	9 20	6 37	8 53	5 42
Pensher or Pen-		7 40	8 51	1137	1 52	4 8	4 59	7 12	9 25	6 40	8 57	5 45
Fencehouses		7 47	8 56	1142	1 57	4 11	5 6	7 17	9 33	6 46	9 2	5 51
Leamside .. arr		7 58	9 2	1148	2 5	4 18	5 15	7 23	9 47	6 58	9 8	6 3
180 ...... dep	6 13	8 10	9 17	12 3	2 15	4 33	5 30	7 36	9 55	7 6	9 20	6 11
Durham 186	6 31	8 23	9 30	1215	2 30	4 46	5 42	7 48	10 7	7 18	9 35	6 25
Brancepeth	....	8 40	....	1227	h	5 3	5 56	....	....	7 30	....	6 38
Willington	6 49	8 49	....	1234	2 49	5 12	6 4	....	....	7 38	....	6 46
Hunwick ....[183	....	8 55	....	1239	....	5 17	6 10	....	....	7 44	....	6 52
Bsh'p. Auckland	7 5	9 5		1246	3 0	5 28	6 18			7 55	....	7 2

Down.	Week Days.								Sundays.		
Frm Penrith, Tebay, Barnard Castle, &c., pp. 182 & 183.	1&2 mail mrn	1&2 gov f g	1&2 ¶ mrn	1&2 gov f a	1&2 clss aft	1&2 gov aft	1,2,3 clss aft	1&2 gov aft	1&2 mail mrn	1&2 gov mrn	1&2 gov aft
Bishop Auckland	....	8 10	10 0	2 5	3 15	6 10	8 30	....	....	8 10	8 15
Hunwick	....	8 16	10 6	2 11	....	6 15	8 36	....	....	8 16	8 21
Willington	....	8 21	1012	2 17	3 27	6 20	8 42	....	...	8 22	8 27
Brancepeth	....	8 29	1020	2 25	....	6 27	8 50	....	....	8 30	8 35
Durham 186	5 15	8 50	1040	2 45	3 50	6 48	9 10	9 30	5 15	8 47	8 55
Leamside .. arr	5 25	9 5	1051	3 0	4 1	7 0	Saturdays only.	9 42	5 25	9 0	9 7
180 ...... dep	5 35	9 15	1059	3 12	4 11	7 11		9 51	5 35	9 8	9 20
Fencehouses	5 41	9 23	11 5	3 18	4 16	7 17		9 57	5 42	9 15	9 26
Pensher 179 or	5 46	9 30	1110	3 24	b	7 22		10 3	5 46	9 20	9 31
Coxgreen (Penshaw	5 50	9 33	1114	3 27	b	7 25		10 7	5 49	9 24	9 34
Hylton	5 55	9 37	1119	3 33	4 27	7 29		1013	5 53	9 29	9 39
Pallion	6 0	9 42	1124	3 37	b	7 34		1018	5 58	9 34	9 44
Millfield	6 3	9 45	1127	3 40	4 32	7 39		1021	6 1	9 38	9 48
Sunderland 189 a	6 8	9 53	1134	3 50	4 37	7 47		1028	6 10	9 46	9 56
179 Sth. Shields a	8 45	1040	1155	4 40	5 45	8 15		1040	8 40	1015	1010
179 Newcastle ..	5 53	10 8	1130	4 0	4 35	7 55		1030	5 58	9 55	10 5

...from Durham. c 3rd class from Brancepeth, Willington, & Hunwick to Bishop Auckland, on Thursdays & Saturdays; returning at 6 10 aft. on Thursdays, and 8¼ aft. on Saturdays. ¶ Gov. from Hunwick, Willington, and Brancepeth to Main Line Stations South of Leamside. e Stops at Frankland and Brandon Sidings. f Stop at Brandon on Sats. g Stops at Frankland on alternate Sats. to take up. h Stops to set down.

SHERBURN JUNCTION

XIII. The Sunderland to Durham via Murton branch passed under the Leamside line and a connecting link was built between Sherburn Junction and Broomside Junction. While this link was primarily for freight traffic, it was used regularly on Durham Miners' Gala Day when passenger specials came into Durham Elvet station. Trains from the north reversed here with the aid of a pilot engine attached at the rear.

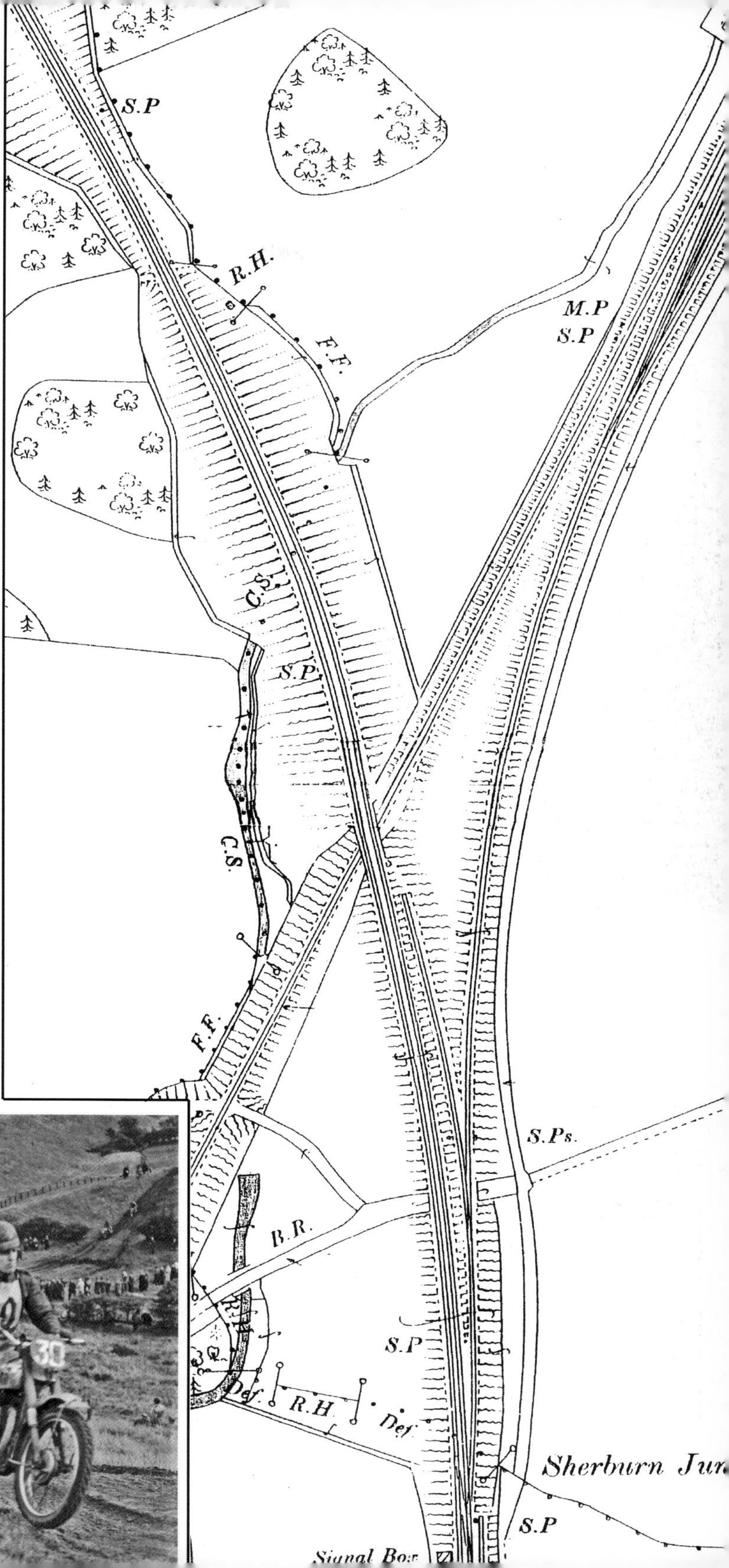

42. A 1950s Motor Cycle Scramble gives an inadvertent view of the Leamside line looking north. The branch to Durham (Shincliffe Town), built in 1837, and extended to Durham Elvet in 1893 is in the top left hand corner. Durham Elvet closed to passengers on 1st January 1931, except for Miners' Gala Day trains that lasted until 18th July 1953. This section of the line closed totally on 11th January 1954, although the link line through to Murton continued until 1963. (Beamish Museum)

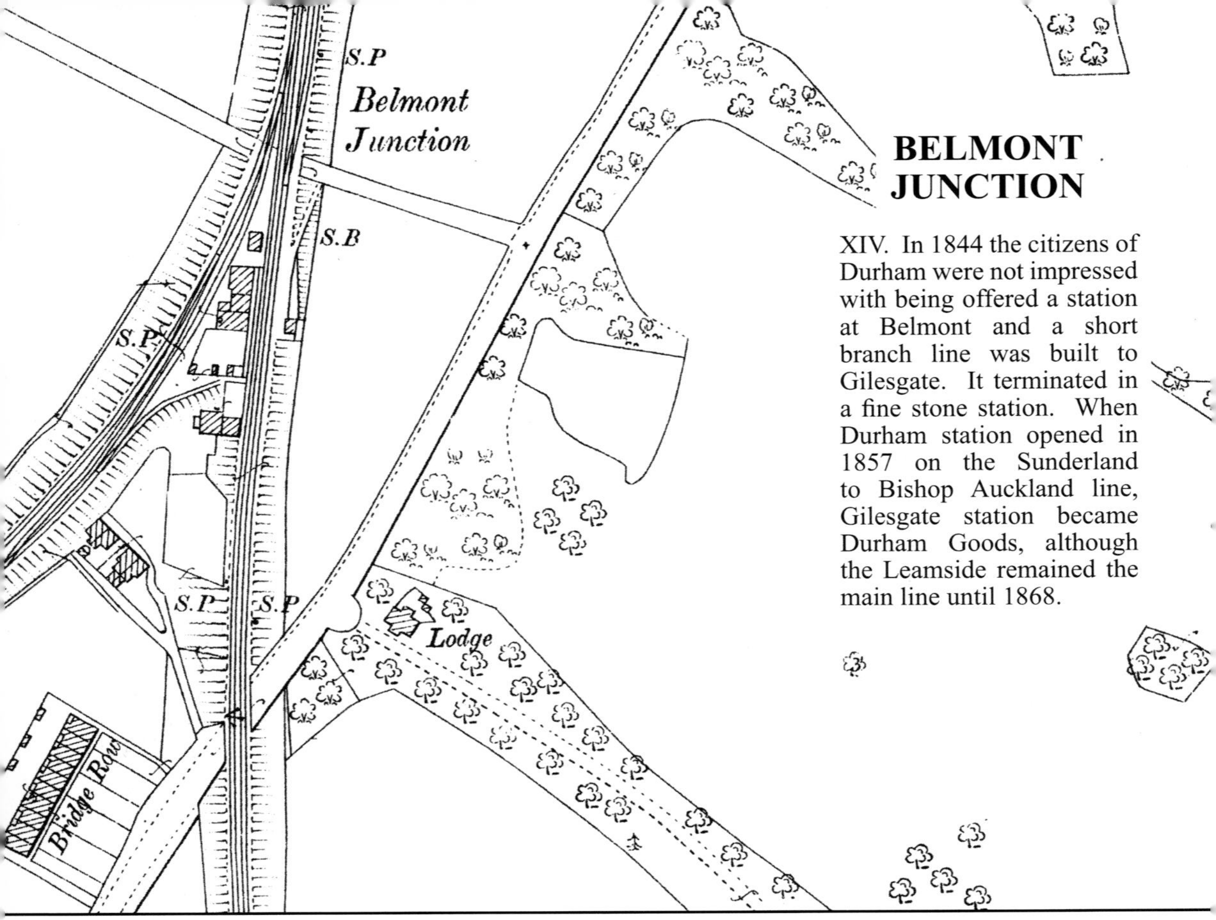

BELMONT JUNCTION

XIV. In 1844 the citizens of Durham were not impressed with being offered a station at Belmont and a short branch line was built to Gilesgate. It terminated in a fine stone station. When Durham station opened in 1857 on the Sunderland to Bishop Auckland line, Gilesgate station became Durham Goods, although the Leamside remained the main line until 1868.

43. Belmont station was open for passengers from 18th June 1844 to 1st April 1857. In this 1950 photograph, the branch to Durham Gilesgate is to the right. Behind the station buildings is the water pumping station with its chimney. In the 1990s the hope was that a new Park and Ride station for Durham City would be built here by the A690 and A1(M) interchange. The Park and Ride car park has been built but not the station. (J.W.Armstrong Trust)

44. The water pumping station with its roof top storage tank was built in 1844 and lasted until 1961. This view is from the Gilesgate branch looking at the water pipe by the Leamside line. (Beamish Museum)

45. Both station building and water tank have gone in this view of the 15th April 1966. Type 2 Bo-BoDE no.D5105 is shunting the Durham Gilesgate goods train at Belmont Junction. (I.S.Carr)

DURHAM GILESGATE BRANCH

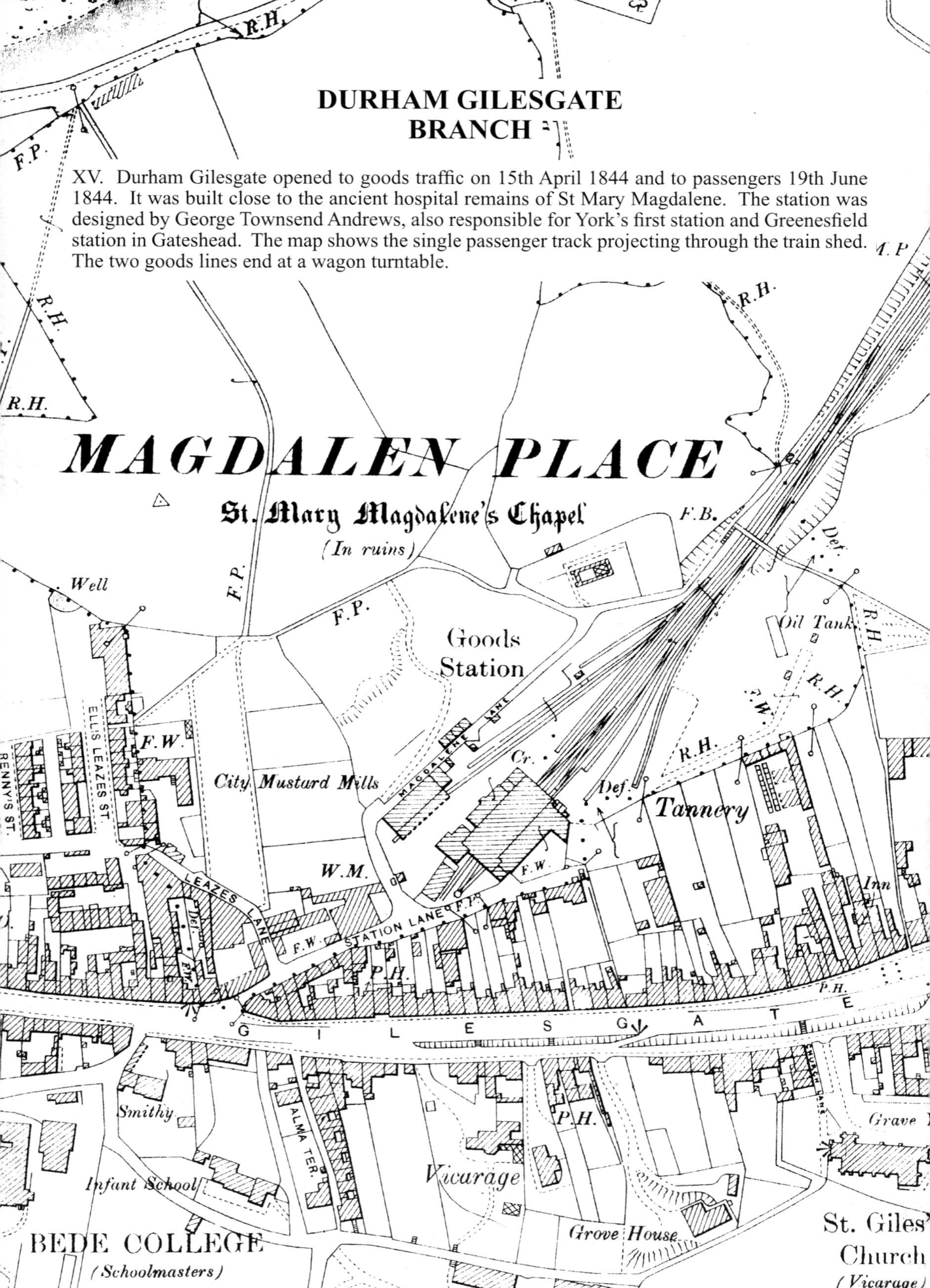

XV. Durham Gilesgate opened to goods traffic on 15th April 1844 and to passengers 19th June 1844. It was built close to the ancient hospital remains of St Mary Magdalene. The station was designed by George Townsend Andrews, also responsible for York's first station and Greenesfield station in Gateshead. The map shows the single passenger track projecting through the train shed. The two goods lines end at a wagon turntable.

46. On 5th August 1966, Bo-BoDE Clayton no.D8590 was working at the goods station. In the background is the magnificent outline of Durham Cathedral. The passenger entrance was the low building behind the two cranes, one of which could lift 10 tons. The double storey offices are at the road entrance. The remains of St Mary Magdalene are beyond the bushes on the right. (I.S.Carr)

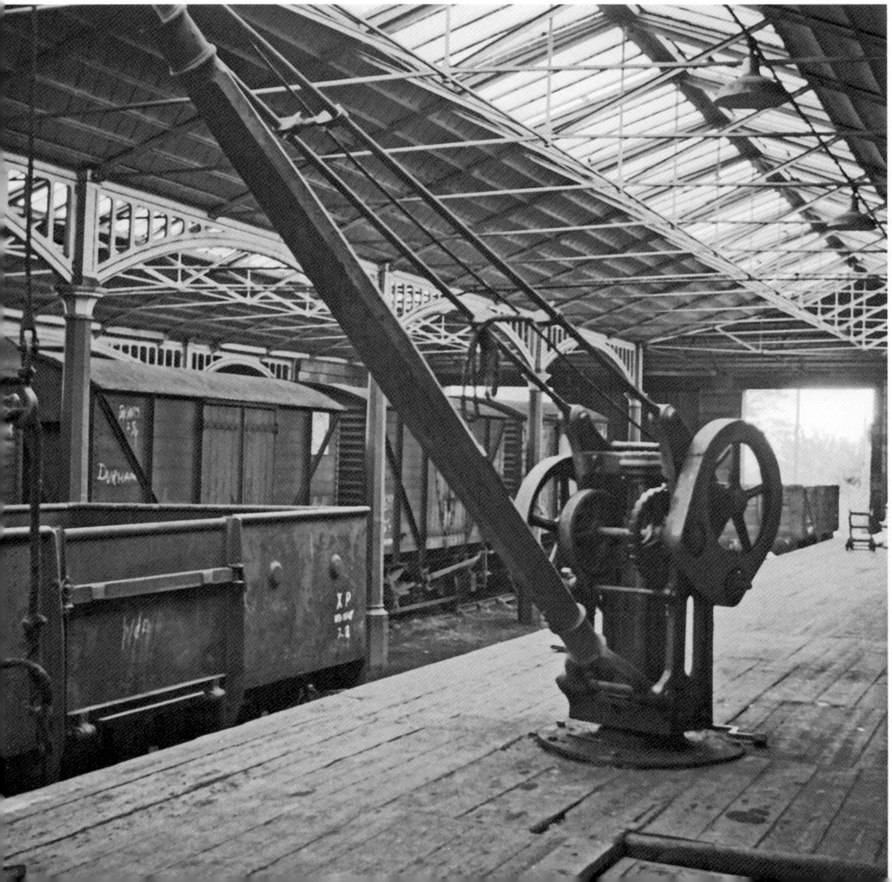

47. This is a 1960s view of the inside of Gilesgate station. The crane is probably on the original passenger platform. The graceful pillars and arches of the roof construction have lasted well. Gilesgate goods station closed on 7th November 1966. On the same date a new distribution depot for domestic coal opened at Durham station on the site of the engine shed at Aykley Heads. (Beamish Museum)

48. The front of the station on 24th March 1966 showed that the station offices had not survived in such good condition, even though at this date, the line still had six months of life left. Large portions of the branch to Gilesgate are now the route of the A690 into Durham. (R.R.Darsley)

49. After closure it was empty until later taken over by Archibalds, the Durham ironmongers. The station has now been modernised and is a Travel Lodge Hotel, which opened in June 1994. This is the passenger entrance and hotel reception on 9th January 2007. (R.R.Darsley)

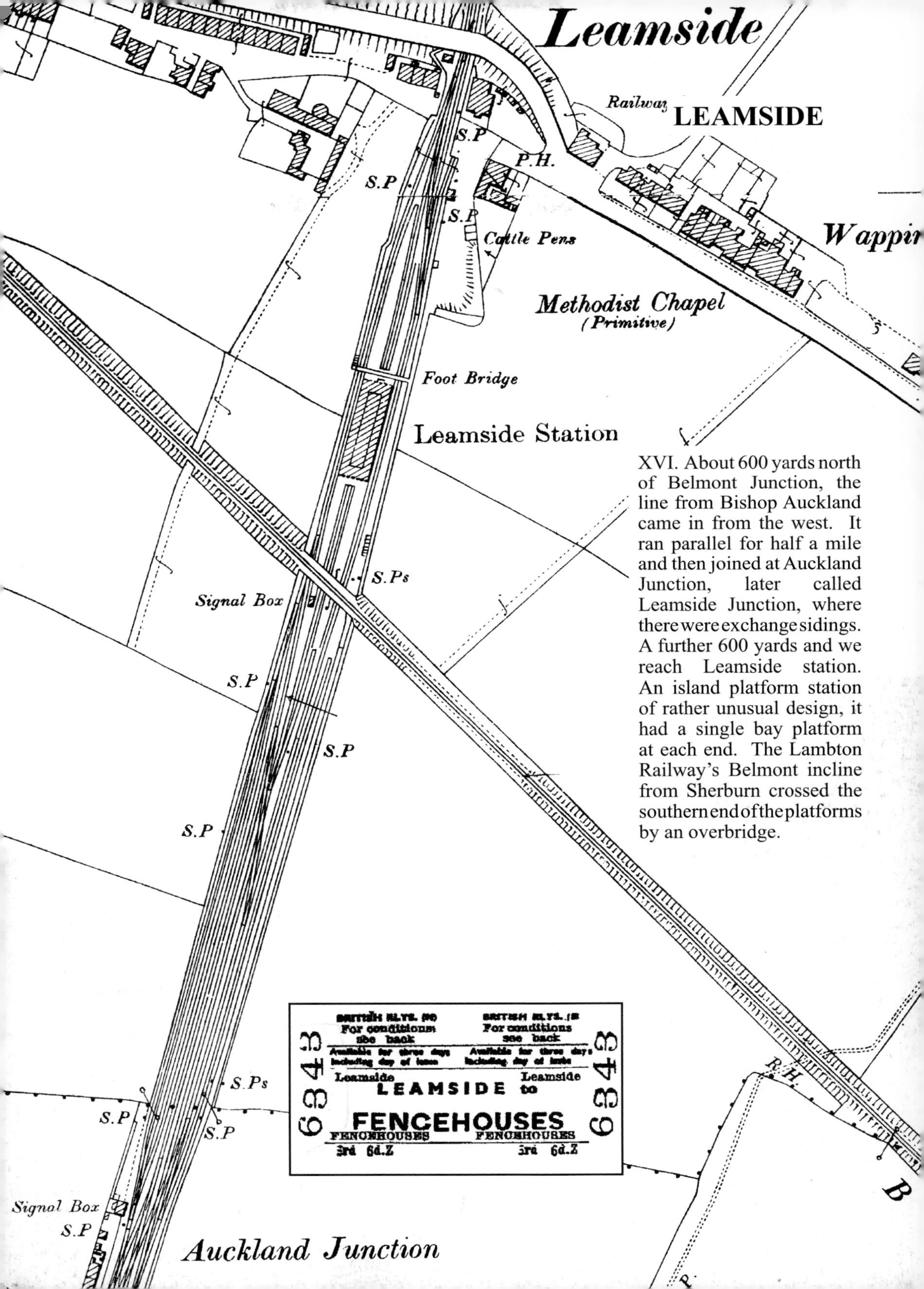

XVI. About 600 yards north of Belmont Junction, the line from Bishop Auckland came in from the west. It ran parallel for half a mile and then joined at Auckland Junction, later called Leamside Junction, where there were exchange sidings. A further 600 yards and we reach Leamside station. An island platform station of rather unusual design, it had a single bay platform at each end. The Lambton Railway's Belmont incline from Sherburn crossed the southern end of the platforms by an overbridge.

50. The station rooms were in the centre under a heavy roof and two towers disguising 4000 and 5000 gallon water tanks. This was the second station. The first station, to the north of the Station Road crossing, opened in 1844 and closed in 1857. The crossing was then replaced by a bridge with a nasty z-bend and the second station built south of the road. The short south bay was used by the passenger service from Ferryhill to Leamside, withdrawn in 1941. The station closed completely on 5th October 1953. (Lens of Sutton coll.)

51. The island platform is viewed from the road bridge looking south. The gates of the old level crossing are in the foreground. The very short bay was for vans and the steam railcars used on services from Sunderland and Newcastle. A typical north east coal cart is being filled from wagons in the goods dock which had a three ton crane. The signals are very tall so that they can be seen on both sides of the road and rail bridges. (Lens of Sutton coll.)

52. At Morton Acre Farm a roped bale of hay is being hand winched onto the two wheeled harvest cart. On the embankment is a Clayton steam railcar thought to be no.2101 *Union* running without the coal rails on the bunker. *Union* entered service in July 1928. Coal rails were fitted from August 1928, which helps date the picture. The Clayton railcars were unsuccessful and although *Union* achieved 109,499 miles, the highest mileage of the N.E. Area allocation, it was the first to be scrapped in April 1936. (Beamish Museum)

53. One mile north of Leamside was Adventure Pit which was sunk in 1817. A stationary engine worked the branch of the Londonderry Railway from here to Meadows Pit. A new Adventure Pit sunk some yards to the south, was served both by the Londonderry Railway and a branch from the Leamside line. The colliery closed in 1896 but was reopened by the Rainton Colliery Co. Ltd. This photograph of 7th March 1914 shows the winding house still under construction. The pit survived until September 1978. Excavations after closure revealed wood boarded tunnels from previous mining that were over 200 years old. (G.Nairn coll.)

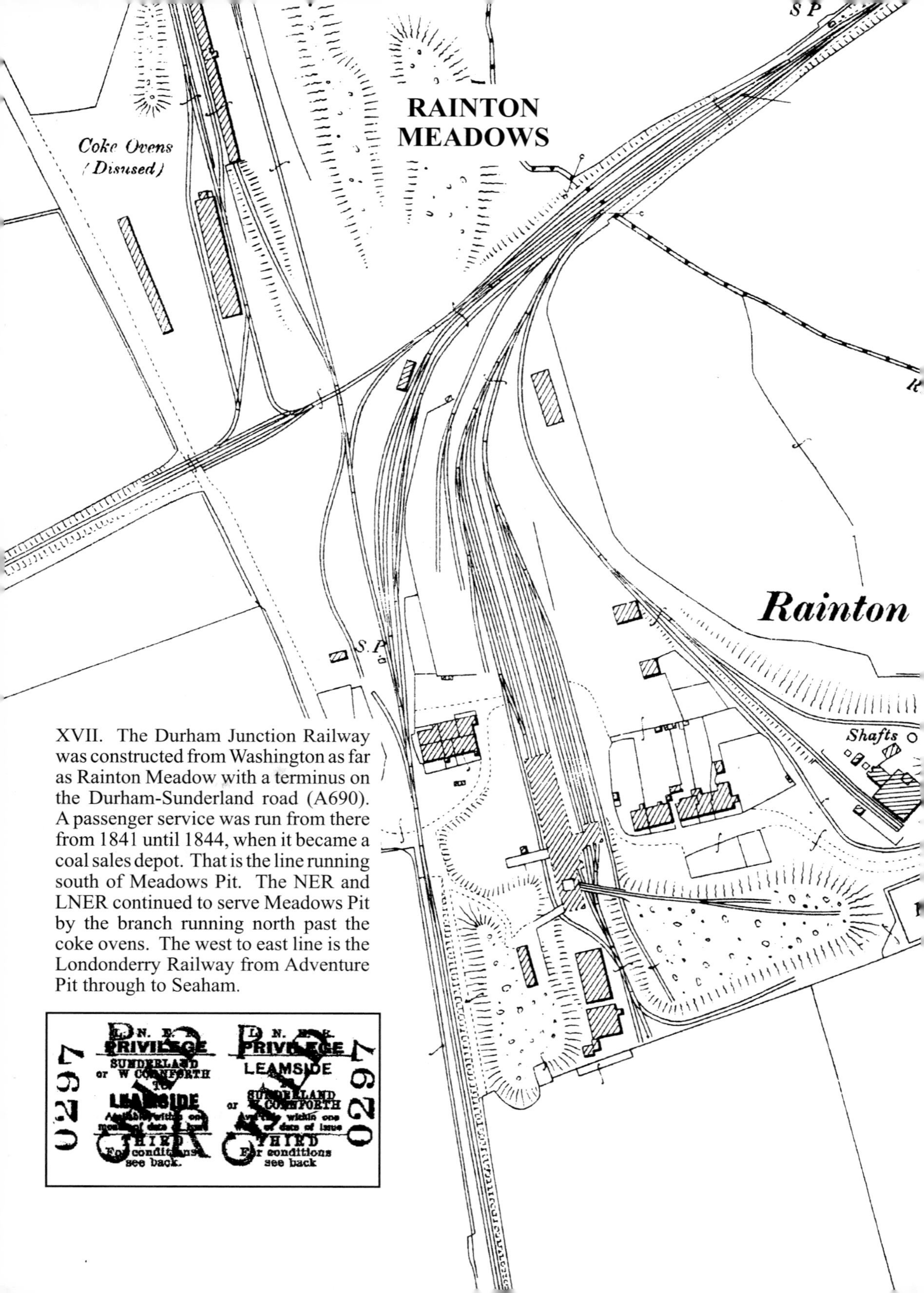

XVII. The Durham Junction Railway was constructed from Washington as far as Rainton Meadow with a terminus on the Durham-Sunderland road (A690). A passenger service was run from there from 1841 until 1844, when it became a coal sales depot. That is the line running south of Meadows Pit. The NER and LNER continued to serve Meadows Pit by the branch running north past the coke ovens. The west to east line is the Londonderry Railway from Adventure Pit through to Seaham.

54. Meadows Pit was sunk in 1824 and served by the Londonderry Railway before the DJR. The pit closed in November 1896 which was a momentous year for it saw the end of Londonderry control in Rainton and the sale of the Lambton empire to Sir James Joicey. Meadow Pit was kept as a ventilation shaft and this photo, taken in 1904, is believed to be the only one of the pit. In 1936 it was reopened for man riding and in 1946 for coal production. The area between it and the site of the nearby Nicholson's Pit, also closed in 1896, became the Lambton Railway's central area for disposal of colliery waste. Known locally as 'Nicholson's', this area was being restored in 2008. (G.Nairn coll.)

FENCE HOUSES
Bowes House
Biddick Lodge
Bowes House Farm
LAMBTON RAILWAY
LAMBTON RAILWAY BOWES HOUSE BRANCH
NEWCASTLE, LEAMSIDE & FERRYHILL
N. E. R.
Boundary Houses
Painshaw Foundry
Union Bdy.
C. Pit (Disused)
A. Pit (Disused)
Stott's Pasture
Bournmoor Farm
Junction Row
Meth. Chap.
Rectory
Bournmoor
School
St. Barnabas's Church
Newbottle
B. Pit (Disused)
BOURNMOOR
Acres
512·871
LAMBTON RAILWAY LUMLEY BRANCH
Coke Ovens
New Lambton
Brick & Tile Works
Firebrick Works
Infant School
D. Pit
Sedgeletch Sewage Works
New Lambton Pumping Engine
Bridge
Mill
Mill Race
Lumley Park Burn
Morton Pumping Engine
Sedgeletch Bridge
Reservoir
Lady Anne Pit
Lumley Sixth Pit
Lumley Brick Wks.
William Henry Pit (Disused)
Old Coal Pit
Pit No. 7 (Disused)
Break Neck Gill
Pity Me
Fence Houses Station
Fence Houses Hotel (P.H.)
Fence Houses
LAMBTON RAILWAY COCKEN BRANCH
MORTON GRANGE
Acres
461·925

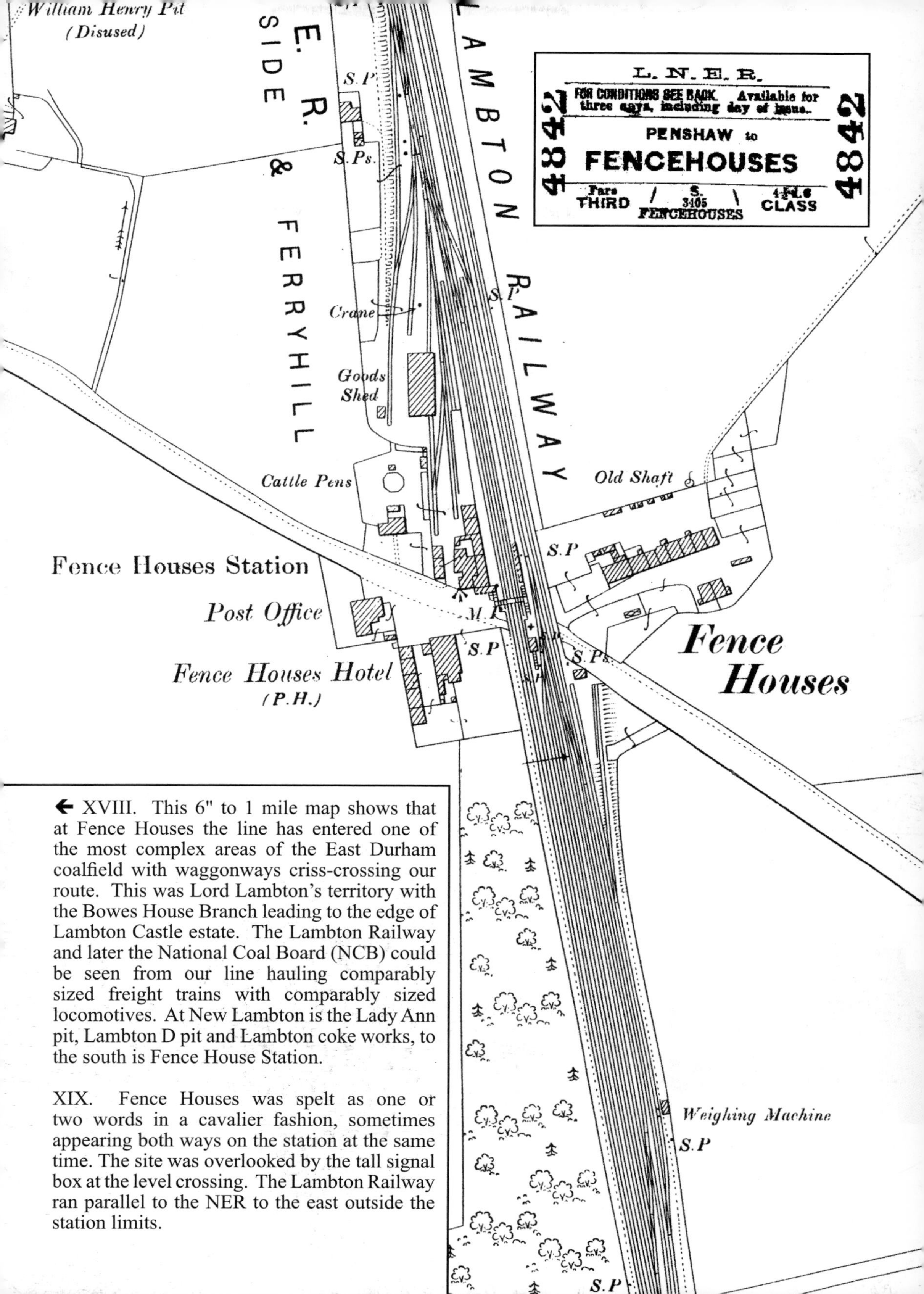

← XVIII. This 6" to 1 mile map shows that at Fence Houses the line has entered one of the most complex areas of the East Durham coalfield with waggonways criss-crossing our route. This was Lord Lambton's territory with the Bowes House Branch leading to the edge of Lambton Castle estate. The Lambton Railway and later the National Coal Board (NCB) could be seen from our line hauling comparably sized freight trains with comparably sized locomotives. At New Lambton is the Lady Ann pit, Lambton D pit and Lambton coke works, to the south is Fence House Station.

XIX. Fence Houses was spelt as one or two words in a cavalier fashion, sometimes appearing both ways on the station at the same time. The site was overlooked by the tall signal box at the level crossing. The Lambton Railway ran parallel to the NER to the east outside the station limits.

55. We are looking south on the down platform which had the main buildings of elegant dressed stone but black from the industry in the area. The staff and a few passengers are waiting for a train to Sunderland in this scene, dated about 1912. (Lens of Sutton coll.)

56. A pitman in his Sunday clothes regards the photographer suspiciously, as he is standing on the Lambton Railway level crossing. The NER crossing gates are closed and the down platform buildings are visible under the footbridge. The short repeater signal by the footbridge appears to be for the signalman. The very tall signal in 55 might not be visible from the signal box. Again the date is about 1912. (Lens of Sutton coll.)

57. This is the signal box and the Lambton Railway crossing with gates only on the east side. The signals protect the interchange sidings and are beside the rear of the up platform shelter. The main station buildings are behind the signal box and behind them is the roof of the goods shed with a 5 ton crane. In the distance a BR train of 21 ton hopper wagons is shunting as it is without its brake van. (C.H.A.Townley/Tyne & Wear Museums)

58. 0-6-2T no.31 was Kitson no.4533 of 1907. It was the last of the first batch of 0-6-2Ts bought by the Lambton Railway and here passes the signal box with a load of empties from the Nicholson's disposal point at Rainton. The angled side sheets to the cab were officially for clearance in the Lambton Staiths tunnel at Sunderland but were more a fashion of Major Lawson, the Lambton Engine Works manager. (V.Wake/J.W.Armstrong Trust.)

59. The station sign is now Fencehouses but little else has changed by 1959, as class A1 4-6-2 no.60129 *Guy Mannering* passes through the station with a diverted Newcastle to Kings Cross express. The NCB lines on the right lead to the New Lambton Coke Works and 'D' pit, which loom large in the background. The station closed to passengers on 4th May 1964. (I.S.Carr)

December 1947

LEAMSIDE and NEWCASTLE

Miles		Week Days																		Sundays			
		a.m			a.m			p.m S			p.m E												
	142 Durham .... dep	8 1	..	..	..	..	..	..	..	..	..	..	..	..	..	..	..	..	..	..	..	..	..
—	Leamside .... dep	8 9	..	..	..	..	..	..	..	..	..	..	..	..	..	..	..	..	..	..	..	..	..
2½	Fencehouses	8 15	..	..	..	..	..	..	..	..	..	..	..	..	..	..	..	..	..	..	..	..	..
4½	Penshaw	8 20	..	..	8 33	..	..	..	..	..	..	..	..	..	..	..	..	..	..	..	..	..	..
6¼	Washington	..	..	..	8 38	..	..	1220	..	..	5 16	..	..	..	..	..	..	..	..	..	..	..	..
7½	Usworth	..	..	..	..	..	..	1224	..	..	5 20	..	..	..	..	..	..	..	..	..	..	..	..
11	Pelaw	..	..	..	..	..	..	1231	..	..	5 28	..	..	..	..	..	..	..	..	..	..	..	..
12¼	Felling	..	..	..	..	..	..	1235	..	..	5 32	..	..	..	..	..	..	..	..	..	..	..	..
13¾	Gateshead East	..	..	..	..	..	..	1240	..	..	5 37	..	..	..	..	..	..	..	..	..	..	..	..
14½	Newcastle .... arr	..	..	..	..	..	..	1243	..	..	5 40	..	..	..	..	..	..	..	..	..	..	..	..

Miles		Week Days																		Sundays			
		a.m A			a.m			p.m E												a.m A			
	Newcastle .... dep	4 30	..	..	8 28	..	..	..	..	..	..	..	..	..	..	..	..	..	..	6 40	..	..	..
¾	Gateshead East	..	..	..	8 31	..	..	..	..	..	..	..	..	..	..	..	..	..	..	6 43	..	..	..
2¼	Felling	..	..	..	8 36	..	..	..	..	..	..	..	..	..	..	..	..	..	..	6 48	..	..	..
3½	Pelaw	..	..	..	8 40	..	..	..	..	..	..	..	..	..	..	..	..	..	..	6 52	..	..	..
7	Usworth	..	..	..	8 48	..	..	..	..	..	..	..	..	..	..	..	..	..	..	7 0	..	..	..
8¼	Washington	4 53	..	..	8 53	..	..	5 40	..	..	..	..	..	..	..	..	..	..	..	7 7	..	..	..
10	Penshaw	4 59	..	..	..	..	..	5 46	..	..	..	..	..	..	..	..	..	..	..	7 14	..	..	..
12	Fencehouses	5 10	..	..	..	..	..	..	..	..	..	..	..	..	..	..	..	..	..	7 20	..	..	..
14½	Leamside .... arr	5 18	..	..	..	..	..	..	..	..	..	..	..	..	..	..	..	..	..	7 27	..	..	..
18½	142 Durham .... arr	5 26	..	..	..	..	..	..	..	..	..	..	..	..	..	..	..	..	..	7 36	..	..	..

A Through Trains between Newcastle and Durham. **E** Except Saturdays. **S** Saturdays only.

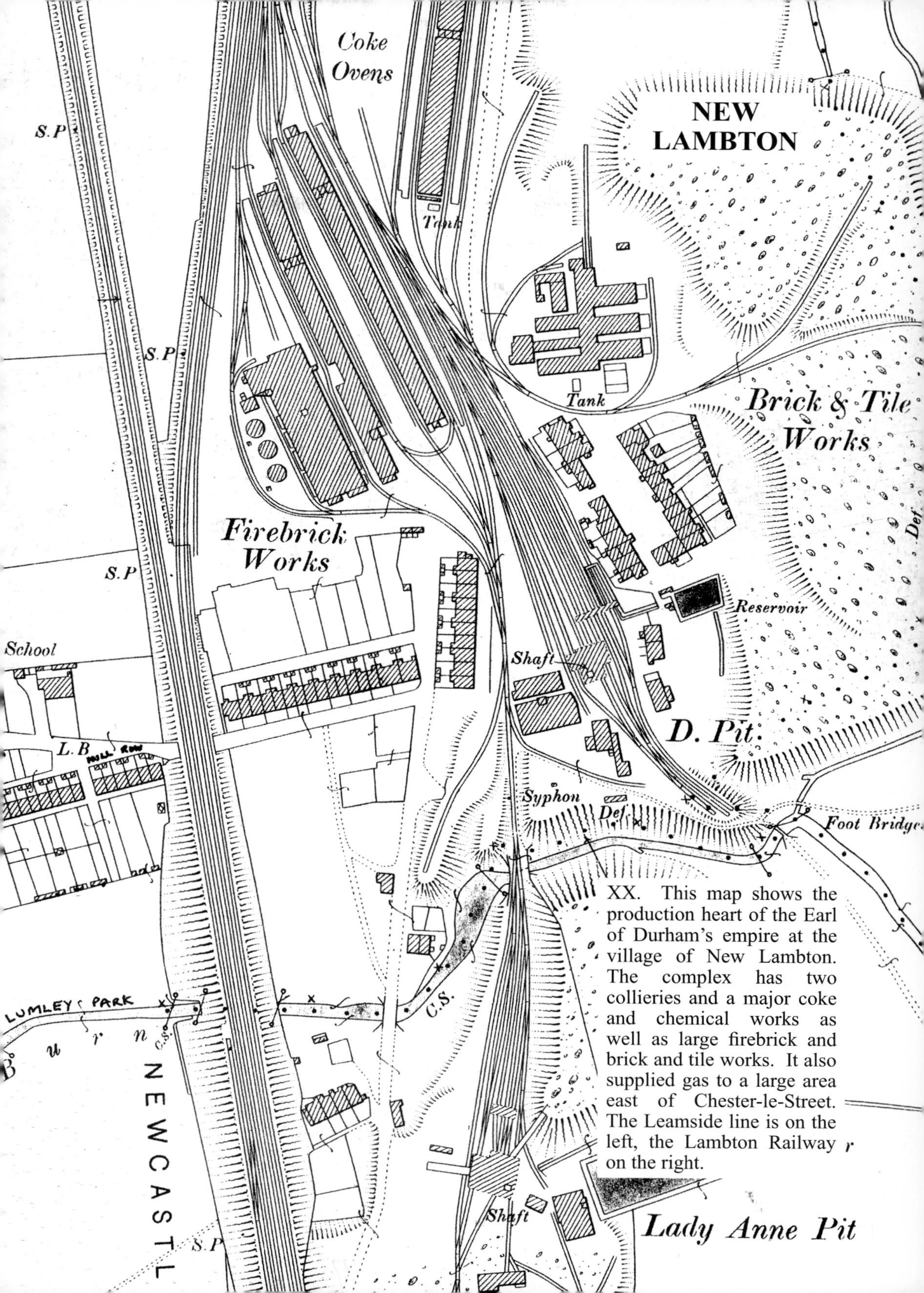

XX. This map shows the production heart of the Earl of Durham's empire at the village of New Lambton. The complex has two collieries and a major coke and chemical works as well as large firebrick and brick and tile works. It also supplied gas to a large area east of Chester-le-Street. The Leamside line is on the left, the Lambton Railway on the right.

60. Lumley Park Burn runs between Lady Anne pit and 'D' pit and then under the railway. A southbound train is hauled by a class 398 0-6-0 with 5ft.8in. wheels and a side window cab. There were four locomotives of this variant, all Darlington built, NER numbers 81, 116, 617 and 626. Off the picture to the left by the railway embankment in the back garden of the first house in Mill Row was an unusual triangular building on stilts – was it a signal gantry, a pigeon loft? Does anyone know? (A.Lynn coll.)

61. A 1955 view of New Lambton, with the firebrick and coke works stretching across the horizon. 'D' pit winding gear is to the right with the flag flying to show that the pit had met its targets. A single deck AEC Regal is in the pit car park, next to a Hillman, but look at the shine on that BSA motorbike! (A.Lynn)

62. The coking plant had a quenching tower into which the cars of hot coke from the ovens were pushed. Usually this was done by an ungainly electric locomotive specially designed to have a cab high above the retort openings but for part of 1977 0-4-0DH Hunslet no.6263 of 1964 was deputising. This locomotive usually worked at Hawthorn Coking Plant. The works opened in 1902 and it closed, with the last section of the Lambton Railway, in January 1986. (Beamish Museum)

63. Lambton' D' pit was sunk between 1789 and 1791 and lasted until 1825. A new pit was sunk in 1854 and this closed on 27th February 1965. The area was being cleared for redevelopment, when 400 metres of 4ft.3in. gauge wooden rails dating from 1780 were discovered. A fan of five tracks and a more sophisticated track with a curved check-rail are shown here on 29th March 1996. They have been re-covered with colliery waste to protect them. The Lambton family had a colliery waggonway in this Bourn Moor area before 1737. It was lengthened and improved in 1770-1780. Iron rails were introduced in 1813 and the gauge changed to 4ft.8½in. with the arrival of steam locomotives. (A.C.Clothier)

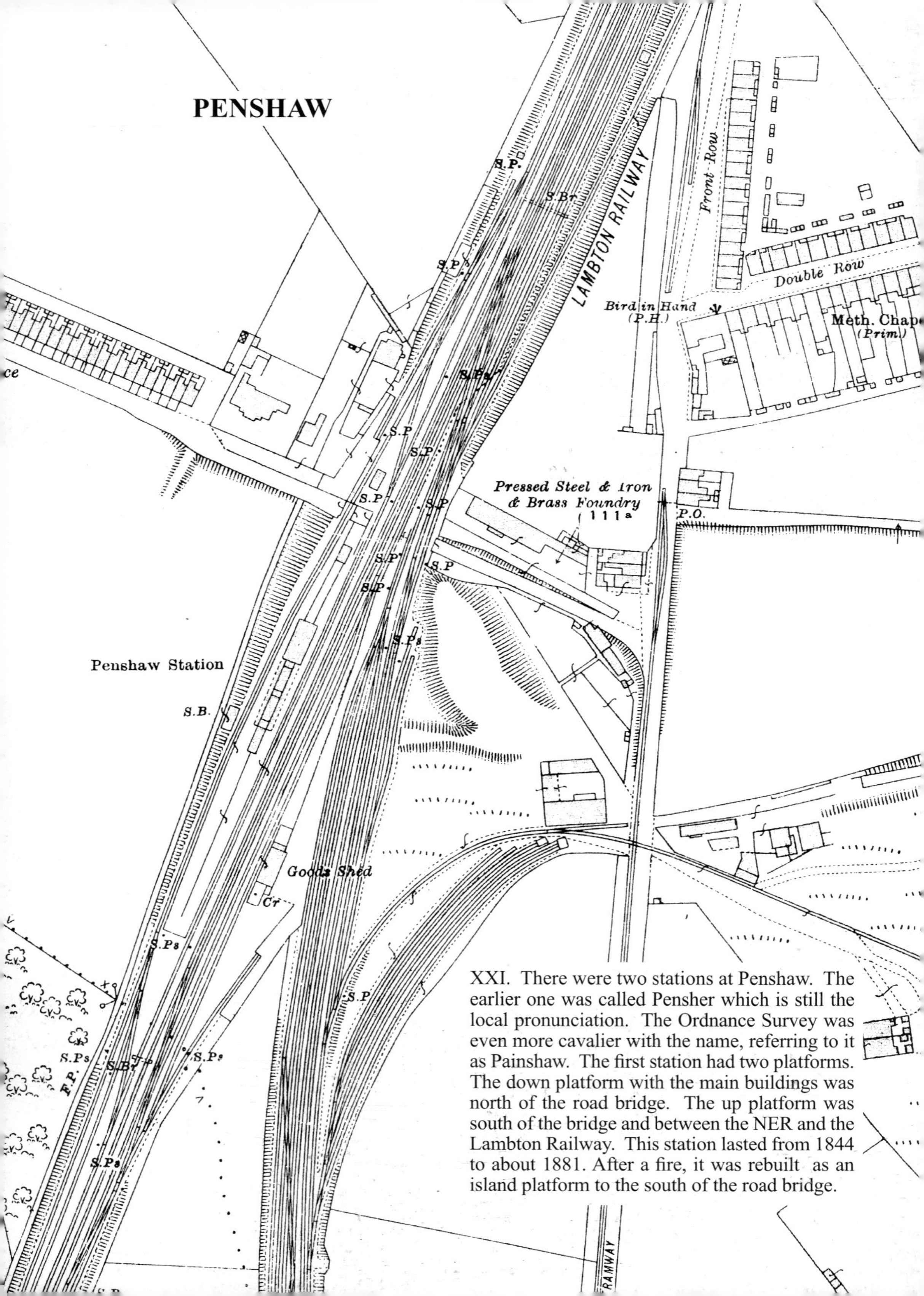

XXI. There were two stations at Penshaw. The earlier one was called Pensher which is still the local pronunciation. The Ordnance Survey was even more cavalier with the name, referring to it as Painshaw. The first station had two platforms. The down platform with the main buildings was north of the road bridge. The up platform was south of the bridge and between the NER and the Lambton Railway. This station lasted from 1844 to about 1881. After a fire, it was rebuilt as an island platform to the south of the road bridge.

64. This 1959 view is to the north from the end of the island platform. The large signal box has a clear view over the single storey station buildings which had glazed awnings on both sides. The stationmaster's house is visible between the two. Access to the platform was from the road that runs underneath the railway. A class 9F 2-10-0 is heading south on a mineral train. (Stations UK)

65. Class A4 4-6-2 no.60007, *Sir Nigel Gresley*, arrives with the 11.05am Newcastle to King's Cross diverted via Leamside on Sunday 23rd August 1959. The glass-topped canopy covers the stairway to the road. The fine array of signals reflect the influence of NER's signal engineer, Mr Hurst, who did not believe in ground disc signals and built huge signal gantries everywhere. (I.S.Carr)

66. The signal is clear for class J27 0-6-0 no.65885 to haul its loaded coal train towards Penshaw Junction. The smoke is drifting over the station which is in the right distance. The Lambton Railway is coming in from the left and from there on, it had running rights to Washington and Sunderland. A row of NCB wagons are on the approach to Penshaw Junction bridge and the line to the Low Lambton staiths. The end wagon is level with the now closed Bird in Hand pub. (I.S.Carr)

67. On 26th August 1964, NCB 0-6-2T no.42 is taking a coal train from Harraton colliery to the Sunderland staiths. The train has exercised running rights from Washington, across the Victoria Viaduct and will take the BR line to Sunderland. The brake van is behind the locomotive because of reversals at Washington and Penshaw. The end of the train is on the line from the viaduct; the Sunderland line is straight ahead. The Low Lambton staiths line has gone but the bridge abutments remain behind Penshaw North signal box. No.42 was built in 1920 by Robert Stephenson, their no.3801. (I.S.Carr)

68. Penshaw had closed to passengers with the Sunderland branch on 4th May 1964. Freight to Sunderland ceased in 1967 and the line has gone with much else, but Deltic class Co-CoDE no.9020 *Nimbus* is heading a train of blue and grey Mark I and Mark II coaches bound for Kings Cross under Penshaw North signal box on a Sunday diversion in 1977. (I.Patterson)

69. This is Penshaw station site on 9th January 2007. In 2004 a gang arrived with lorries, cranes and cutters. Wearing high visibility jackets and hard hats, they cut up nearly two miles of double track for scrap. They were apprehended when a resident made enquiries and the gang leader received a three year jail sentence. The Tanfield Railway Association salvaged the ruined rail for Network Rail in exchange for useable 60ft. track panels. Later in 2007 Network Rail recovered the concrete sleepers, stating that to replace the track would cost £2 million. (R.R.Darsley)

NORTH OF PENSHAW

Washington Chemical Works
Washington Station
Gasometer
Reservoir
Coke Ovens
Blast Furnace
Biddick Row
Victoria Place
Washington Iron Works
The Railway Tavern
Old Station
Signal Ho.
Waggon Way
Old Waggon Way
Wesleyan M. Chapel
Washington Staith
Ship Building Yard
The Earl of Durham Inn
Washington Wood Side
Old Quarry
Wood House
S W O R T H
(Detached)
537·097 Acres
North Biddick
Viaduct
Low Lambton Quarry
Low Lambton Staiths
Botany Bay
Victoria Br.
Bore Hole
Old Quarry
Old Brick & Tile Works
Old Clay Pit
Old Coal Pit
Lane House
Spring
Hill Top
Reach Wood
Long Reach
River Wear
Low Lambton Farm
Drifts & Levels
Clay Shaft
Fire Brick Works
Engine
Painshaw Junction Br.
Painshaw Junction
Signal Ho.
Cow Roads
Dog Hole
The Bird in Bush Inn
Painshaw Staiths
Coal Staiths
Rope Walk
Biddick Brewery
Worm Hill
The Biddick Inn
Quarry Well
North Biddick
The Main Engine
Lampblack Works
Painshaw Engine
New Painshaw Pit
Old Coal Pit
Pit Row
Painshaw Br.
Waggon Hill
Painshaw Tile Works
New Painshaw
Front Row
Double Row
Londonderry Railway
Fatfield
Biddick
Lampblack Works
Haugh
Biddick Ferry
South Biddick
Charlershaugh Colliery
Biddick Ford
The Bird in Hand P.H.
Signal Post
Painshaw Station
Wooden Br.
Telegraph
P A I N
1085·

← XXII. This 6" to 1 mile map of 1856 shows the route from Penshaw to Washington across the River Wear. The first Penshaw station is shown north of the road to Waggon Hill. The line to Sunderland goes right at Painshaw Junction, with a Lambton Railway line to Low Lambton staiths. The first station at Washington was at the junction with the Stanhope and Tyne Railway. The second station is opposite the Chemical Works. Fatfield was the height of navigation, where the earliest waggonways came down to the river.

70. A NER class 38 4-4-0 crosses Victoria Viaduct on an up train in about 1902. Alexander McDonnell followed Edward Fletcher whose last passenger locomotive was the 901 class 2-4-0. McDonnell made many changes including bogies, left-hand drive, no exhaust cocks, and a different chimney taper! Unfortunately his locomotives were inferior to the 901 and rapidly disappeared from express work though they lasted some thirty years on secondary work. Through the second arch can be seen the colliery at North Biddick. (G.Nairn coll.)

71. There are four main arches, the outer two of 100ft. span and the inner two of 144ft. over land and 160ft. over the river. The length is 811ft. and the height above the high water mark is 135ft. It was designed by Benjamin Green, engineered by T.E.Harrison, and built by Gibb & Son from Aberdeen. The last stone was laid on the day of Queen Victoria's coronation, 28th June 1838. Hence the name. 1-Co-Co-1DE no.40106 is heading north on a Manchester to Newcastle train in the summer of 1980. On the hill is Penshaw Monument (see 78). (N.E.Stead)

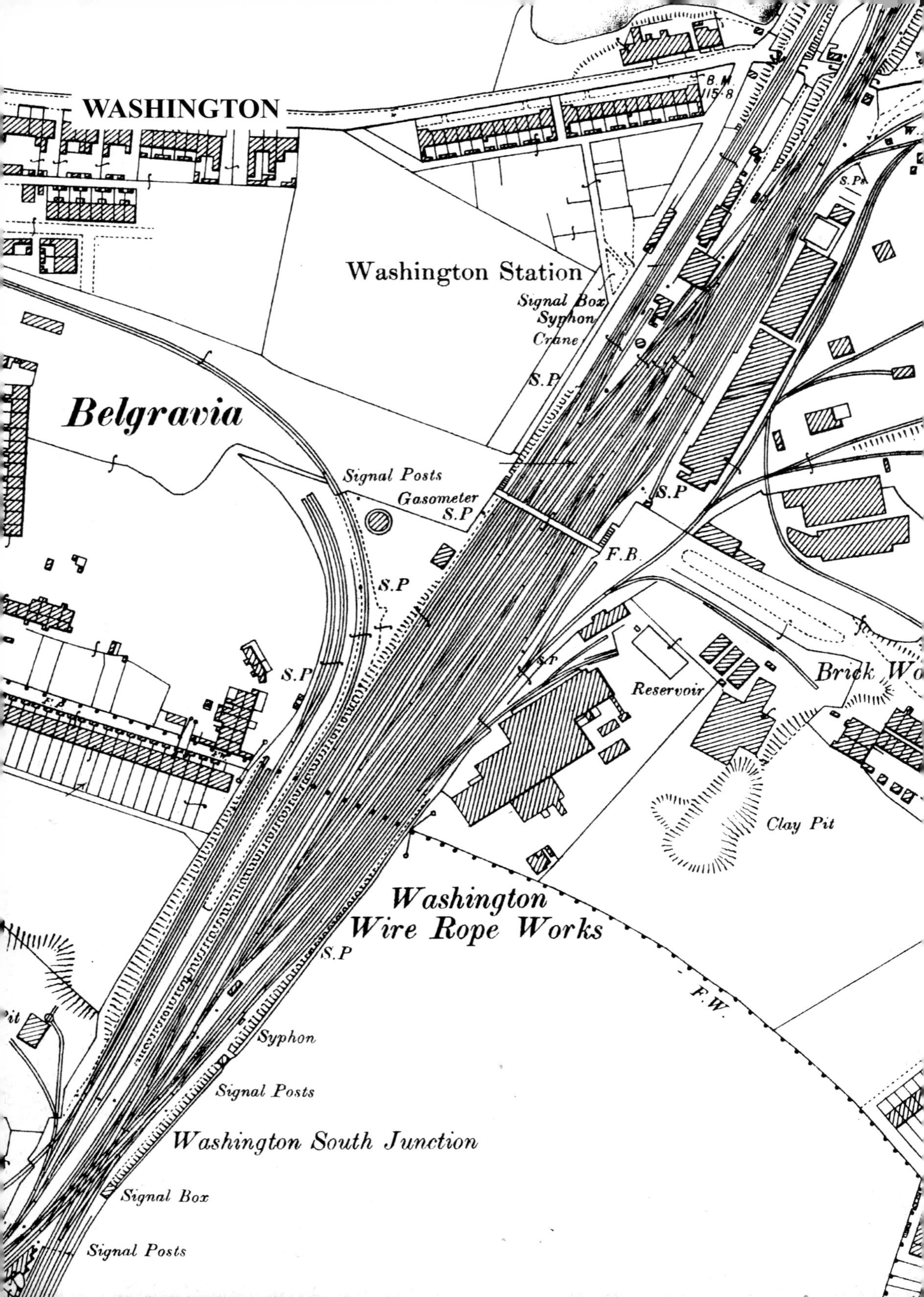

WASHINGTON
B.M. 15·8
Washington Station
Signal Box
Syphon
Crane
S.P
Belgravia
Signal Posts
Gasometer
S.P
S.P
F.B
S.P
S.P
S.P
Reservoir
Brick Wo
Clay Pit
Washington
Wire Rope Works
S.P
F.W.
Syphon
Signal Posts
Washington South Junction
Signal Box
Signal Posts

← XXIII. The first station, used from 1835 to 1869, is the building in the bottom left corner opposite the "signal posts". The second station was more convenient to the village. Washington Old Hall was the family seat of George Washington, first President of the United States of America. In the 1960s the Leamside line became the south eastern boundary of the new town of Washington. The population increased from 6,200 in 1901 to 19,500 in 1961 and rose to 55,000 in 2007.

72. South of the station was an $1\frac{3}{4}$ mile branch line to Washington Glebe and Washington 'F' collieries. Glebe was the scene of a fire-damp explosion on February 20th 1908, killing 14 miners and injuring more. 'F' pit still exists as a colliery museum. A road to the north provided access to the station as the main buildings were on the up line with freight lines passing behind them. In about 1905 a northbound train is at the platform complete with an NER clerestory brake van. (G.Nairn coll.)

73. Crowds gather on the station platform as class V3 2-6-2T no.67691 arrives with a special train from Usworth taking miners and their families to the Miners' Gala at Durham on 19th July 1958. Passenger services continued until 9th September 1963. (I.S.Carr)

74. The Washington Chemical Works started in 1842. In 1872 it was bought by R.S.Newall. Under his son, it became the largest producer of magnesia in the world by 1900. Here the plant is under construction and behind the towers are the chimneys of the brick works. The station is on the embankment to the right of Washington North signal box. (Beamish Museum)

75. The Washington Brickworks forms the background for a team photograph of locomotive crew and shunters. NER 0-6-0WT (LNER class J76) no.609 was one of Fletcher's class 124 developed from the very successful 0-4-4 Bogie Tank Passenger. Built in 1881, no.609 was the first to be withdrawn in July 1911. No.124 of this class worked the Coxhoe passenger trains until 1902. (Beamish Museum)

76. In 1920 Frederick Newall joined with Sir Samuel Turner to form Turner & Newall. In the 1960s the asbestos insulation business was more important than the chemicals and the firm became Newall's Insulation and Chemical Co. Ltd. Various industrial steam and diesel locomotives were used at the works. This is *Margaret*, an English Electric 0-4-0DH no.D1126 of 1966. Rail traffic ceased in 1971. *Margaret* went to Scotland and her sister locomotive, *Muriel,* DH1123, is preserved at the Nene Valley Railway. In 1980 the works was sold to Cape Insulation Ltd. It was closed and reclaimed in about 2002. (I.S.Carr)

77. The famous iron ore trains from Tyne Dock to Consett steelworks passed through Washington on the Pontop & South Shields Railway. On 8th August 1955, class O1 2-8-0 no.63712 arrives with a 448-ton train. The locomotive's Westinghouse pumps were used for opening the bogie wagons which were vacuum braked. Class O1 was a Thompson rebuild of the Great Central O4 class 2-8-0. No.63712 was one of five sent to Tyne Dock in 1951, where they remained until withdrawn in 1962. (N.E.Stead coll.)

NORTH OF WASHINGTON

Brockley Whins Junction

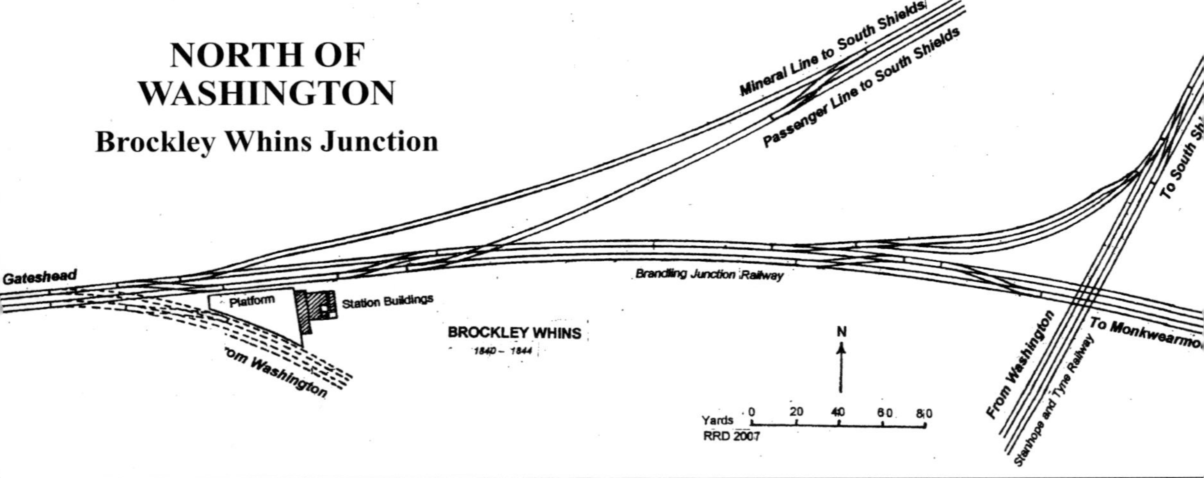

XXIV. The line from Washington to Pelaw via Usworth was built in 1849. Before that trains used the Pontop & South Shields line to Brockley Whins. This crossed the Brandling Junction Railway from Monkwearmouth to Gateshead on the level. Between 1840 and 1844 trains from Rainton Meadows were fly shunted at the junction. The engine was detached while still moving, half a mile before the crossover. It steamed ahead into the loop. The carriages followed the locomotive across the crossover, sailed past towards South Shields and the engine came out of the loop behind them. The guard applied the brake, the engine recoupled and went tender first towards Gateshead. Trains in the other direction were more sedate. They were pulled into the loop on the curve. The engine ran around, pushed them north of the junction, then pulled them south to Rainton Meadows. In 1844 the new curve connecting the P&SSR with the BJR removed the need for these antics and provided Brockley Whins station with another platform face. The first record of signalling at a junction was also here. At the approach to the crossing were three posts in succession. At the first post the driver whistled, at the second, he reduced speed and at the third, if a red flag was hoisted at the crossing a P&SSR train could cross at half speed. If a white flag, a BJR train could pass. If both flags were up and waved or there were no flags, then all trains had to stop.

USWORTH

XXV. Usworth was a small village and merited only a small station. There were no goods facilities, as the Usworth Colliery branch was half a mile to the north of the station, going one mile to the west to reach the pit.

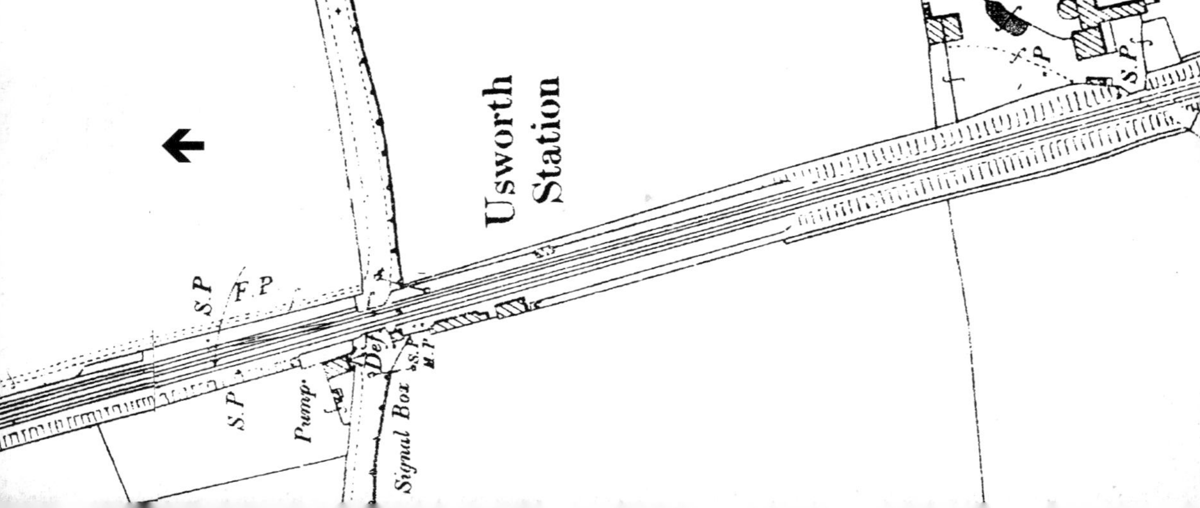

78. The station had the single storey buildings on the down platform shown here. There was only a small cabin on the up line. The view is south from the level crossing in 1958. On the hill in the distance is Penshaw Monument, built in 1844 to the style of the Temple of Theseus in Athens to honour the first Earl of Durham. It can be seen from most directions for many miles. (Stations UK)

79. Class A4 4-6-2 no.60029 *Woodcock* was passing the up platform with the 1.15pm Edinburgh to Kings Cross diverted via Leamside on Sunday, 23rd August 1959. The roof of the signal box guarding the level crossing can be seen over the second coach. (I.S.Carr)

80. The Nissan factory is about half a mile from the trackbed near Usworth station. Usworth opened in 1863 and closed on 4th May 1963. The station was demolished and in 2007, although the track was left, it was cut at the level crossing and the tarmac of the road re-laid. On 31st July 1966 Type 5 Co-CoDE D1971 is passing with the 10am Edinburgh to Kings Cross train. (N.E.Stead)

NORTH OF USWORTH

81. Usworth pit was sunk in 1845 and shunted by horses, steam locomotives and at times by the NER and LNER. It ended belonging to the Washington Coal Co. Ltd which also owned Washington F and Washington Glebe collieries, both served by the NER branch from Washington station. In 1959 it was joined with Follonsby and Wardley No.2 collieries underground and became solely a man riding shaft. (A.Lynn coll.)

82. Follonsby pit was on the east side of the line, as it approached Pelaw Junction. This mine was sunk in 1911. It was also served by the Bowes Railway and in 1940 was sold to the Washington Coal Company. It was properly known as Wardley No.1 and in 1959 became part of the Wardley/Usworth pit complex which from 1969 was known as Usworth Colliery, though some way from the original Usworth shaft. Wardley No.2 shaft closed in 1971 and Usworth on 8th August 1974. (G.Nairn coll.)

83. A Freightliner terminal was built on the west side of the line opposite Follonsby Colliery opening on 31st July 1967. The Ordnance Survey spells the area Follingsby and that became the name of the terminal. To the left is the Freightliner crane and to the right is the Follonsby/Wardley No.1 headstock and coal handling plant. (Beamish Museum)

84. 1-Co-Co-1DE no.45066 is leaving the Follingsby Freightliner terminal with 4V73 overnight to Pengam on 30th August 1985. In a rationalisation of Freightliner depots, the yard closed from Monday, 6th April 1987. (N.E.Stead)

85. In the 1980s the site of Swalwell coal concentration depot was required for the MetroCentre development. The British Coal Opencast Executive built a replacement at Follonsby/Wardley No.1. Known as Wardley Coal Disposal Point, it opened on 14th May 1989. Here Co-CoDE no.56119 is leaving on a test train on 25th May 1989. (I.S.Carr)

PELAW JUNCTION

86. This shows Pelaw Junction before the construction of the Tyne Wear Metro. The Leamside line is coming in from the right. The line to Sunderland is in the centre with the site of the second Pelaw station and the line to South Shields curving to the left. It is 17th May 1959 and class A3 4-6-2 no.60074 *Harvester* is on a Whit Sunday Leeds to Newcastle excursion. (I.S.Carr)

87. In 1981 tracklaying on the flyover to take Metro trains over the Leamside and Sunderland lines was underway. 0-6-0DE WL3 Brush BT803 of 1977 was on a Metro works train on 4th November as the up "Aberdonian" High Speed Train is diverted via the Leamside line. Pelaw Junction's modern signal box was closed in 1980 and the area other than the Metro came under the Gateshead box until replaced by the Tyneside IECC at Chaytor Bank, Gateshead in April 1991. (I.S.Carr)

PELAW

XXVI. Counting the Tyne Wear Metro station, there have been four stations at Pelaw on three sites. The site of the first station's only platform was between FP and FB by the junction with the Pelaw Main waggonway. This was used between 1839 and 1857. The 1896 map shows the second station with construction underway for the third station which was, and still is, a large island platform. The station was known as Pelaw Main until January 1886.

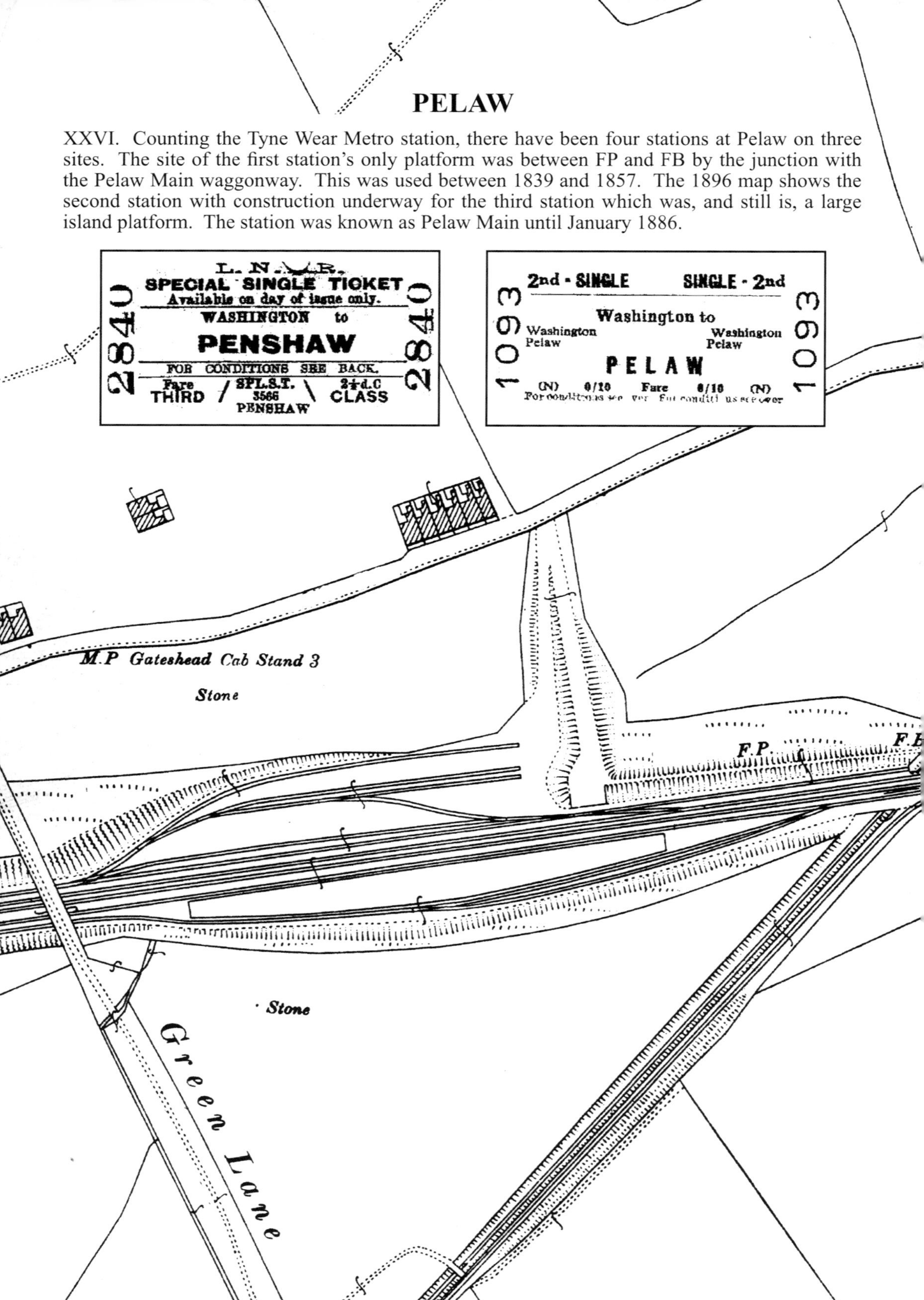

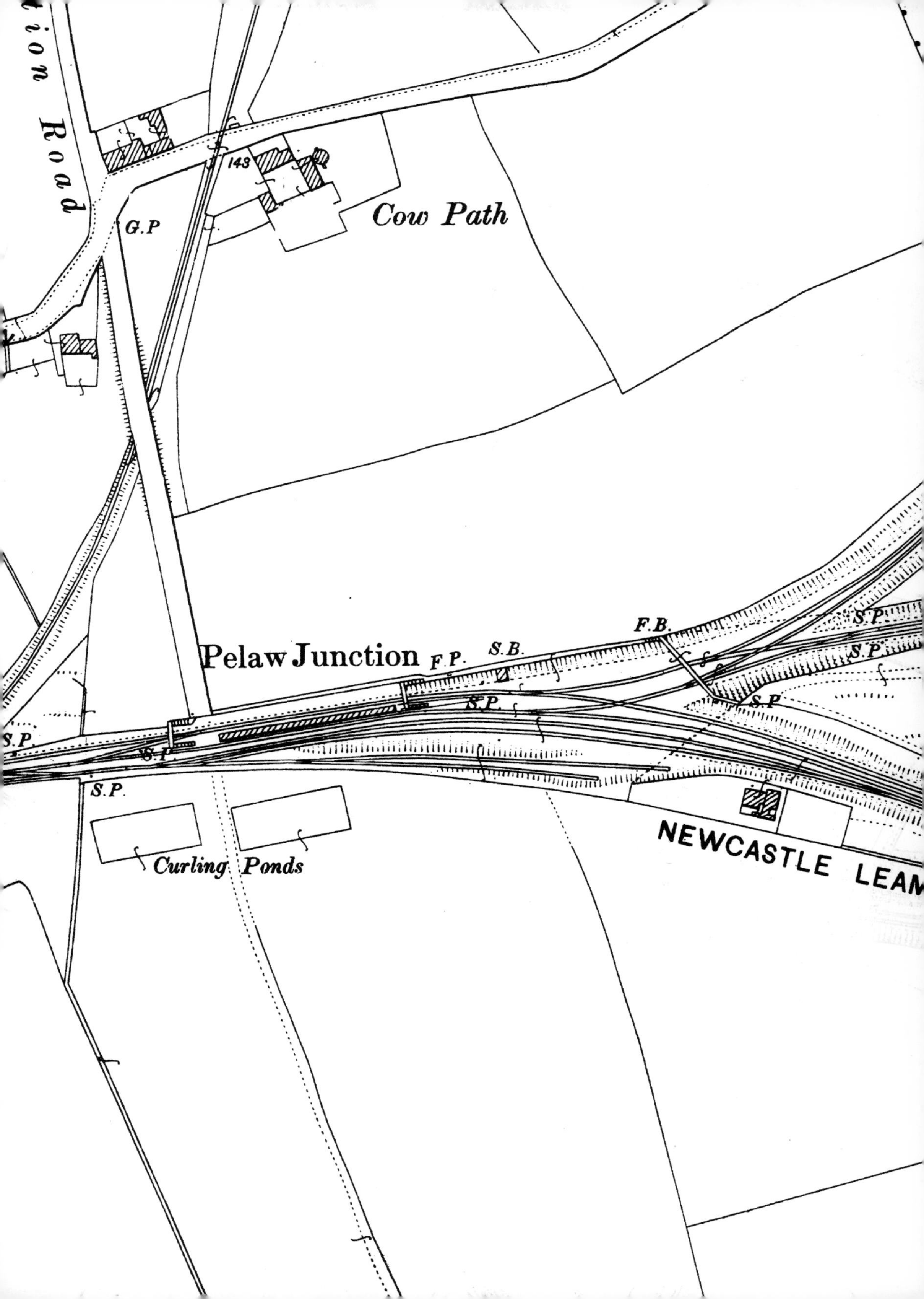
tion Road
143
Cow Path
G.P
Pelaw Junction
F.P.
S.B.
F.B.
S.P.
S.P
S.P
S.P.
S.P
S.P.
Curling Ponds
NEWCASTLE LEAM

88. The third Pelaw station is in all its NER glory. Behind the station is one of the Co-operative Wholesale Society (CWS) factories which were built between the Shields Road and the railway from 1902 onwards. There were factories for drugs, clothing, quilts and bedding, cabinet making, engineering and printing. (Lens of Sutton coll.)

89. The photographer is looking east from the Green Lane overbridge. Access to the island platform is by the covered footbridge. Besides the platform signal box there is an elevated cabin beyond the footbridge. A coal train hauled by NER class P3 0-6-0 (BR J27) is waiting for the signal. In the foreground is a class T2 0-8-0 (BR class Q6). On the left is the goods yard and access to the CWS sidings. (G.Nairn coll.)

90. This is the CWS Cabinet and Upholstery factory at Pelaw and the western end of the goods yard in about 1911. 'Pelaw Polish' was a well known brand from 1912 onwards. In WWII, the factory made gliders and aircraft parts. Most of the factories closed by 1980, though the printing works survived to 1993 and the shirt factory to the new millennium. (G.Nairn coll.)

91. No part-made or finished goods were used in the cabinet factory. The furniture making process started with the arrival of logs by rail. The works electric crane is posed on its embankment and a selection of NER wagons are below. The approach bridge to the station can be seen under the log. (Beamish Museum)

92. A snowy December 27th in 1962 shows a two coach electric train from South Shields about to depart for Newcastle. The line from Newcastle to South Shields was electrified in March 1938 using a 600v DC third rail system. The 15 2-EBP class electric multiple units were built by Eastleigh in 1954/55. One unit is preserved in Coventry. (I.S.Carr)

93. The future of the electrified lines on Tyneside was reviewed by BR in 1960 and on 7th January 1963 diesel multiple units replaced electric trains south of the Tyne with the 2-EBP stock going to the Southern Region. Metropolitan Cammell's Driving Trailer Composite no.E56050 leads Motor Brake Second no.E50225. Another economy has been the replacement of all the station buildings by a brick 'bus shelter'. (Lens of Sutton coll.)

94. The Tyne Wear Metro is not really considered in this book but as a counter to the depressing view in 93, this photograph taken from the footbridge shows the present Pelaw Metro station. The Metro built a new station in the place of the island platform and opened that in 1979. However, the buildings were restyled and re-opened on 22nd May 2006. (R.R.Darsley)

HEWORTH

95. There was no station at Heworth until the Tyne Wear Metro built its interchange station which comprises of a Metro train station, a BR station, a bus station and large car parks. Metrocar units 4090+4088 are arriving on the first day of trial running, the 19th June 1981. On the BR station side Co-CoDE no.37082 heads a down train of coal wagons. (I.S.Carr)

FELLING

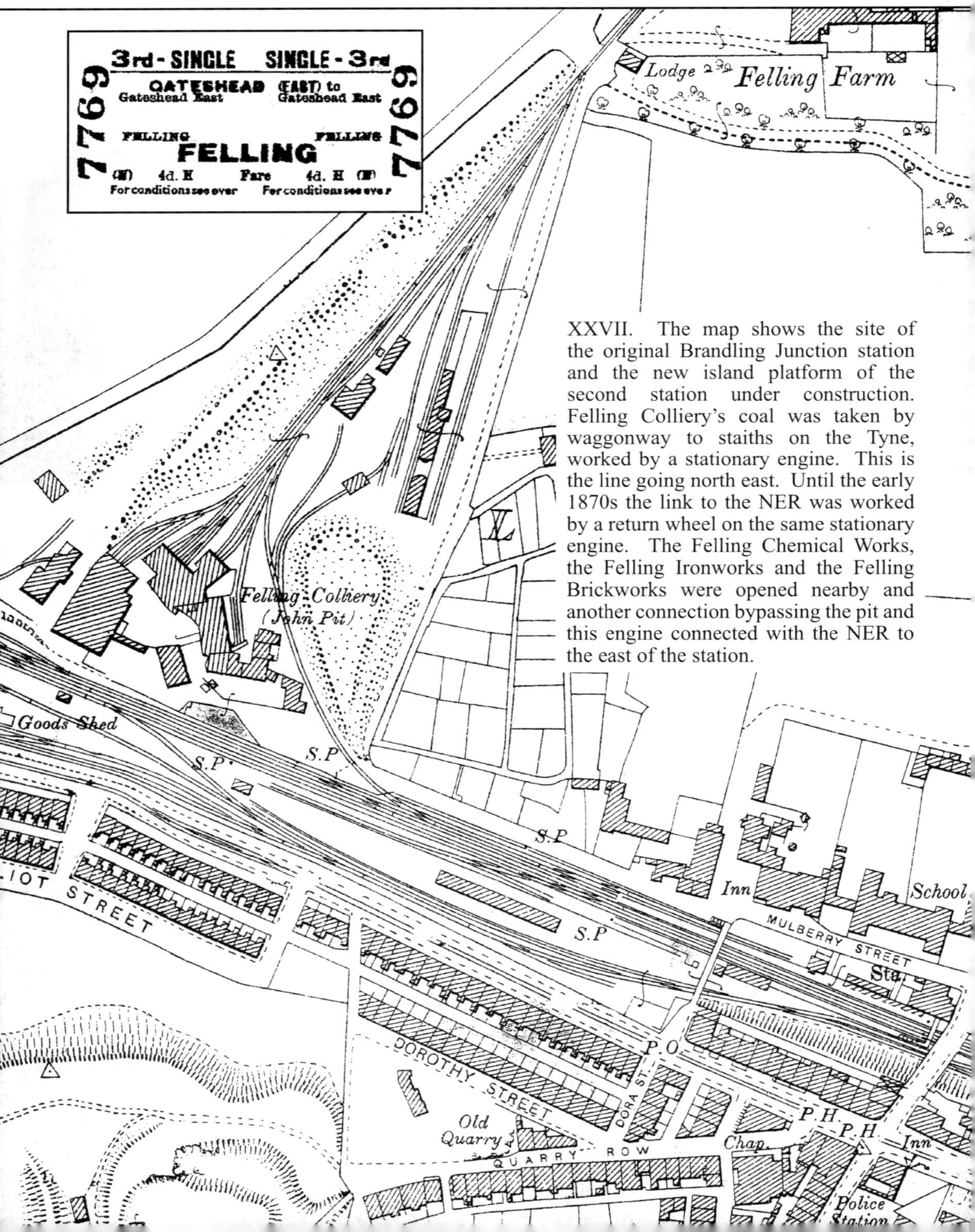

XXVII. The map shows the site of the original Brandling Junction station and the new island platform of the second station under construction. Felling Colliery's coal was taken by waggonway to staiths on the Tyne, worked by a stationary engine. This is the line going north east. Until the early 1870s the link to the NER was worked by a return wheel on the same stationary engine. The Felling Chemical Works, the Felling Ironworks and the Felling Brickworks were opened nearby and another connection bypassing the pit and this engine connected with the NER to the east of the station.

96. The Brandling Junction station is the small gabled building to the north of the running lines. It still exists as an office. It opened in 1842. More conventional NER wooden buildings were added later. This station closed in 1896 and in this 1950s picture, the platforms have been removed and some attempts at landscaping made. Behind is the Mulberry Street school. (Beamish Museum)

97. The 1896 station was a far grander affair with glass ends and large valances. However, the stone embankment and the general surroundings always made it seem a gloomy station – so gloomy that you can only just see a 2-EPB electric unit leaving for Pelaw. The whitewash and the neat flower pots show that somebody is trying. The present Metro station, though utilitarian, is more pleasing and was upgraded in 2008. (Stations UK)

98. Felling colliery added to the gloom. The pit had a long history. The first colliery opened in 1779 and closed in 1811 when a new shaft, the John pit, was sunk. In 1812 it was the place of the then worst mining disaster when 91 people lost their lives. This led directly to the invention of the miners' safety lamp. The pit was sold to John Bowes and partners in 1883 and was finally abandoned in December 1933. (Beamish Museum)

99. Another disaster at Felling occurred on 26th March 1907, when class R (later D20) 4-4-0 no.725 was derailed because the rails had buckled from the heat of the sun (in March!). The locomotive was working a train of LNWR stock on the Liverpool to Newcastle service. A deaf and dumb pedestrian on the overbridge pointed out the buckled rail to the driver of a passing steam roller. He ran along the top of the cutting to Heworth signal box but the signalman took no action. Eight passengers were seriously injured and two later died. (A.Betteney coll.)

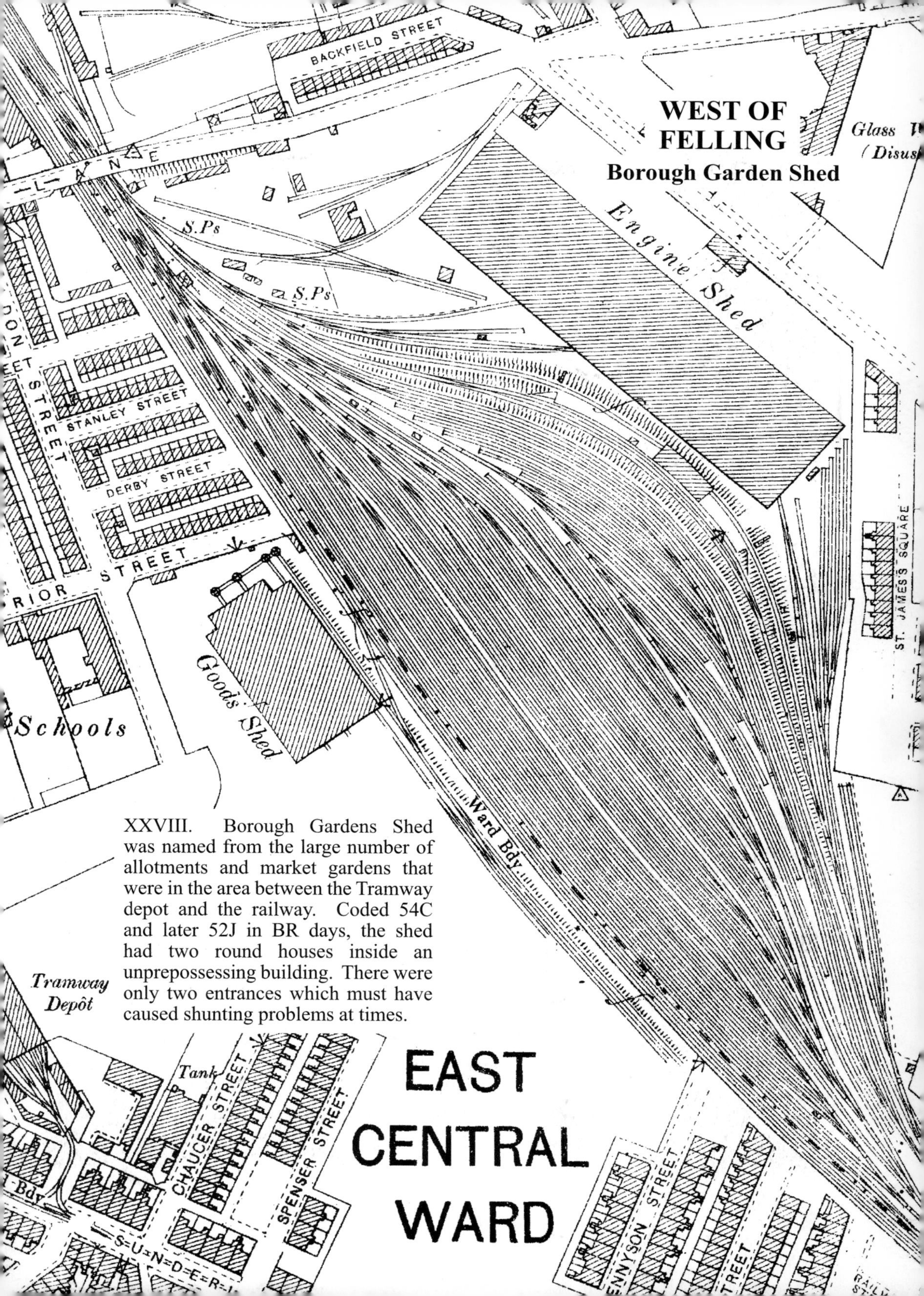

XXVIII. Borough Gardens Shed was named from the large number of allotments and market gardens that were in the area between the Tramway depot and the railway. Coded 54C and later 52J in BR days, the shed had two round houses inside an unprepossessing building. There were only two entrances which must have caused shunting problems at times.

100. The approach to the shed from the south east shows the storage roads parallel to St. James Square. Behind B1 class 4-6-0 no.61321 are two class J39 0-6-0 with another, no.64700, on its right and class Q6 0-8-0 no.63354 by the boundary wall. The scene is about 1956. (N.E.Stead coll.)

101. The long wall of the shed had a single exit road from one of the turntables. Class Q6 0-8-0 no.63384 is stabled with two others of the class. After Borough Gardens Shed was closed, it and the adjacent Gateshead Park Lane goods yard were used for the Tyneside Central Freight Depot (TCFD), which opened on 15th October 1963. That, with the Tyne Marshalling Yard replaced all the Newcastle and Gateshead goods yards. It closed on 8th July 1991 and only the office block remains. (N.E.Stead coll.)

102. This view from the cab of class A3 4-6-2 no.4472 Flying Scotsman was taken on the SLS/MLS Durham Coast Railtour of 7th September 1968. Borough Gardens shed was on the left under the approaching bridge. On the right are the sidings for the coal depot, later a Redland's materials yard, and for Close Works which included a large part of the former locomotive works of Chapman & Furneaux and of Black, Hawthorn & Co Ltd. Later the works was Armstrong Whitworth Rolls Ltd. Rail traffic ceased in 1970, when it became the Davy Roll Co Ltd. (I.S.Carr)

GREENESFIELD

103. Designed by George Townsend Andrews and constructed by Charles John Pearson, a leading Gateshead builder, the station was a terminus. Trains from Carlisle coming up the Redheugh incline from the west reversed into it. The station had a single platform, stepped so that there were different lines for arrival and departure but passengers did not have to cross the tracks. Greenesfield station was elegant as was Andrew's Gilesgate station. It opened 18th June 1844 and closed 30th August 1850. It was converted to the YNB loco repair shed by adding two more roof spans of similar design in 1851-2. The NER used it for the construction of new locomotives until 1910, though repairs continued to 1932. It reopened in the war and lasted to 1959. The station remained part of the workshop, with the hotel as offices until 1968. In 2008 only the shell of the hotel remained. (Gateshead Library)

THE GATESHEAD STATION OF THE NEWCASTLE-UPON-TYNE AND DARLINGTON RAILWAY.

The complete station frontage, recorded in Douglas's 'Records of Remarkable Events connected with the Borough of Gateshead', 1844. Gateshead Central Library.

GATESHEAD WORKS

104. No.1 Erecting shop inside Gateshead Works shows the Greenesfield station roof and awning tracery. The left hand wall is the platform side of the station buildings. This postcard was posted 11th December 1908. Under construction are NER class S (later class B13) 4-6-0s. These were the first 4-6-0 passenger locomotives in the country. Forty were built between 1899 and 1909 and one lasted in service stock until 1951. The works closed on 5th March 1959 but steam locomotive repairs continued until 1964. (R.Johnston/G.Nairn coll.)

GATESHEAD EAST

105. The Gateshead tram terminus was in Wellington Street and Gateshead East station with its elevated down platform is on the right. Tram no.41 to Heworth is about to turn right into Hills Street. In the background another tram is by the entrance to the High Level Bridge under an advertisement for Nestlé's milk. (R.Johnson/G.Nairn)

XXX. The first terminus of the Brandling Junction Railway, was at Oakwellgate. Originally there was a 1 in 23 incline from Oakwellgate to Redheugh and a self-acting incline plane down to the Gateshead Quayside. The new Gateshead station was built clinging to the viaduct that was the approach to the High Level bridge. Designed by John Dobson, it was renamed Gateshead East when Thomas Prosser designed and built Gateshead West for the Team Valley line (ECML) in 1868.

106. NER class R (D20) 4-4-0 no.1236, built in Gateshead in 1907, is heading towards Felling through Gateshead East station. No.1236 was withdrawn in 1947 as LNER no.2393. The down platform was much longer than the up platform, possibly as an emergency platform if the High Level bridge should be blocked. The date is around 1930. (Stations UK)

107. Both up and down platforms are shown in this photograph of 17th April 1955. The wooden platform surface lasted until the station was closed in 1970. The conductor rail for the 600v DC electric line to South Shields is clearly visible as class A8 4-6-2T no.69887 arrives on a train from Sunderland. (J.W.Armstrong Trust)

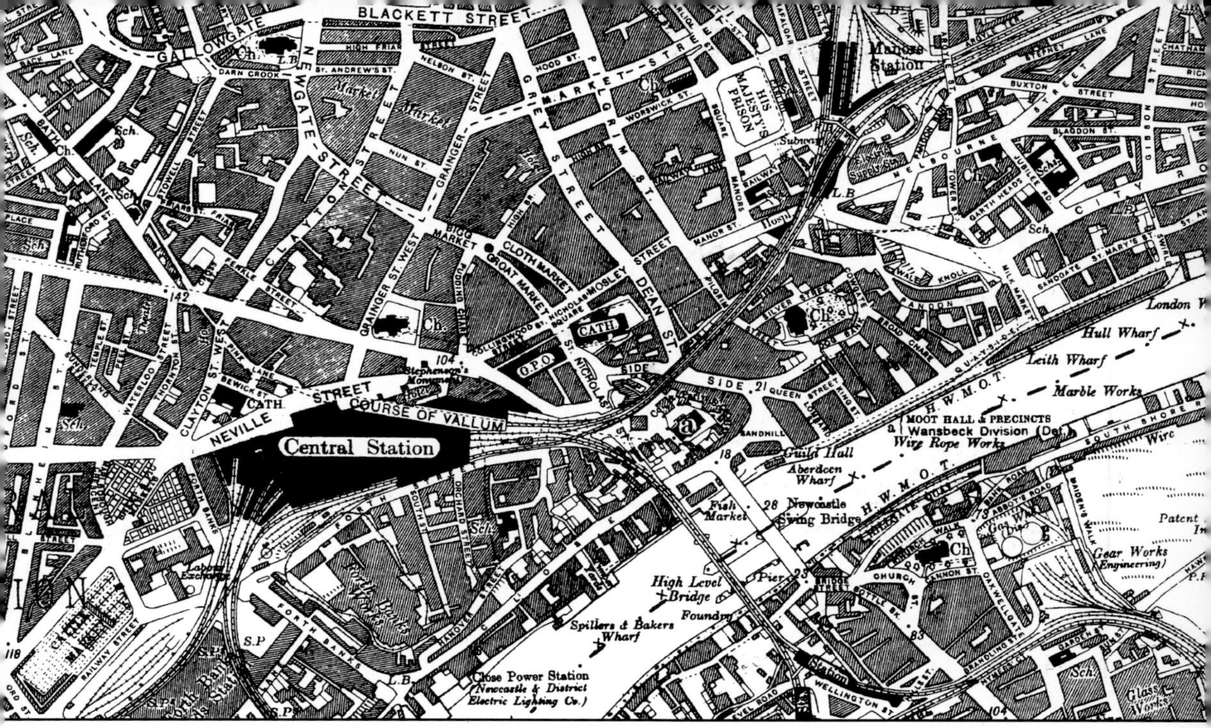

XXXI. Gateshead has a population of 105,000 and Newcastle of 276,000. In 2008 they are being branded as a joint city with major developments along the riverside. On the 6" to 1 mile map of 1896, our line comes in lower right. The coal and lime sidings fan out to the north on stone arches – now built into the Sage Music Centre car park. The area by the Patent Hammer Inn was the site of Gateshead Park Ironworks and is now another major development area. Gateshead East station is prominent before the line crosses the High Level Bridge into Newcastle Central station, the terminus of our journey.

High Level Bridge

108. The road and rail bridge was opened by Queen Victoria on 28th September 1849, though passengers as well as goods trains had travelled across on a temporary wooden viaduct from 29th August 1848. George Stephenson died on 12th August 1848 and there was a proposal to name it 'Stephenson Bridge'. Both entrances to the road deck were to have three magnificent triumphant masonry arches with a statue of George Stephenson on the Newcastle side but these ideas went in the economies following Hudson's downfall. (Ward Philipson/R.R.Darsley coll.)

109. The bridge is 1338ft long and 40ft wide with six major arches. The railway tracks are 112ft above high water mark. This is the view from the Gateshead end with the keep of the 'new castle' and the flying spire of St Nicholas Cathedral in line. An 0-6-0T of NER class E (later J71) is waiting to cross the bridge having probably come off Gateshead shed. (Beamish Museum)

110. In 1955-59 the wooden rail deck was replaced with steel troughs and the way beams replaced by conventional ballasted track. The electric trains to South Shields ran from 1938 to 1963. Here a class 101 DMU replacement is crossing towards Newcastle on 12th August 1977. The eastern track was for 'up' southbound trains, the two other tracks were 'down' with the western one for freight only. (R.R.Darsley)

111. A class 220 DMU is crossing under the wires on 6th January 2005. When the bridge was electrified, special Fine Arts Commission designed masts were used and the number of tracks was reduced to two. In February 2005 the roadway, which is hung from the rail deck on wrought iron tension rods, was closed for repairs which finished in May 2008. Network Rail spent £42m to give the bridge an extra 60 years life. May Gurney were their main contractors. Road traffic is southbound public transport only, and limited to 20mph. (R.R.Darsley)

NEWCASTLE CENTRAL

For more maps and photographs of Newcastle, see ***Darlington to Newcastle via Durham*** **nos 111-120 and** ***Newcastle to Hexham*** **nos 1-12 and 118-120.**

112. Reputed to be the largest in the world, the east end diamond crossings came from the 1893/4 track quadrupling and reorganisation of the station. In 1904 it was simplified; in 1912 high steel manganese rails were used. The sets were renewed in 1924, 1938, 1949, 1956 and 1963. In 1970 the rail shape reverted to the 1893 bullhead design. In 1991, with electrification, it was simplified to three double slip switch diamond crossings. The locomotives are, left to right, class C (J21) 0-6-0, class R (D20) 4-4-0 and class E (J71) 0-6-0T. (Newcastle Central Libraries)

113. Newcastle Central station, designed by John Dobson, was opened 29th August 1850, but the portico was not completed until 1861. The three original train shed spans were curved. Between 1894 and 1895 two additional spans to the south were added. The fourth span was curved to the north but straight to the south and the fifth span was straight. Three class C Newcastle Corporation tramcars were passing in Neville Street in this 1904 photograph. (A.Betteney coll.)

114. Both Newcastle Corporation and Gateshead & District tramways stopped at their sides of the High Level Bridge until its roadway was strengthened in 1922. At the east end of Central station it was possible to see trams of both companies as they worked joint routes such as that to Low Fell. In this 1940s picture, Gateshead car no.30 is ahead of Newcastle's car no.80. Newcastle changed from trams to trolleybuses in 1949. Some single deck rebuilt class C trams like no.80 were sold to Gateshead whose trams were replaced by buses in 1951. (Beamish Museum)

115. Here is the concourse of Central station looking east in 1903. At this time all north-south trains were still reversing at the station. Behind the office cabin are the suburban platforms that were used eventually by the NER electric trains to the coast, north and south of the river. (Beamish Museum)

116. This viewpoint seems to be from one of the NER famous signal gantries (and not from the castle keep). We are looking towards the east end of the Central station. A class R (D20) 4-4-0 is leaving with an up express either via Leamside or Sunderland and an NER coastal electric train of 1904 stock is heading for Monkseaton via South Gosforth. (D.G.Charlton)

117. Class A4 4-6-2 no.60009 *Union of South Africa* on the up "Flying Scotsman" is passing under Newcastle no.1 signal box in January 1949. In 1906 the signal boxes were converted to electro-pneumatic control – there had been 613 manual levers! Box 1, 2 and 3 were replaced in 1959 by an electric control box in the centre of the station and in 1999 this was replaced by the Tyneside IECC. (A.W.V.Mace/Milepost 92½)

118. The view south from platform 10 included the carriage sidings and the freight avoiding lines. Austerity 8F 2-8-0 no.90451 passes by on 20th June 1955 with a through mixed freight. The locomotive is ex-works from Darlington and its workmanlike condition contrasts markedly with that of the station roof. (N.E.Stead coll.)

119. Type 4 Co-CoDE no.1832 is on a northbound express and the Metro-Cammell DMU is for South Shields on 28th August 1972. The station awnings have lost their attractiveness and this was not restored until 1989. The suburban platforms closed with the opening of the Metro on 11th August 1980. The area became the station car park. (T.Heavyside)

120. In the 1989 refurbishment, the simple grandeur of the roof was brought back into view. The ticket office was built in the form of a futuristic glass pod. In the 2007 National Rail Awards, the station won 'Best Station Award' in the large station category and 'Best Station Overall'. That was a fitting tribute to the staff, especially those of GNER who worked in the ticket office in the final year of their franchise. (R.R.Darsley)

Gateshead Libraries
Gateshead
Council
Gateshead Libraries

LANDMARK JUDGMENTS that changed India

LANDMARK JUDGMENTS that changed India

Justice Asok K. Ganguly

RUPA

Published by
Rupa Publications India Pvt. Ltd 2015
7/16, Ansari Road, Daryaganj
New Delhi 110002

Sales Centres:
Allahabad Bengaluru Chennai
Hyderabad Jaipur Kathmandu
Kolkata Mumbai

ISBN: 978-81-291-3508-7

Second impression 2016

10 9 8 7 6 5 4 3 2

Printed and bound in India by Replika Press Pvt. Ltd.

To my parents

CONTENTS

PREFACE

A Just Social Order

When writing about the Constitution, one has to take on the duty of familiarizing readers with what it is all about. It is true that these days the noise about the Constitution and Constitution courts is far more than what it used to be, say, fifteen years ago. Even then, the concept of a Constitution is shrouded in mystery for most people. To dispel this, it is worthwhile to start with a very acceptable and workable definition of a Constitution by A. King: '[A Constitution is] *The set of the most important rules and common understandings in any given country that regulate[s] the relations among that country's governing institutions and also the relationship between those governing institutions and the people of that country.*'[1]

'People of the country' obviously means the common people, who are always high on the agenda for any Constitution, at least on paper. Our Indian Constitution, and the oldest written Constitution of the world, the American Constitution, start with the famous expression 'We the people'. Thus, people occupy centre stage in the constitutional scheme of any modern democracy. Therefore, the Constitution should not be something alien to the people; rather, they are the most important dramatis personae in the arena of constitutional governance. Our Constitution is, therefore, for the people and of the people, even though it may not strictly be by the people.

As soon as we talk of people, we have to think of their rights.

Rights are the products of historical experiences of the people themselves and they have been earned through struggle, strife and sacrifice.

In India, the demand for a written Constitution was made more than a century and two decades ago, in 1895 by Bal Gangadhar Tilak in his Constitution of India Bill, 1895. About three decades later, it was reiterated by Sir Tej Bahadur Sapru. As leaders in our freedom struggle, both felt the pulse of the masses and in their demand for constitutional governance, they were actually voicing a popular cause.

Netaji Subhas Chandra Bose, who was the first amongst our national leaders to demand swaraj (or self-rule), in his Haripura Presidential address delivered in February 1938 in the fifty-first session of the Indian National Congress, clarified the Congress policy on fundamental rights. Even though Bose was not a member of the Constituent Assembly, the policy formulated by him as Congress president[2] bears striking resemblance with the chapter on fundamental rights presently in our Constitution.

Ultimately, Bose's ideas were shaped by Pandit Jawaharlal Nehru, Dr Bhimrao Ramji Ambedkar and various other luminaries, who were highly inspired by and fought for these noble ideas, which form the core of our national struggle for freedom. That is why, in our Constitution, one of the fundamental duties of our citizens is to cherish and follow the noble ideas which inspired our national struggle for freedom[3]. Our fundamental rights for both citizens and persons can be best appreciated if they are read conjointly with the fundamental duties mentioned in Article 51A of the Constitution. Therefore, apart from it being the product of a national upsurge and struggle, the very framing of the Constitution is a revolution in itself. It is invariably directed against the authority of the state, be it a monarchy or a colonial power or a democratically elected government.

The Constitution seeks to protect the basic rights of the people and the spirit of human liberty against encroachment by the state. Hence one discerns some conflicts between the rule of law on the one hand—which very often matures into due process of law in view of judicial review provided under the Constitution—and the authority of state-building on the other. This tension of state-building often threatens the concept of individual liberty and freedom in view of the authoritarianism of the rule of law. It is here that the judiciary, thanks to its independence from state control, strikes the proper balance between the contradicting trends. That is why independence of the judiciary is an inalienable attribute in every Constitution, so that the Constitution may have both authoritative and legitimate ends for the welfare of the people and provide for them opportunities to enjoy a quality of life which is conducive to the development of the faculties of even the humblest of citizens.

In this context, the balance of rights between private persons and public bodies must be upheld. Both are subject to rule of law. A private person may do anything which is not prohibited by law. In the absence of a legal bar, his actions need no justification from the law. For public bodies the position is not the same. This has been explained with remarkable lucidity below:

> A public body has no heritage of legal rights which it enjoys for its own sake; at every turn, all of its dealings constitute the fulfillments of duties which it owes to others; indeed, it exits for no other purpose. I would say that a public body enjoys no rights properly so called, it may in various contexts be entitled to insist that this or that procedure be followed, whether by a person affected by its decision or by a superior body having power over it; it may come to court as a judicial review applicant to complain of the decision of some other public authority; it may maintain

> a private law action to enforce a contract or otherwise protect its property. But in every such instance, and no doubt many others where a public body asserts claims, or defences in court it does so, [sic] if it acts in good faith, only to vindicate better performance of the duties for whose fulfillment it exists. It is in the sense that it has no rights of its own, no axe to grind beyond its public responsibility; a responsibility which defines its purpose and justifies its existence. Under our laws, this is true of every public body. The rule is necessary to protect the people from arbitrary interference by those set in power over them.[4]

This clear statement admirably sums up the concept of rule of law in all democratic countries and is very relevant in the Indian context. It meshes with the vision in the Preamble of our Constitution, which places the dignity of the individual on the same footing as the unity and integrity of the nation, thus rejecting the concept of a totalitarian state.

So it is most crucial in such a state to usher in a just 'social order' which is 'fundamental in the governance of the country'.[5]

A just social order cannot exist without inclusive and sustainable economic growth. In the last twenty years, in terms of the growth of gross domestic product (GDP)—which was about 6 per cent in the 1990s and rose to 7 per cent in the first decade of this century—it has to be admitted that India is possibly the world's second fastest growing economy after China. However, the difficulty lies elsewhere. It is accepted by all impartial bodies that the societal reach of economic progress in India is remarkably limited. The distribution of income has not been fair and there is no rise in the real wage of workers in view of spiralling inflation. All essential services like health, schooling, sanitation, drinking water, etc. have become scarce, costlier and beyond the reach of the common man. In these matters India is possibly the second worst among the South Asian countries, being only ahead of strife-ridden Pakistan. Though India has progressed further on per capita income than countries such as Bangladesh, Sri Lanka, Nepal and Bhutan, so far as social indicators are concerned, it is found deficient. This sordid situation has come about primarily due to erroneous prioritization of economic policy. Admittedly, the neo-liberalist economic policy of the government has been at variance with the constitutional goal of equal society, which aims at preventing the concentration of wealth in a few hands.

We cannot afford to forget that the formation of a welfare state motivated India's freedom struggle, based as it was on a vision of swaraj. This was achieved by the silent revolution of framing a Constitution which, in the words of Pandit Nehru, 'will free India through a new Constitution, to feed the starving people and clothe the naked masses and give every Indian fullest opportunity of his capacity'[6]. This explains the radical message of social and economic justice in our Constitution, starting from the grand design of the Preamble and running through the entire gamut of the provisions in the fundamental rights and directive principles.

This was pressed home by an amendment to the Constitution[7] in 1976 by which the words 'socialist' and 'secular' were added to the Preamble along with the pre-amendment words, 'sovereign democratic republic', and the expression 'unity of the nation' was amended to 'unity and integrity of the nation'. Till today, this is the only amendment to the Preamble.

Thus, what was latent during the framing of the Constitution was made patent by these amendments. The message of such amendments must be fully cherished to mobilize strong public opinion in our democratic polity to guide and monitor the governance of the country, in which economic development is of the essence. Economic development and empowerment of the people must be compatible with constitutional values, which are the foundational blocks of our civilized society. The judiciary, by its interpretation of the Constitution, plays a significant role in changing the destiny of the nation and which it has done remarkably, as we will see in the chapters of this book.

I have also tried to show that both our Constitution and the pre-existing legal regime are based on the broad principles of the English common law. However, over the years, they have absorbed and been enriched by Indian traditions and verdicts of our judiciary.

Eminent jurist Fali S. Nariman very aptly describes it[8]: 'Originally an English transplant with Anglo-Saxon roots, the legal system in India has grown over the years, nourished in Indian soil; what was intended to be an English oak has turned into a large, sprawling Indian banyan whose serial roots have descended to the ground to become new trunks.'

This huge banyan tree of our legal system must give shelter to us, including the humblest and weakest person, in our pluralistic society.

NOTES

1. Anthony King, *The British Constitution*, (Oxford University Press, 2009), p. 3.
2. *Congress President's Speeches, Articles and Letters (January 1938-May 1939)*, (Netaji Research Bureau), pp. 9-10.
3. Constitution of India, Article 51A(b).
4. *Regina v. Somerset County Council, Exparte*, reported in 1995 *WLR* 1037.
5. Articles 37 and 38 of the Constitution.
6. *Constituent Assembly Debates*, Vol. 1, p. 316.
7. Constitution (42nd Amendment) Act, 1976, w.e.f. 3 January 1977.
8. Fali S. Nariman, *India's Legal System: Can it be saved*, (Penguin, 2006), p. 206.

FOREWORD

Our democratic Constitution, as expected, has given due emphasis to the concept of separation of powers, in which apart from the legislature and the executive, the judiciary occupies a very important positions, specially in the important task of not only deciding inter-party disputes but also in the exposition of the Constitutional and legal principles by the Supreme Court of India, which will be binding on the High Courts and the judiciary as a whole as well as on all citizens of India. In due course, our apex court has dealt with several fundamental concepts of our constitutional law, which need to be duly studied and appreciated.

In this respect, a great service has been rendered by Hon'ble Justice Asok Kumar Ganguly in his treatise titled *Landmark Judgments that Changed India*.

The credentials of Justice Ganguly are well-known. He has been one of the legal luminaries of our country and one of our eminent judges, who has added laurels to the judiciary by his well-considered exposition of constitutional law, in which he has an abiding interest.

In this book, he has discussed various landmark judgments of the Supreme Court, dealing with different fundamental concepts of constitutional law, which, as the author, he has dealt with very lucidly and in a manner which will be readable not only to lawyers but also to the discerning sections of our citizens.

Dealing with the evolution of the 'basic structure' doctrine in the backdrop of constitutional values, Justice Ganguly has analysed some of the important judgments of the Supreme Court with an incisive approach. He has dealt with the development of constitutional law on the concept of basic structure and on the power of Parliament with admirable precision and with a sense of history in the development of constitutional jurisprudence in India.

In different chapters of his book, the author has dealt with the evolving mosaic of constitutional interpretation in the several judgments of the Supreme Court to emphasize that the judicial power of the apex court has strengthened the roots of democracy in India.

The author has also dealt with a series of decisions of the Supreme Court endorsing affirmative state action by way of reverse discrimination by giving protection in favour of the Scheduled Caste and Scheduled Tribe candidates in the state service.

With his deep knowledge of law and of our Constitution, Justice Ganguly has covered, in a short compass, the role of the Supreme Court in the development of our constitutional law in the areas of personal liberty, human rights, constitutional amendments and the core concept of judicial review with admirable clarity.

I must compliment the author also for dealing with the well-known dissent of Justice Khanna in the case of *ADM Jabalpur v. S.S. Shukla Etc. Etc.* and his contribution to the cause of personal liberty in the dark days of Emergency.

I am confident that the treatise will be of considerable interest to everyone—students, academicians, lawyers and all those who are interested in following the absorbing development of the constitutional law in our country.

Somnath Chatterjee

INTRODUCTION

Concept of Limited Government, Fundamental Rights, Natural Law, Higher Law and the Impact on Judicial Review of Constitutional Courts

The very concept of judgments bringing about wide-ranging social changes presupposes that the courts not only interpret laws, but that in the process of interpretation they also declare laws, which has the effect of making laws. This process of constitutional interpretation, better known in constitutional parlance as judicial review, is inevitable in India, where we have a written Constitution with a chapter on fundamental rights. These features of the Constitution automatically lead to the concept of a limited government.

Our Constitution is based on three fundamentals, which form the core of constitutionalism. They are:

(1) A written Constitution
(2) A chapter on fundamental rights
(3) Limited government

The concept of a limited government is the obvious corollary of two other fundamental tenets. This concept is based on the postulate that the powers of governmental authorities are limited by law. Neither the executive nor the legislature can act beyond the limits of the law.

Article 73 of the Constitution clearly stipulates that, subject to the Constitution, the executive power of the union shall extend to matters in respect of which Parliament has the power to make laws. Article 162 of the Constitution subjects the executive power of the state to the same limitations. The executive power is thus coterminous with legislative power. That is why it is said in all representative democracies that the government is one of laws and not of men. This principle was first incorporated in the Constitution of Massachusetts, 1780[1] and was subsequently followed in the celebrated decision in *Marbury v. Madison*. Chief Justice Marshall, delivering the judgment, expressly said: 'The Government of the United States has been emphatically termed a government of laws and not of men'.[2] This doctrine introduced in American jurisprudence has been phrased beautifully in the words of Woodrow Wilson: 'The history of liberty is a history of the limitation of governmental power, not the increase of it.'[3]

In the Indian context also, any talk of the Dicean concept of omnipotence of Parliament is totally misplaced. The parliamentary system, which is introduced in our Constitution, subjects Parliament to various limitations. One of them is the control exercised by the Constitution over the distribution of legislative power. In view of Article 245 of the Constitution, Part XI thereof provides that Parliament may make laws, subject to 'the other provisions in the Constitution'. This limitation has many facets and unfolds itself in the form of subject-wise demarcation between the union and the states in the matter of making laws. This is specifically spelt out in Article 246 and its various sub-articles which talk of three lists—union, concurrent and state. There are other provisions in this part, mandating which law will prevail in case of any repugnancy between union and state laws. And our Constitution, in view of its dominant unitary character, has leaned in favour of the union laws. However, it is clear that in its own field each legislature is supreme. The next limitation on the power is already indicated in Article 245: 'the other provisions of the Constitution'. The other provisions would obviously include Part III of the Constitution, which is the chapter on fundamental rights.

The expression 'fundamental right' was first used in the US Supreme Court by Justice Washington, sitting on circuit, in the case of *Corfield v. Coryell*.[4] The learned judge explained the concept by saying:

> [W]e feel no hesitation in confining these expressions to those privileges and immunities which are, in their nature, fundamental, which belong, of right, to the citizens of all free governments and which have, at all times, been enjoyed by the citizens of the several States which compose this Union…[5]

But it was not until 1937 that Justice Curdozo of the US Supreme Court formulated for the first time the concept of fundamental rights as a doctrine in *Palko v. Connecticut* and held that some rights are fundamental as they 'represent the very essence of a scheme of ordered liberty… principles of justice so rooted in the traditions and conscience of our people as to be marked as fundamental'.[6]

The framers of the Indian Constitution represented the people of India who were suffering from oppression, deprivation and discrimination for about two centuries of colonial rule. They realized that a chapter on fundamental rights is an essential safeguard against the recurrence of such an experience in the future. The Americans did the same after succeeding in their struggle for independence against British domination. While referring to the Bill of Rights in the Indian Constitution, Ivor Jennings pointed to these features, saying: 'The Indian reaction (in enacting the Bill of Rights) like the American reaction, is in a large measure a product of the British rule'.[7] In the Constituent Assembly debates in India, a sub-committee on fundamental rights deliberated on the contents of these rights and the distinguished members of that august body knew that fundamental rights were the basic human rights, without which a free democracy was impossible. A number of the members of the assembly expressed their opinions as these rights being permanent and inalienable.

Dr B.R. Ambedkar talked of these rights as principles that have become 'the silent, inarticulate premise of our outlook'[8].

Dr S. Radhakrishnan, participating in the debates over these rights, said, 'The declaration, which we make today, is of the nature of a pledge to our own people and a pact with the civilized world.'[9]

The reasons why fundamental rights are in the nature of natural rights and why these rights cannot be changed by law, and all laws made by the state have to respect these rights, have been explained by the American Supreme Court in the case of *Board of Education v. Barnette*:

> …the very purpose of a Bill of Rights was to withdraw certain subjects from the vicissitudes of political controversy, to place them beyond the reach of majorities… and to establish them as legal principles to be applied by the court. One's rights to life, liberty and property, to free speech, a free press, freedom of worship and assembly, and other fundamental rights may not be submitted to the vote; they depend on the outcome of no elections.[10]

On fundamental rights there are some misconceptions, of which the most widespread is that these rights are granted by the state. In fact, fundamental rights are nothing but natural rights. These are based on the primary instincts of human beings, as shaped by their inherent perception of what is right and wrong. These rights are universal in all ages and inhere in every human being. The first corollary of this theory is that these rights, being inherent in human beings, existed even before the evolution of the state.

However, with the growth of the state by way of social control, the ambit of these inherent rights is limited by the collective interests of the society or state in which a person lives. Therefore, any civilized state will have to recognize these rights, not in an unbridled form, but regulated in the larger and collective interests of the state. As it is often said, I have a right to swing my arm, but I must not hurt someone's nose while doing so. It is on these postulates that we now have six basic rights which are in the nature of natural human rights and are grouped as fundamental rights in Part III under Article 19(1)(a), (b), (c), (d), (e) and (g), but they are all subject to reasonable restrictions imposed on them by laws on certain grounds enumerated in articles 19(2), (3), (4), (5) and (6). Therefore, these fundamental rights are not granted by the state or the legislature, but are natural rights of human beings and have been recognized by the state as fundamental but not absolute, and the power of the legislature is subject to these rights. Most of these fundamental rights under Part III of our Constitution are natural law rights.

The second question which has to be clarified about the nature of fundamental rights is whether these rights are antecedent to the formation of the state as inalienable rights of human beings. They are the irreducible, minimum conditions for the free existence of man. These rights stand above the law of the land and, being universal in nature, are common to civilized society everywhere in the world. Thus, they are known as higher laws.

About the concept of these natural rights which are enumerated as fundamental rights, Alexander Hamilton had said long ago, in 1775: 'The sacred rights of mankind are not to be rummaged for, among old parchments or musty records. They are written, as with a sun beam, in the whole *volume* of human nature, by the hand of the divinity itself; and can never be erased or obscured by mortal power.'[11]

John Adams, the second president of the United States, articulated the principles behind these rights succinctly:

> You have rights antecedent to all earthly government—rights that cannot be repealed or restrained by human laws—rights derived from the great Legislature of the Universe... British liberties are not the grants of princes or parliaments, but original rights, conditions of original contracts coequal with prerogative and coeval with government.

There is thus a distinction between natural rights and civil rights. Civil rights are those rights which are available to human beings in view of his/her being a member of a civil society. But every 'civil right', as rightly pointed out by Thomas Paine, 'has for its foundation some natural right pre-existing in the individual, but to the enjoyment of which his individual power is not, in all cases, sufficiently competent'.[12]

Civil rights being man-made are thus distinct from natural rights. This dichotomy has been tersely put in *Jowitt's Dictionary of English Law* by defining natural rights as 'rules derived from God, reason or nature, as distinct from man-made law'.[13]

William Blackstone explained the distinction and correlation between natural law and civil law or man-made law with great clarity.

> This law of nature, being coeval with mankind, and dictated by God himself, is of course superior in obligation to any other. It is binding over all the globe in all countries and all times; no human laws are of any validity, if contrary to this; and such of them as are valid derive all their force and all their authority, mediately or immediately, from this original.[14]

Natural laws over the centuries have made an invaluable contribution to the development of positive law in many countries. The origin and development of equity in England owed much to natural law. It is this concept of natural law which influenced the drafting of the Constitution of the United States and of various states. It is the starting point of modern international law and international conventions, covenants and declarations.

This is the concept of constitutionalism with limited government under a written Constitution. It is clear from what is discussed above that a written Constitution has its philosophical roots in the idea of natural law and is based on the hypothesis of a 'higher law'. This concept of a higher law became very pronounced with the adoption, in 1787, of the American Constitution, which is possibly the first written Constitution of a confederation in the true sense of the term. After that the democratic and the civilized world understood that a written Constitution has to always be in tune with democratic principles, as it incorporates in an organic law the fruits of natural law, which are the inalienable rights of human beings. These natural laws are to act as limitations upon the organs of the state and cannot be left at the mercy of the majority in a Parliament.

In our country, after full deliberations and debates in the Constituent Assembly, the written Constitution was adopted with a provision for judicial review and limited government. It will be an antithesis of constitutionalism in India if, ignoring these basic features, the concept of parliamentary sovereignty is asserted. This has been laid down by the Supreme Court in the case of *Golaknath* to the following effect: 'No authority under the Constitution is supreme: the Constitution is supreme and all the authorities function under the supreme law of the land.'[15]

Insofar as England was concerned, its parliamentary supremacy rests on the good sense of the people in the system of responsible government. These principles were aptly summed up by Lord Wright in *Liversidge v. Anderson*: 'In the Constitution of this country there are no guaranteed rights. The safeguard of the British liberty is in the good sense of the people and in the system of representative and responsible government which has been evolved.'[16]

However, subsequent opinion of the jurists in England leant towards imposing restrictions on parliamentary supremacy. In the Hamlyn lecture delivered by Richard O'Sullivan, one of the senior-most king's counsel of England, titled 'The Inheritance of the Common Law' (1950), it is said:

> It is perhaps not good for the health of a political community that the acts of the Legislature should be allowed to prevail over fundamental moral and ethical principles. Nor is it good that the people of any realm should (even in theory) be without any constitutional guarantee of fundamental human rights.[17]

The learned author reiterated the same position further:

> It is, you may think, a little odd that the people who gave to the world the inheritance of the Common Law should be compelled to rely upon a Declaration of Convention of International Law for the safeguarding of their fundamental human rights. One way or another it is essential that these rights shall be safeguarded.[18]

The position in England substantially changed with the coming into force of the Human Rights Act (HRA), 1998, on 2 October 2000. It is one of the twists of history, a quirk of fate, that the said act came into effect in England on 2 October, the birthday of Mahatma Gandhi, who fought for the cause of human rights in India during the British rule.

However, the act has brought about a sea change in the administration of justice in England. About the impact of the HRA on British jurisprudence, Lord Irvine said: 'No measure of law reform has had such wide and profound effects on administrative law as has the HRA.'[19]

When HRA came into force, Jack Straw, the home secretary of England, described it as 'the first Bill of Rights this country has seen for three centuries'.[20] Section 3 of the act enjoins that the courts should interpret all laws compatibly with conventional rights 'as far as possible'. Section 4 of the act provides that the court 'may' issue a declaration of incompatibility if any primary or subordinate legislation is found incompatible with convention rights, which are mentioned in Schedule 1 of the act in terms of Section 1 (3). The schedule provided the United Kingdom, for the first time, a list of codified human rights enforceable in domestic courts.

This interpretative power of the court has been called a strong adjuration[21] and applies to both pre- and post-HRA laws. Similarly, Article 13 of our Constitution mandates that unless both pre- and post-constitutional laws comply with fundamental rights, they will be declared void. But unlike Article 13, by the Section 3 interpretation, courts in England cannot invalidate a statute even if it is found incompatible with convention rights.

Section 2 of the act gives an indication of the materials to be taken into account by the court in the determination of a question of incompatibility. Judgments, decisions, declaration and even the advisory opinion of the European Constitution of Human Rights are relevant in such determination.

However, both sections 3 and 4 of the act make it clear that interpretation of incompatibility by a court or even a declaration to that effect does not affect the validity, continuing operation or enforcement of the provision in respect of which the declaration is given.

But such declarations are not mere empty rituals, as Section 10 of the act provides for remedial action under which Parliament may respond to such a declaration by amending the offending law in a normal way. And Section 10 (2) fast-tracks the amendment strategy by empowering the minister to remove the incompatibility taint from the law if the minister finds that there are 'compelling' reasons to do so.

In order to ensure that post-HRA laws are convention-compliant, Section 19 of the act provides that while introducing the bill to the Parliament, the concerned minister, before the second reading of the bill, may give a statement that in his view the law is convention-compatible; or he may say that he is unable to make such a statement but the House may proceed with the bill.

Section 19 was initially believed to be a 'parrot provision' but with the establishment of the Parliamentary Joint Committee on Human Rights (JCHR) in 2001, the working of Section 19 is monitored. The Joint Committee also reports to Parliament on the convention-compatibility, or the lack of it, in the bills. Now, it has become a government practice to include an outline of the government's view on compatibility, by way of explanatory notes to every bill.

The act has thus acquired the status of a constitutional law[22] and has exalted both the profile and influence of higher courts, giving the judiciary a newly invigorated position…in matters of public law[23].

Professor Sir William Wade in *Administrative Law* (Ninth Edition) traced the new concept of compatibility in English law by which the courts try to reconcile the convention rights, which are akin to fundamental rights in our country, with the laws made by Parliament. Thus, the twin concepts of limited government and higher law became the two most emerging trends in British jurisprudence.

Lord Chancellor Lord Irvine said:

> We believe that it is right as a matter of principle for the courts to have the duty of acting compatibly with the Convention not only in cases involving other public authorities but also in developing the common law in deciding cases between individuals. Why should they not?[24]

The question posed by the lord chancellor has been admirably answered by Professor Wade in his treatise on administrative law:

> Human rights under the Convention may conflict with the Acts of Parliament, as already mentioned, and have done so frequently. The Act addresses this problem with a remarkable amalgam of judicial, legislative and administrative procedures, designed to respect the sovereignty of Parliament while at the same time protecting human rights. In the first place, the court must strive to avoid conflict by benevolent construction. But if that proves impossible, the court may make a 'declaration of incompatibility', whereupon it is for the government and Parliament to take 'remedial action' if they think fit. This is a very different policy from that of the European Communities Act, 1972, which incorporated the law of the European Union by providing simply that it should prevail with paramount effect, overriding the sovereignty of Parliament whenever necessary.
>
> The rule of construction is that legislation, both primary and subordinate, and whenever enacted, must be 'read and given effect in a way which is compatible with the Convention rights' 'so far as it is possible to do so'. In other words, instead of seeking the true intention of Parliament at the time of the enactment, the court must

> adopt the interpretation which is the more favourable to a Convention right.[25]

The consequence of a declaration of incompatibility by the court of a parliamentary statute has also been discussed by Wade:

> Where a declaration of incompatibility is made, and no appeal is pending, or where incompatibility is revealed by a later decision of the European Court of Human Rights, the appropriate minister must consider whether there are 'compelling reasons' for amending the conflicting legislation. If so, he may by order make such amendments to the legislation as he considers necessary to remove the incompatibility.[26]

The doctrine of compatibility which was evolved in England is a typical example of British compromise between competing claims of parliamentary sovereignty and the jurisprudential concept of a higher law articulated in convention rights. Even though constitutionalism in Britain has not accepted the doctrine of basic structure, after the HRA, constitutional jurisprudence in Britain virtually veered round to something akin to the said doctrine, and the court's power of judicial review over laws made by parliamentary statute was firmly established.

Admittedly, the court's power in the United States encompassed the power of judicial review, including the power to nullify any legislation which is unconstitutional. This is based on the theory that if a law is made inconsistent with power vested in the Parliament, then the judges, in view of their independence and in view of the defined power of the Parliament, can declare such a law to be void, in order to guard the Constitution. It is axiomatic that any law enacted by the Parliament, contrary to the Constitution, has no force.

Therefore, the judicial review has been endorsed by Alexander

Hamilton in 'The Federalist' in the following terms:

> The interpretation of the laws is the proper and peculiar province of the courts. A Constitution is, in fact, and must be regarded by the judges as, a fundamental law. It therefore belongs to them to ascertain its meaning as well as the meaning of any particular act proceeding from the legislative body. If there should happen to be irreconcilable variance between the two, that which has the superior obligation and validity ought, of course, to be preferred, or, in other words, the Constitution ought to be preferred to the statute, the intention of the people or the intention of their agents.[27]

The jurisdiction of judicial review, which has been vested in the judges by the Constitution, argued Hamilton, represents the will of the people, and Parliament, consisting of the representatives of the people, virtually acts in the position of peoples' delegates. No act of the delegate can overthrow the will of the people. Hamilton further clarified by saying that in nullifying an act of Parliament, the judiciary does not assume a position superior to the Congress. Hamilton explained:

> Nor does this conclusion by any means suppose a superiority of the judicial to the legislative power. It only supposes that the power of the people is superior to both, and that where the will of the legislature, declared in its statutes, stands in opposition to that of the people, declared in the Constitution, the judges ought to be governed by the latter rather than the former. They ought to regulate their decisions by the fundamental laws rather than those which are not fundamental.[28]

According to Hamilton, it is only the judiciary which can police on this limitation on the legislature and he made this very clear by the following argument:

> Limitation of this kind can be preserved in practice [in] no other way than through the medium of courts of justice, whose duty it must be to declare all acts contrary to the manifest tenor of the Constitution void. Without this, all the reservations of particular rights or privileges would amount to nothing.[29]

In India, we have accepted the American concept of limited government, judicial review and the idea of higher law under Part III of the Constitution. Apart from that, the Indian Constitution specifically provides in Article 13 that the state cannot make any law which 'takes away' or even 'abridges' the rights under Part III. In case it does, such a law will be void. It is only the judiciary which can declare a law void. This is a unique feature in our Constitution and is not found elsewhere.

Similarly, on the several fundamental rights in Article 19, discussed above, reasonable restrictions can be imposed by law. The obvious question is who can decide whether or not the restriction is reasonable? Only the courts can decide the same. Article 32 of the Constitution is another provision which fortifies the court's power of judicial review, as any person can enforce his/her fundamental right by moving the Supreme Court—this right conferred on a person under Article 32 is itself a fundamental right. The importance of this article was lucidly explained by Dr Ambedkar in the Constituent Assembly when he said:

> If I was asked to name any particular article in this Constitution as the most important article without which the Constitution would be a nullity—I could not refer to any other article except this one. It is the very soul of

> the Constitution and the very heart of it and I am glad that the house has realised its importance.[30]

Article 226 of the Constitution, which empowers the High Courts in this country to exercise the power of judicial review in case of complaints of violation of fundamental rights or any other legal right, also entrenches the power of judicial review. About the sweep of the court's power under articles 32 and 226, what the Supreme Court said, as early as in 1955, is very pertinent and worth remembering:

> The language used in Articles 32 and 226 of our Constitution is very wide and the powers of the Supreme Court as well of all High Courts in India extend to issuing all orders, writs or directions, including writs in the nature of habeas corpus, mandamus, quo warranto, prohibition and certiorari as may be considered necessary for enforcement of fundamental rights, and in the case of High Courts for other purposes as well. In view of the express provision of our Constitution we need not now look back to the early history or the procedural technicalities of these writs in English law nor feel oppressed by difference or change of opinion expressed in particular cases by English judges.[31]

In view of these constitutional provisions, the power of judicial review in India is much more deep-rooted than it is in England. Of course, recent trends in the English court, as pointed out earlier, indicate a strengthening of the powers of judicial review.

Articles 141 and 142 of the Constitution empower the Supreme Court that in exercise of its power of judicial review it can declare a 'law' which shall be binding on all courts in India. It has been held that the power of declaring law is wider than the power of making law. This is a unique power of the Indian

Supreme Court, not to be found in other Constitutions. What has been very thoughtfully explained by President Roosevelt in his speech is virtually true of the Supreme Court's power under Article 141. The American president said:

> The chief lawmakers in our country may be, and often are, the judges, because they are the final seat of authority. Every time they interpret contract, property, vested rights, due process of law, liberty, they necessarily enact into law parts of a system of social philosophy; and as such interpretation is fundamental, they give direction to all law-making.[32]

Article 142 enables the Supreme Court to pass such decrees or orders as are necessary for doing complete justice in any cause or matter pending before it. This provision, along with Article 136 of the Constitution, authorize the Supreme Court to exercise the widest possible discretion while acting in exercise of its power of judicial review. This is also a unique feature of our Constitution, which strengthens the court's power of judicial review.

In the epoch-making decision in the case of *Kesavananda Bharati*,[33] the Supreme Court held that judicial review is one of the basic features of the Constitution. In the subsequent Constitution decision by the Supreme Court in the case of *L. Chandra Kumar v. Union of India*[34], the Supreme Court, after an analysis of the ratio in the case of *Kesavananda Bharati* and some other decisions, came to the conclusion that judicial review is the basic feature of the Constitution of India.

In view of this clear constitutional dispensation, the Supreme Court of India has delivered many judgments, discussed in the subsequent chapters, which have impacted not only our laws but also greatly influenced the social life of India. Those judgments, being delivered by the last court in a country of over 1.2 billion people, the largest democracy in the world, have also influenced jurisprudential trends in other countries.

NOTES

1. Article XXX of the Constitution of Massachusetts, 1780.
2. Lawyers' edition 60.
3. Woodrow Wilson, 'History of Liberty', Address to the New York Press Club, 9 September 1912.
4. 6. Fed. Cases 546 (No 3230) (1823)
5. Ibid.
6. (1937) 302 US 319.
7. Ivor Jennings, *Some Characteristics of the Indian Constitution*, (Oxford University Press, 1953), p. 34.
8. *Constituent Assembly Debates Vol. I,* pp. 99–100.
9. *Constituent Assembly Debates Vol. II,* p. 273.
10. (1943) 319 US 624.
11. Richard B. Morris (ed.), *The Basic Ideas of Alexander Hamilton*, (Pocket Library, 1957), p. 9.
12. Thomas Paine, *Rights of Man (1791–92)*, (Penguin, 1984), pp. 44–45.
13. *Jowitt's Dictionary of English Law,* 2nd Edition, (Sweet & Maxwell Ltd, 1977).
14. Blackstone's *Commentary on the Laws of England*, quoted by Supreme Court in *Union of India v. Tulsi Ram Patel* (AIR 1985 SC 1416–1454).
15. AIR 1967 SC 1643–1655.
16. (1942) AC 206.
17. Richard O'Sullivan, 'The Inheritance of the Common Law', *The Hamlyn Lectures*, Second Series, (Stevens and Sons Limited, 1950), pp. 83–89.
18. Ibid.
19. Lord Irvine, 'The Human Rights Act Two Years On: An Analysis', (*Public Law* 308, 2003).

20. Speech at the Institute of Public Policy Research, 13 January 2000.
21. *Regina v. Director of Public Prosecutions Ex Parte Kebeline and Ors* (2000) 2 AC 326 per Lord Coke at page 373 of the report.
22. Vide the opinion laws LJ in *Thoburn v. Sunderland City Council* (2003) QB 151, para 62.
23. A. Tomkins, 'Defining and Delimiting National Security', (*118 Law Quarterly Review*, 2002), 200 at 202.
24. William Wade and Christopher Forsyth, *Administrative Law* (Ninth Edition), (Oxford University Press, 2004), p. 168.
25. Ibid., p. 170.
26 Ibid., p. 171.
27. Alexander Hamilton, James Madison and John Jay, 'Federalist No. 78', *The Federalist Papers*, ed. Clinton Rossiter, (Penguin Books, 1961), p. 467.
28. Ibid.
29. Ibid., pp. 467–68.
30. *Constituent Assembly Debates, Volume VII*, p. 957.
31. Justice B.K. Mukherjee (as His Lordship then was) in *Basappa T.C. v. T. Nagappa* (1955) 1 SCR 250–256.
32. *43 Congressional Record*, Part I, p. 21.
33. (1973) 4 SCC 225.
34. AIR 1997 SC 1125.

I

THE BASIC STRUCTURE DOCTRINE EVOLVED TO PROTECT CORE CONSTITUTIONAL VALUES

Fundamental Rights and Parliament's Power of Amendment of the Constitution

IN LOCATING THE landmark judgments which change India, I have decided to club them under separate groups. The first group deals with judgments on the controversy between Parliament's power to amend the Constitution and the Supreme Court's power of judicial review of those amendments In this controversy, the key issue is whether Parliament, in the name of amending the Constitution, can destroy its basic features. This controversy emerged prominently in at least the following six judgments:

(1) *Sri Shankari Prasad Singh Deo v. Union of India and State of Bihar* (AIR 1951 SC 458)
(2) *Sajjan Singh v. State of Rajasthan* (AIR 1965 SC 845)
(3) *I.C. Golaknath and Ors v. State of Punjab and Anr* (AIR 1967 SC 1643)
(4) *Kesavananda Bharati Sripadagalvaru and Ors v. State of Kerala and Anr* ([1973] 4 SCC 225)
(5) *Indira Nehru Gandhi v. Shri Raj Narain and Anr* (1975 Supp SCC 1)

(6) *Minerva Mills Ltd and Ors v. Union of India and Ors* (AIR 1980 SC 1789)

The amending power of a Constitution, more often than not, indicates the nature of the Constitution. For instance, the Constitution of England, being mostly unwritten, is like a tapestry, deftly woven and developed over centuries. Its warp is monarchy and the woof is possibly the indomitable self-esteem of the descendants of the first Anglo-Saxon invaders. This Constitution is mostly impacted by constitutional values and doctrine and is amendable by a simple majority of the legislature or by judicial decisions not challenged by the state. International agreements, custom and traditional usage which has acquired constitutional status, can also amend the Constitution. Recently, the Human Rights Act (HRA), 1998, articulating European Convention Rights, has acquired the status of a constitutional document and is a major influence on English constitutional jurisprudence, as discussed (supra).

Insofar as the American Constitution is concerned, it can be amended under Article 5, when two-thirds of both houses of Congress propose amendments or when Congress is required by two-thirds of the state legislatures to call a constitutional convention. Amendments have to be ratified by three-fourths of the state legislature or conventions made on the mode of ratification proposed by Congress. No amendment, however, can deprive any state of equal voting rights in the senate without its consent.

Down under, the Australian Constitution posits under Chapter 8 that a proposed amendment has to be initiated by an absolute majority in each house, and after it is passed, a referendum has to be held. If only one house passes a proposed amendment, the governor general may also submit it to a referendum. The provision for dual majority of votes is necessary for approval—a national majority and then majority in four of the six states make constitutional amendment rather difficult.

Under the Indian Constitution there are various provisions dealing with amendments. Here we are dealing with Article 368 of the Constitution, which requires a majority of the total membership of both houses of Parliament and a majority of not less than two-thirds of the members, present and voting. Ratification by not less than half the state legislatures is required in respect of a few chapters of some parts of the Constitution. Our Constitution has by now been amended about a hundred times. It is very significant that parts III and IV, which respectively deal with fundamental rights and directive principles of state policy, can be amended without any ratification by the state. This has given rise to a lot of controversy, right from the very inception of the debate on Constitution amendment in the case of *Shankari Prasad*[1].

Article 13(2), which is in Part III of the Constitution, the chapter on fundamental rights, mandates that the state, which includes the Parliament, cannot make any law which abridges or takes away rights conferred by Part III, and that any law so made would be void.

Now the question is whether a constitutional amendment would be 'law' within the meaning of Article 13 of the Constitution. In *Shankari Prasad*, Justice Patanjali Shastri (as His Lordship then was) held that 'in the absence of a clear indication to the contrary' it is difficult to hold that fundamental rights are 'immune from Constitutional Amendment' and further held that the terms of Article 368 are general and empower the Parliament 'to amend the Constitution without any exception'. On the aforesaid reasoning it was held unanimously in *Shankari Prasad* that in the context of Article 13 'law' would not mean amendment to the Constitution made in exercise of constituent powers. The apparent conflict between articles 368 and 13(2) of the Constitution was resolved by the Supreme Court by relying on the principles of harmonious construction. That is how the 1st Amendment of the Constitution, introducing the 9th Schedule, was upheld by the Supreme Court. Almost identical questions, but in a different context, came up for consideration before the Constitution Bench of the Supreme Court in *Sajjan Singh*, wherein the constitutional validity of the Constitution (17th Amendment) Act, 1964, (henceforth referred to as the 17th Constitution Amendment Act), was up for scrutiny. The most significant part of this judgment is the formulation by Chief Justice Gajendragadkar, wherein the learned chief justice held that the dictionary meaning of 'amend' cannot be relied on for construing the word 'amend' in Article 368. It was held that the power to 'amend' in the context of Article 368 'is a very wide power' and cannot 'be controlled by the literal dictionary meaning'.[2]

It is observed, with respect, that while making such sweeping observations the learned chief justice did not support it with any discernible line of reasoning except by relying on the reasons in *Shankari Prasad* which upheld the 1st Amendment to the Constitution.

With due respect, the reasoning of the learned judge in *Shankari Prasad* is far from being cogent. By quoting Dicey, the learned judge gave an inane perception of constituent power. The reasoning of the learned judge is marked by what Mr Nariman described[3] as a lack of 'a positivist approach' by not attempting 'to plumb the depths' of the silences of the Constitution and not to probe its 'crevices'. That is why the learned judge was constantly ruing the absence of clear intention in the text of the Constitution, and this led the learned judge to hold that fundamental rights are not immune from constitutional amendments. The learned judge resolved the conflict between articles 13 and 368 by following harmonious construction—a canon of statutory interpretation, without possibly appreciating that constitutional interpretation is a different ballgame.

Unfortunately the learned judge did not follow the mode of constitutional interpretation contemporaneously advanced by Justice Vivian Bose. His Lordship formulated that the words in the Constitution 'are not just dull lifeless words static and hidebound as in some mummified manuscripts, but living flames...tongues of dynamic fire potent [enough] to mould the future as well as guide the present'[4]. Justice Felix Frankfurter, in the Steel Seizure Case, adhered to the same principle by saying, '[I]t is an inadmissible narrow conception of American Constitutional Law to confine it to the words of the Constitution and to disregard the gloss which life has written upon them.'[5]

In the opinion of Lawrence H. Tribe, the famous jurist, a true interpretation of the Constitution by judges must echo their cognizance of its 'dark invisible matter'[6]. This is true of Indian Constitutional Law and I would venture to say, again with the highest respect, that a rather limited interpretation of constitutional values was given by the Supreme Court in *Shankari Prasad* (supra).

In *Sajjan Singh*, the Supreme Court held that the constituent power of amendment can be exercised both prospectively and retrospectively. By following the principle in *Shankari Prasad*, the majority opinion in *Sajjan Singh* affirmed that the word 'law' in Article 13 should be taken to exclude constitutional amendment under Article 368, as it is made in exercise of constituent power. In *Sajjan Singh*, even though the 17th Constitution Amendment Act was upheld by Justice Hidayatullah (as His Lordship then was), His Lordship recorded his express dissent with the reasoning in *Shankari Prasad* and opined that fundamental rights are far too fundamental to be made a plaything of a special majority.

His Lordship refused to accept that the chapter on fundamental rights, being a solemn part of the Constitution, could be on less firm ground than the articles and parts of the chapter mentioned in the proviso to Article 368, as amendment of these provisions require ratification. His Lordship also referred to the anomaly of not ratifying an amendment of Article 32 while doing it for an amendment of Article 226, and declined to play a 'grammarian's role' in interpreting the Constitution. Thus, His Lordship refused to express a final opinion on the question of whether the law of amendment of the Constitution is outside the purview of Article 13(2).

Justice Mudholkar also upheld the 17th Constitution Amendment Act, but refused to accept that the view of the Supreme Court in *Shankari Prasad* was the last word. His Lordship, possibly for the first time while dealing with the fundamental rights, raised a question of basic features of the Constitution and argued for giving them 'permanence'[7], opining that otherwise amending them would amount to rewriting the Constitution.[8]

Therefore, the seeds of the later doctrine in *I.C. Golaknath v. State of Punjab and Ors,* of unamendability of fundamental rights, were sown in the opinions of Justices Hidayatullah (as His Lordship then was) and Mudholkar.

The earlier conflicts between the parliamentary power and judicial protection of fundamental rights took final shape in the majority opinion in *Golaknath*[9]. In delivering the verdict, the learned chief justice relied on a lecture given by German scholar Dieter Conrad in India on 'Implied Limitations of the Amending Power'.

The majority opinion in *Golaknath* was rendered by a majority of six to five. The validity of the 1st, 4th and 17th Constitution Amendment Acts came under scrutiny in the case. The majority held that these amendments abridged the scope of fundamental rights but since they were declared valid by previous decisions of the Supreme Court, they would, in view of the doctrine of prospective overruling, 'continue to be valid' and the decision in *Golaknath* would have prospective operation. But from the date of the said decision, Parliament would not have any power to amend any provision of Part III of the Constitution or 'to take away or abridge fundamental rights enshrined therein'.[10]

The decision in *Golaknath* was a turning point in the political, social and constitutional history of our country. It is clear that the Supreme Court, by changing its interpretative 'methodology', donned the lawmaking role. In *Golaknath*, the majority opinion overruled the decisions in *Shankari Prasad* and *Sajjan Singh* and held that constitutional amendment is law within the meaning of Article 13(2) and is therefore void if it contravenes the fundamental rights. Thus *Golaknath* started the great war, as opposed to earlier skirmishes in *Sajjan Singh*, between parliamentary and judicial supremacy.

The majority judgment in *Golaknath* held that the power to amend the Constitution was not in Article 368. It merely provided for the procedure as the marginal note to Article 368 indicated. It also held that the power to amend the Constitution emanated from Entry 97, List I of Schedule VII. Therefore, any amendment to the Constitution was 'law' for the purpose of Article 13(2).

However, the ratio in *Golaknath* clearly restricted Parliament's amending power and thus imposed the constraints on legislative majority. In a way, the ratio in *Golaknath* was openly counter-majoritarian and based on the premise that fundamental rights are nothing but natural rights and no power exists in defiance of these rights anywhere in the Constitution, and not even in the largest majority.[11] Therefore the majority opinion in *Golaknath* gave a literal and positivist interpretation of articles 13(2) and

368 of the Constitution. However, the then central government considered the judgment in *Golaknath* a stumbling block for its march towards socialism.

To virtually get over the judgment in *Golaknath*, the Constitution (24th Amendment) Act, 1971, (henceforth the 24th Constitution Amendment Act) was introduced, bringing about, inter alia, some amendments to Article 368 of the Constitution. In the 24th Constitution Amendment Act, it was made clear that Article 13(2) would not apply to constitutional amendment and the marginal note to Article 368 was also changed. This amendment empowered Parliament to take away or abridge all or any of the fundamental rights and gave unlimited plenitude to the amending power of Parliament.

In 1970, His Holiness Swami Kesavananda Bharati, pontiff of a Kerala math, challenged the land reforms of the Kerala government by filing a petition before the Supreme Court under Article 32 to vindicate the fundamental rights of religious institutions to manage their properties. During the pendency of this writ petition before the Supreme Court came the 24th Constitution Amendment Act, followed by the Constitution (25th Amendment) Act, 1971, and the Constitution (29th Amendment) Act, 1972, (henceforth 25th and 29th Constitution Amendment Acts, respectively). The Kerala Land Reforms Act was included in the 9th Schedule by the 29th Constitution Amendment Act. The validity of these amendments was challenged in an Article 32 proceeding which was pending before five judges. In August 1972, the matter was transferred to a thirteen-judge bench at a time when the Supreme Court had fifteen judges. The case was heard by the thirteen-judge bench from November 1972 to April 1973.

In the case of *Kesavananda Bharati*, out of thirteen judges, ten held that *Golaknath* was wrongly decided and had to be overruled and was, in fact, overruled. Chief Justice Sikri and Justice Shelat, who were part of the majority led by Chief Justice Subba Rao in *Golaknath*, held otherwise.

In *Kesavananda Bharati*, the majority decided that the amending power of Parliament is distinct from legislative power and this power is wide enough to reach every part of the Constitution. However, this proposition was qualified by holding that the basic structure of the Constitution is unamendable. In formulating the notion of basic structure we find that the judgment highlighted the concept of constitutional entrenchment in order to insulate certain constitutional provisions from amendment. The majority virtually held that there is some moral reality in the form of inherent principles which the Constitution purports to represent. The constitutional fundamentals being included in the map of a moral terrain, there are limits to which it can be changed so as not to snap the constitutionalism of the moral principles which are entrenched in the Constitution. The idea of basic structure is, thus, resting on constitutionalism as against democratic values.

In this monumental decision, thirteen judges gave eleven judgments. The consensus of opinion upheld the amending powers of the Constitution in the 24th Constitution Amendment Act. Of the thirteen learned judges, six judges (Chief Justice Sikri, Justice Shelat, Justice Grover, Justice Hedge, Justice Mukherjee and Justice Jagmohan Reddy), even while upholding the amending powers under the 24th Constitution Amendment Act by relying on the principles of implied limitations of the amending power, opined that the said power could not be utilized to emasculate the basic structures of the Constitution which, inter alia, include the fundamental rights.

Eleven separate and rather longish opinions of the Supreme Court in *Kesavananda Bharati* have unfortunately created some doubts on many vital issues. Nevertheless, the decision in *Kesavananda Bharati* is a watershed in the development of constitutional law in India. The judgment in this case has to be considered as the greatest contribution of the Supreme Court to constitutional jurisprudence. However, in this case, the Supreme Court accepted the plenary amending powers of Parliament and lifted the stumbling block of Article 13, placed there by the ratio of *Golaknath*. At the same time, the decision in *Kesavananda Bharati* widened the scope of judicial review on the notion of basic structure to which all valid exercise of amending powers must conform, as stated by Upendra Baxi.[12]

The Theory of Implied Limitation on the amending powers of the Constitution, as formulated in *Kesavananda Bharati*, some commentators suggest, fortified the basics of the *Golaknath* ratio in a way.

If we look at the amending powers under the Constitution, we find that apart from Article 368, the word 'amendment' occurs in various parts of the Constitution, for example, in articles 4(1), 107, 111, 161(2) and 372. Also in Paragraph 7 Part D of the 5th Schedule and in Paragraph 21(1) of the 6th Schedule. These amendments are different from the provisions of Article 368 and the concept of basic structure is only relatable to the power of Parliament under Article 368.

The doctrine of basic structure which is not mentioned in the Constitution has its genesis in the concept of implied limitation on the power of amendment under Article 368 of the Constitution. The words in the Constitution are not 'just dull, lifeless words static and hidebound as in some mummified manuscript but are living flames intended to give a life to a great nation and... tongues of dynamic power potent to mould the future as well as to guide the present'. These are the prophetic words of Justice Vivian Bose in *State of West Bengal v. Anwar Ali Sarkar*[13] when our constitutional jurisprudence was at a nascent stage.

Subsequently, also in *Kesavananda Bharati*, Chief Justice Sikri echoed the same principle by saying that words in the Constitution cannot be construed in a vacuum. In saying so, the learned chief justice relied on the speech of Lord Green in *Biede v. General Accident Fire and Life Insurance Corporation*[14]. The learned chief justice also referred to the formulations of Justice Holmes in *Towne* v. *Eisner*[15] where he held that 'a word is not a crystal, transparent and unchanged, it is a skin of living thought and may vary in colour and content according to the circumstances and the time in which it is used'. The learned chief justice also referred to an observation of Lord Gowyer and Lord Wright that 'a grant of power in general terms standing by itself no doubt be construed in the wider sense, but it may be qualified by other express provisions of the same enactment, by the implications of the context and even by...the general scheme of the Act'.[16]

From what is discussed above, it is apparent that the concept of implied limitation on the amending power of Parliament under Article 368 of the Constitution virtually emanated from the silences of the Constitution. Michael Foley, in his treatise *The Silence of Constitutions*[17], explained that what is said in the Constitution is important but what is not said, but is implied in the silence from what is said, is equally important.

Now, if the basis of the majority verdict in *Kesavananda Bharati* is analysed, we would find that Chief Justice Sikri opined that the word 'amendment' is not to be given the widest meaning.

As His Lordship upheld the Theory of Implied Limitations of Amending Power, the chief justice argued that unlimited amending power may lead to totalitarianism and thus would enslave the people and ultimately make the Constitution unamendable and rigid. The learned chief justice had the noble and grand design of the Constitution in view and held that Article 368 of the Constitution had to be interpreted in the background of the said vision. He upheld the 24th Constitution Amendment Act, but made it clear that it would not enable Parliament to change the fundamental features of the Constitution by destroying fundamental rights and the identity of the Constitution.

Chief Justice Sikri did not consider the directive principles of state policy to be an integral part of the basic features of the Constitution. The learned chief justice, on scrutiny of the 25th Constitution Amendment Act, held that Article 31C is invalid. In doing so, he adopted a rights-based approach and opined that the directive principles cannot be given primacy over fundamental rights. However, the learned chief justice upheld the validity of Article 31(2).

Justice Shelat and Justice Grover also were in favour of implied limitation of amending powers. According to these judges, our Constitution had been erected to bring about an egalitarian society which provides for development of the country in social, economic and political fields, without affecting the basic freedoms. Both Justice Shelat and Justice Grover upheld the 25th Constitution Amendment Act, except its Section 3, which introduced Article 31C. This article, according to the learned judges, was unconstitutional as it enabled the negation of the basic rights protected under articles 14, 19 and 31; second, the power of amendment which was exclusively given to the Parliament could not be delegated to any other legislative body of the country.

Highlighting the structural unity of the Constitution, both Justice Shelat and Justice Grover concurred with Chief Justice Sikri by holding that amendment power could not be controlled by the proviso to Article 368 alone. Both the learned judges held that Article 368 must be construed narrowly, and in construing the purport of the amendment, the judges were to consider other 'aids of interpretation', especially the Preamble. Both judges opined that the powers under the Constitution and its representative character could not be equated with the power of the people who framed the Constitution. The learned judges held: 'It cannot be overlooked that basic theory of our Constitution is that "pouvoir constituent" is vested in the people and was exercised, for and on behalf by the Constituent Assembly for the purpose of framing the Constitution'[18].

Justices Shelat and Grover indicated the following to be the basic features of the Constitution:

(1) The supremacy of the Constitution.
(2) The republican and democratic form of government and the sovereignty of the country.
(3) The secular and federal character of the Constitution.
(4) The demarcation of power between the legislature, the executive and the judiciary.
(5) The dignity of the individual secured by the various freedoms and basic rights in Part III and the mandate to build a welfare state contained in Part IV.
(6) The unity and integrity of the nation.

But the judges maintained that basic features could never be exhaustively indicated.

Justices Hegde and Mukherjee held that there could be no restriction on amending power under Article 368 of the Constitution and that it could reach each and every part of the Constitution. However, Their Lordships were of the opinion that the meaning of 'law' in Article 13(2) must be construed harmoniously with Article 368 of the Constitution. Accordingly, Justices Hegde and Mukherjee opined that the identity and nature of the Constitution must remain unchanged and there was danger in acknowledging the unlimited amending power of Parliament. The learned judges argued that the substance of the original Constitution must be sustained and could not be done away with. Their Lordships also said that under Article 60 of the Constitution, the president of India had taken an oath to 'preserve, protect and defend the Constitution', so he could not assent to any amendment changing the basic features of the Constitution, which are permanent, and the fundamental features of the Constitution could not be emasculated. The learned judges similarly held that clause (c) of the 25th Constitution Amendment Act, which introduced Article 31C, was invalid.

Relying on the concept of 'popular sovereignty', Justices Hegde and Mukherjee decided that a close look at the Preamble would demonstrate that the people of India had conferred the Constitution on themselves. This cannot be challenged before a court, which is a creature of the Constitution. The judges also held that even though Parliament is vested with amending powers, being the creature of the Constitution, the ultimate sovereignty lies with the people. They expressly opined: 'When a power to amend the Constitution is given to the people, its contents can be construed to be larger than when that power is given to a body constituted under that Constitution.'[19]

The judges also held that our Constitution is based on a social philosophy and that like religion, such a philosophy has some basic and circumstantial features. Some features of our Constitution are so basic that they cannot be destroyed, at least from within.[20]

This is how the learned judges evolved the concept of implied limitation on amending powers.

Justice Jagmohan Reddy, while agreeing with Chief Justice Sikri on the main points, held that the main issue before the Bench was to determine the scope of Parliament's amending power under Article 368 of the Constitution.

The learned judge suggested two alternative methods to explore the problem. The first was to assume that the amending power was 'omni-sovereign'. In formulating this principle, the learned judge referred to the views of Justice Holmes. The alternative view was to place on the amending power a structural-cum-teleological interpretation as opposed to an analytical/literal construction. The learned judge, however, leaned in favour of the latter view and held that to understand the purport of the constitutional provisions, one had to consider the following: (1) our national aspiration; (2) the objectives discussed in the Constituent Assembly and adopted in the Constitution, giving it the character of a democratic republic; (3) various other features, such as rights of individual citizens; (4) the duties of the state; (5) the distribution of legislative powers; and (6) the amending powers of the state. Therefore, Justice Reddy argued: 'The edifice of our Constitution is built upon and stands on several props. Remove any of them, the Constitution collapses. These are: (1) Sovereign Democratic Republic; (2) Justice, social, economic and political; (3) Liberty of thought, expression, belief, faith and worship; (4) Equality of status and opportunity.'[21]

The opinion of Justice H.R. Khanna is of crucial import in formulating the ratio in *Kesavananda Bharati*. It is his opinion, with which none of the other twelve judges fully agreed, that has become the law of the land. However, the golden common link between the opinions of Justice Khanna and the aforesaid six judges who opined in favour of citizens is that Parliament cannot, while amending the Constitution, alter the basic framework of the Constitution, like abolishing the free democratic character of the republic. Nor can it dilute the integrity or unity of India or abolish the states.

On Article 368 of the Constitution, Justice Khanna opined that there are certain limitations inherent in the concept of amendment. His views are as follows:

> It may at this stage clarify that there are certain limitations which inhere and are implicit in the word 'amendment'.

> These are limitations which flow from the use of the [word] 'amendment' and relate to the meaning or construction of the word 'amendment'. This aspect has been dealt with elsewhere while construing the word 'amendment'. Subject to this clarification, we may not advert to the two facets of the concept of implied limitations referred to above.[22]

Justice Khanna made it further clear that by a process of amendment the Constitution could not be abrogated nor could its identity be lost. In the lucid exposition of this doctrine, he opined:

> We may not deal with the question as to what is the scope of the power of amendment under Article 368. This would depend upon the connotation of the word 'amendment'. Question has been posed during the arguments as to whether the power to amend under the above article includes the power to completely abrogate the Constitution and replace it by an entirely new Constitution. The answer to the above question, in my opinion, should be in the negative. I am further of the opinion, that amendment of the Constitution necessarily contemplates that the Constitution has not to be abrogated but only changes have to be made in it. The word 'amendment' postulates that the old Constitution survives without loss of its identity despite the change and continues even though it has been subjected to alterations.[23]

His Lordship posed a question, asking what was meant by retaining the old Constitution, and answered it himself by saying that it meant 'the retention of the basic structure or framework of the Constitution.'[24]

His Lordship held very unerringly that 'the language of Article 368 lends support to the conclusion that one cannot, while acting under that Article, repeal the existing Constitution and replace it by a new Constitution.'[25]

His Lordship also held that to uphold the second part of Article 31C, which excludes judicial review, is opposed to the basic structure of the Constitution and is beyond 'the permissible limits of what constitutes amendment under Article 368'[26]. However, Justice Khanna held that the right to property is not a part of the basic structure.

The jurisprudence evolved by Justice Khanna in his opinion in *Kesavananda Bharati* had a high moral content. He introduced what can be termed as the best moral interpretation of the Constitution and he was in favour of both process-based and substance-based review. In a process-based review, only the procedural propriety in reaching the decision is examined by the court; however, in a substance-based review, the probe by the court is much deeper.

Ultimately Justice Khanna recognized, in his opinion, the non-derogability of the basic structure of the Constitution. He accepted that the Constitution is sovereign, and since it has been adopted by the people, the sovereignty of the people merged with the constitutional sovereignty clothes it with non-derogable moral features, which constitute the basic structure and are beyond the amending power under Article 368.

In appreciating the jurisprudence of the majority ratio in *Kesavananda Bharati* one has to keep in mind a basic distinction. This is between constitutional interpretation and construction of a constitutional text in such a way as to design a new approach to constitutional values by weaving it out of the text of the written Constitution.

Of course, the principles of construction cannot ignore the text, nor can they be dehors the text of the Constitution, but they cannot rest at merely discovering a pre-existing deeply hidden meaning in the text. This is the difference in approach in *Kesavananda Bharati*, as compared to the approach of the Supreme Court in its previous decisions in *A.K. Gopalan v. State of Madras*[27], *Shankari Prasad* and *Sajjan Singh*. In order to attempt a construction of the constitutional document, the judge or the jurist has to rely on the value-based vision of a judicial statesman rather than bank on the 'governing wit' of a judge who considers himself bound by the black letter of the text. Construction of the constitutional text is therefore an embellishment and an addition to the fabric of constitutional fundamentals. It is creative, whereas interpretation is not necessarily creative. Interpretation is textual, but construction is conceptual.

For a proper perception of the basic structure doctrine, we may refer to Ronald Dworkin's precepts when he argues that the judicial review leading to construction does not present any serious counter-'majoritarian' difficulty at all. According to him, constitutionalism is meant to control the majorities. Dworkin further elaborates: 'The Constitution, and particularly the Bill of Rights, is designed to protect individual citizens and groups against certain decisions that a majority of citizens might want to make, even when the majority acts in what it takes to be the general or common interest. Such protection is rooted in the moral rights which individuals possess against the majority'.[28]

In *Law's Empire*,[29] Dworkin claims that his vision of rights is based on commitment to democracy. By democracy Dworkin, of course, does not mean majoritarianism only.

This view of Dworkin is borne out from the written Constitution of any free democracy, which normally has an inbuilt content of counter-majoritarian values. Our Constitution is not an exception. Our Constitution recognizes certain fundamental freedoms in respect of every person, even if he is not a citizen. This gives our Constitution the complexion of an international charter of human rights. Apart from that, it expressly assures the minorities of several basic guarantees in the chapter on fundamental rights. Therefore, when the court has to uphold core constitutional values, it has to fashion its jurisprudence on a counter-majoritarian basis. Thus, in adjudication of constitutional questions, the highest court has to conjoin the jurisprudence of the original intent with constitutionalism, which in turn ushers in a just social order. Therefore, judges have to reach beyond the apparently impenetrable sphere of meaning by adopting the strategy of unravelling meaning in the constitutional text. This is why Alexander M. Bickel correctly pointed out that 'the root difficulty is that judicial review is a counter-majoritarian force in our system'[30].

If we seek any support for justification of the basic structure doctrine from the text of our Constitution, we may refer to Article 38 that casts on the state—which includes the higher judiciary—a duty to promote the welfare of the people by securing and protecting social order in which justice—social, economic and political—is to inform all the institutions of national life. This reflects the preambular vision. We find resonance of the same view in Larry Simon's approach when he says, 'At a heuristic level, the basic criterion for evaluating the arguments supporting the various methodologies or interpretations is the extent to which those methodologies and interpretations promote a good and just society… The evaluative standards must come from the external perspectives of political and moral theory'.[31]

However, the basis of a changed approach in *Kesavananda Bharati* sprang from a realization by the judiciary that the powers of Parliament can be plenary but they can never be arbitrary and the highest court may sometimes find that the constitutional text is 'incurably incomplete', as was suggested by H.L.A. Hart. Hart visualized that the uncoding of such a text presents 'problems of penumbra'. He argued that to resolve such disputes 'the purely cognitive interpretation by jurisprudence is…unable to fill alleged gaps. The filling up of a so-called gap in the law is a law-creating function and can only be performed by a law-applying organ; and the function of creating law is not performed by jurisprudence interpreting law'.[32]

In filling up these gaps, the silence in the Constitution, as discussed (supra), with significant overtones, has a major role in conferring unstated discretion on the judges.

Dworkin accepted that such an interpretation is a Herculean task, but it can be performed by integrating the form of natural law into positive law. In order to achieve this the judge, as suggested by Dworkin, has to draw upon moral principles in order to put the law in the 'best light' and make it complete.[33]

This mammoth task was performed by the Supreme Court in *Kesavananda Bharati*, and its far-reaching jurisprudence of basic structure can be traced to the aforesaid juristic strands of thought.

This concept of basic structure again came up for further consideration in the case of *Indira Nehru Gandhi* v. *Raj Narain*, widely known as the Election Case.[34] The factual background to the case is of some relevance to the social and political history of our country. Indira Gandhi, the prime minister of India (the appellant), appealed before the Supreme Court impugning a judgment dated 12 June 1975 of the High Court of Allahabad, which held the appellant guilty of electoral malpractices. The judgment was immediately appealed to the Supreme Court and Justice Krishna Iyer, sitting during vacation, gave a temporary stay of the High Court judgment on the condition that the appellant would be refrained from casting her vote or participating in parliamentary debates and would draw her remuneration as a Member of Parliament (MP) till the appeal is finally heard. On 26 June 1975, the president declared a General Emergency in the whole of India.

Before the appeal could be heard, Parliament enacted the Election Laws Amendment Act with effect from 6 August 1975. Then, on 7 August 1975, there was a bill to amend Article 71 and to introduce the Constitution (39th Amendment) Act, 1975, (henceforth 39th Constitution Amendment Act) by inserting Article 329A, making special provisions for election to Parliament in the case of prime minister and speaker. That bill was passed by Parliament on 7 August 1975, and on 8 August 1975 it was passed by the Council of States. Then, by 9 August 1975, several state legislatures ratified the bill. It was gazetted on 10 August 1975 as the 39th Constitution Amendment Act. The hearing of the appeal was fixed on 11 August 1975. All this happened within a span of five days.

Never before in the history of any democracy in the world was a constitutional amendment expedited in such a manner to help the cause of one individual litigant. To say the least, this was a mockery of constitutional functioning.

For the first time a constitutional amendment was made not in respect of rights of property or for advancing social welfare but with reference to electoral law purporting to decide an election dispute between two contesting parties. The amendment was virtually directed towards the disposal of the pending appeal by holding that the election of the appellant is declared valid in terms of Article 329A(4).

It was for the first time that Parliament introduced, through constitutional amendment, the concept that it can exercise judicial power.

When the appeal came up for hearing, the Supreme Court unanimously set aside the judgment of the Allahabad High Court. However, on the validity of Article 329A of the Constitution, the Supreme Court invalidated the same by holding that it violated the basic structure of the Constitution even though the judges, while returning the said finding, differed on their reasoning. All the five judges in the Election Case unanimously held that the court was bound by the majority opinion in the *Kesavananda Bharati* judgment on basic structure, even though four of them (Chief Justice A.N. Ray, Justice Beg, Justice Mathew and Justice Chandrachud) had not shared the majority opinion on basic structure in *Kesavananda Bharati*.

Chief Justice A.N. Ray, while upholding the election of the appellant, held that clause (4) of Article 329A suffered from various infirmities and is opposed to the rule of law. The learned Chief Justice also held that clause (4) was in the nature of an exercise of judicial power.[35]

Justice Khanna, who was a party to the majority opinion in *Kesavananda Bharati* and held that no constitutional amendment can mutilate or emasculate the basic structure of the Constitution. The learned judge reiterated that the opinion of the majority in *Kesavananda Bharati* is that democratic set-up was a part of the basic structure of the Constitution.[36] Following the same ratio, Justice Khanna struck down as unconstitutional all the clauses of sub-article (4) of Article 329A, introduced by the 39th Constitution Amendment Act. In his own words, Justice Khanna held:

> As a result of the above, I strike down clause (4) of Article 329A on the ground that it violates the principle of free and fair election which is an essential postulate of democracy and which in its turn is a part of the basic structure of the Constitution in as much as (1) it abolishes the forum without providing for another forum for going into the dispute relating to the validity of the election of the appellant and further prescribes that the said dispute shall not be governed by any election law and that the validity of the said election shall be absolute

> and not consequently to be liable to be assailed, and (2) it extinguishes both the right and the remedy to challenge the validity of the aforesaid election.[37]

Justice Mathew also held that the majority opinion in *Kesavananda Bharati* was that Parliament's power under Article 368 is not absolute. His Lordship also said that the consensus among judges in *Kesavananda Bharati* was that democracy is a basic structure of the Constitution.[38]

Following the aforesaid ratio, Justice Mathew held that clause (4) of Article 329A, introduced by the 39th Constitution Amendment Act, was performing a function which had traditionally been in the province of the court[39] and the declaration of validity of appellant's election by clause (4) of the Amending Act was a fiat of a sui generis character of the amending body.[40]

Noting that at the time when the constitutional amendment was passed the appellant's appeal was pending before the Supreme Court, Justice Mathew opined that the amendment by clause (4) was legislation 'ad hominem' (for the person), and was a direct interference with the decision of these appeals by the Supreme Court on their merits by a legislative judgment.[41]

Justice Mathew clearly held that the amending power under clause (4) was exercised in violation of the principles of natural justice and the amending power, under that clause, by evolving new norms for adjudging the validity of a particular election, was exercising a 'despotic power' and that would damage the 'democratic structure of the Constitution.'[42]

Justice Beg (as His Lordship then was), in an extremely elaborate judgment, held that the claim of the counsel supporting the impugned clause (4) of Article 329A, that the constituent power was an undifferentiated amalgam of judicial, legislative and executive power enabling the constituent body to bring about any amendment in the Constitution and was not tenable.

His Lordship held that this could not be ignored in view of the majority judgment in *Kesavananda Bharati*, which could not be overruled. After discussing various treaties and the decisions of various courts, the learned judge held that clause (4) of Article 329A does not operate to oust the jurisdiction of the Supreme Court to decide the appeal on merits by applying the Representation of People's Act. His Lordship also held that perhaps the 'Doctrine of Reading down' could be applied to clause (4) to hold that the jurisdiction of this court to hear the election appeal on merits had not been ousted, but His Lordship noted that no such argument was made by the counsel arguing in support of the said clause.[43]

However, His Lordship did not uphold the validity of clause (4) of Article 329A, even though His Lordship expressed the opinion in very guarded language.[44]

Justice Chandrachud (as His Lordship then was) also struck down clauses (4) and (5) of Article 329A, but His Lordship did so for different reasons. His Lordship held that democracy is an essential feature of the Constitution, but just as one swallow does not make a summer, similarly the impugned amendment does not destroy the democratic structure embedded under the Constitution.[45]

His Lordship, however, held, relying on the ratio of *Anwar Ali Sarkar*[46], that the classification of prime minister or the speaker for excluding any challenge to their election under the impugned amendment did not satisfy the Doctrine of Reasonable Classification and amounted to favoured treatment, and that may outrage the sense of justice of common men which sustains a democracy. Therefore, clauses (4) and (5) of Article 329A were arbitrary and destructive of the rule of law. His Lordship also held that the amending power could not be an amalgam of all powers—legislative, executive and judicial—and this was opposed to the concept of our Constitution, which postulates a well-planned legal order.[47]

The importance of this election case is that it puts the validity of the majority ratio of *Kesavananda Bharati* beyond doubt and also sheds new light on the concept of constituent power by subordinating it to the primacy of the constitutional structure.

The decision in *Minerva Mills* is another milestone, which prevented Parliament from overriding the basic structure doctrine in *Kesavananda Bharati* by enacting the Constitution (42nd Amendment) Act, 1976, (henceforth 42nd Constitution Amendment Act) which came into effect from 3 January 1977 virtually for dislodging the said doctrine.[48]

The challenge to the nationalization of Minerva Mills, a textile undertaking, could not be made in view of the 42nd Constitution Amendment Act, which barred a challenge to the law of nationalization, as the impugned Nationalization Act was included vide entry 105 to the 9th Schedule to the Constitution,

Minerva Mills, by filing an Article 32 writ petition, challenged the constitutional validity of sections 4 and 55 of the 42nd Constitution Amendment Act, inter alia, on the touchstone of the basic structure theory.

For a proper appreciation of the questions, sections 4 and 55 of the 42nd Constitution Amendment Act are set out below:

Section 4. Amendment of Article 31C: In Article 31C of the Constitution, for the words, brackets, letters and figures 'the principles specified in clause (b) or clause (c) of Article 39, the words and figures "all or any of the principles laid down in Part IV"' shall be sustained.

Section 55. Amendment to Article 368: In Article 368 of the Constitution after clause (3) the following clauses shall be inserted namely:

> (4) No amendment of this Constitution (including provisions of part III) made or purporting to have been made under this article whether before or after the commencement of Section 55 of the Constitution (42nd Amendment Act), 1976, shall be called in question in any court on any ground.
>
> (5) For removal of doubts, it is hereby declared that there shall be no limitation whatsoever on the constituent power of the Parliament to amend by way of addition, variation or repeal the provisions of this Constitution under this article.

In *Minerva Mills* the majority judgment was rendered by Chief Justice Chandrachud on behalf of himself and Justices Gupta and Kailasam on 30 July 1980. Both sections 4 and 55 of the 42nd Constitution Amendment Act were held unconstitutional. Justice Bhagwati (as his Lordship then was), in a separate judgment, concurred with the majority about the unconstitutionality of Section 55 but gave his dissent by upholding Section 4 of the 42nd Constitution Amendment Act.

Even though (then) Justice Chandrachud was in the minority in *Kesavananda Bharati*, in *Minerva Mills* the learned chief justice assured that the power under Article 368 of the Constitution could not be exercised by Parliament to damage its basic structure and he summed up the *Kesavananda Bharati* ratio in *Minerva Mills.*[49]

In delivering the majority judgment, the chief justice first took up for scrutiny Section 55 of the 42nd Constitution Amendment Act by which clauses (4) and (5), set out above, were added to Article 368.

Reiterating the doctrine of the basic structure in *Kesavananda Bharati*, the chief justice held that Parliament could not, under Article 368, expand its amending power to destroy the basic essential features of the Constitution. The donee of a limited power cannot by exercise of that power convert the limited power into an unlimited one.[50]

The Supreme Court went on to state that the addition of clauses (4) and (5) of Article 368 were ultra vires the amending power of Parliament. The rationale being that they removed the limitations on the power of amendment to render the *Kesavananda Bharati* verdict ineffective. Furthermore, the court stated that the language of clause (4) would render the fundamental rights a 'mere adornment', as no recourse could be taken to any court, which is against the principles of the Constitution.[51]

The court, through the chief justice, reiterated the position of *Kesavananda Bharati* by stating that clause (4) was invalid, to the extent that it took away rights conferred under articles 14 and 19. The Court pointed out that the amendment to Article 31C in effect abrogated articles 14 and 19, which virtually tears away the heart of basic fundamental freedoms enshrined in the two provisions.

Justice P.N. Bhagwati disagreed with the majority on the amendment to Article 31C. His Lordship stated that where protection to a law has to be given under Article 31C, the court would have to establish a direct connection between the intended effect and the protection sought. His Lordship placed the onus on the court to determine which portions of the legislation were not pushing forth the intended directive principle. The trouble with such a stance is that it gives the court a much more overt policymaking role, which is contrary to the law established earlier.

Minerva Mills developed the premise of basic structure further by analysing the 'core conscience' and the 'scheme' of our National Charter and this was done by Chief Justice Chandrachud even though His Lordship had previously dissented from the basic structure doctrine in *Kesavananda Bharati*. By invalidating

Section 55 of the 42nd Constitution Amendment Act, the majority opinion in *Minerva Mills* affirmed that there can be no ouster of judicial review even in cases of constitutional amendment. Thus, due process strategies were firmly entrenched in our constitutional jurisprudence.

In doing so, the court travelled beyond the territories reached in *Kesavananda Bharati* in the arena of judicial access. While striking down Section 4 of the 42nd Constitution Amendment Act, the Supreme Court made it clear that fundamental rights have primacy over directive principles. It was thus asserted that courts could be approached for enforcing fundamental rights which cannot be subordinated to directive principles. In this way, the Supreme Court enriched the core substantive values of our Constitution, as against the procedural ones.

NOTES

1. AIR 1951 SC 458.
2. AIR 1965 SC 845, para 19, p. 854.
3. Fali S. Nariman, *The State of the Nation*, (Penguin Books, 2014), p. 183.
4. J. Bose in *The State of West Bengal v. Anwar Ali Sarkar,* AIR 1952 SC 75, p. 103.
5. *Youngstown Sheet & Tube Co. v. Sawyer*, 343 US 579, p. 610.
6. Professor Emeritus Lawrence H. Tribe, *The Invisible Constitution,* (Oxford University Press, 2008), p. 115.
7. AIR 1965 SC 845, para 57, p. 864.
8. Ibid., para 58, p. 864.
9. AIR 1967 SC 1643.
10. Ibid.
11. Ibid., p. 1698.
12. Upendra Baxi, *The Indian Supreme Court and Politics* (Eastern Book

Co., 1980), p. 22.

13. AIR 1952 SC 75.
14. (1968) 2 AER 995, p. 998.
15. 245 US 418.
16. (1939) FCR 18, p. 42.
17. Michael Folly, *The Silence of Constitutions*, (Routledge, 1989).
18. (1973) 4 SCC, para 539.
19. (1973) 4 SCC 225, para 652.
20. Ibid., para 651.
21. (1973) 4 SCC 225, para 1124.
22. Ibid., para 1445, p. 776
23. Ibid., para 1426, p. 767.
24. Ibid., para 1427, p. 768.
25. Ibid., para 1426, p. 767.
26. Ibid., para 1537, p. 768 and pp. 824–25.
27. AIR 1950 SC 27.
28. Ronald Dworkin, *Taking Rights Seriously*, (Harvard University Press, 1978), p. 133.
29. Ronald Dworkin, *Law's Empire*, (Harvard University Press, 1986).
30. Alexander M. Bickel, *The Least Dangerous Branch: The Supreme Court at the Bar of Politics*, (Bobbs-Merrill, 1962), p. 16.
31. Larry Simon, 'The Authority of the Constitution and its Meaning: A Preface to a Theory of Constitutional Interpretation', (*Southern California Law Review*, 1958), 58 612.
32. H.L.A. Hart, *The Concept of Law*, (Oxford University Press, 2012), p. 124.
33. Dworkin, *Taking Rights Seriously*, op. cit., pp. 1–130; Dworkin, *Law's Empire*, op. cit., pp. 176–275.
34. 1975 Supp SCC 1.
35. Ibid., para 59, p. 44.
36. Ibid., para 198, p. 87.
37. Ibid., para 213, p. 94.

38. Ibid., para 264, p. 119.
39. Ibid., para 266, p. 120.
40. Ibid., para 267, p. 120.
41. Ibid., para 302, p. 128.
42. Ibid., para 305, p. 128.
43. Ibid., paras 520–521, pp. 197–98.
44. Ibid., para 635, p. 241.
45. Ibid., para 676, P. 256.
46. AIR 1952 SC 75.
47. (1975) Supp SCC 1, paras 680–681, pp. 257–58.
48. (1980) 3 SCC 225.
49. (1980) 3 SCC 625, para 12, p. 641.
50. Ibid., para 17, p. 643
51. Ibid., para 16, pp. 642–43.

2

DISSENT IN THE LAST COURT, CHANGING CONSTITUTIONAL VALUES

Upholding Individual Liberty and Opposing the State's Encroachment of the Same During the Emergency

ADM JABALPUR V. SHIVKANT SHUKLA ETC. ETC.[1]

The importance of this judgment lies in its monumental dissent by Justice Hans Raj Khanna, in which the learned judge, during the dark days of that phoney Emergency, kept the flickering candle of individual liberty burning. This minority judgment also paved the way for the future development of the 'Due Process' doctrine in *Maneka Gandhi v. Union of India and Others*[2], which rests on the concept that anything arbitrary is an antithesis of the guarantee of equality in Article 14. The judgment also resulted in a far-reaching constitutional amendment, vide the Constitution (44th Amendment) Act, 1978, (henceforth the 44th Constitution Amendment Act), by which it was made clear that proceedings for enforcement of rights under articles 20 and 21 of the Constitution, even during an Emergency, can never be suspended by a Presidential Declaration under Article 359 of the Constitution.

The decision arose in the background of the following facts: Various persons who were detained under Section 3 (1) of the

Maintenance of Internal Security Act (MISA) petitioned before different High Courts for habeas corpus, praying for their release. At the hearing of those petitions, the state governments raised the preliminary objection to their maintainability on the ground that the plea for release of the detenues, being substantially based under Article 21, could not be entertained by the High Courts, as the rights of the petitioners to move any court for enforcement of freedom under Article 21 had been suspended by the Presidential Order dated 27 June 1975, issued under Article 359, as a sequel to the Emergency declared in the country. Therefore, the state governments in various High Courts contended that the petitions should be dismissed at the threshold.

The High Courts of Allahabad, Bombay, Delhi, Karnataka, Madhya Pradesh, Punjab and Rajasthan held that it was open to the detenues to challenge the detention if they could show the same was ultra vires MISA or that the power of detention had been exercised in breach of conditions prescribed in the act. However, the High Courts of Andhra Pradesh, Kerala and Madras upheld the preliminary objection.

Various state governments and the Union of India challenged before Supreme Court the orders of the High Courts which overruled the preliminary objection of the government. During the pendency of the proceeding before the Supreme Court, the president issued a further order on January 8 1976 under Article 359(1) of the Constitution, declaring the right to move any court for enforcement of rights under Article 19 and that any proceeding pending in any court for the enforcement of those rights would remain suspended during the Proclamation of Emergency dated 3 December 1971 and 27 June 1975.

The case was heard by a Constitution Bench of the Supreme Court consisting of Chief Justice A.N. Ray and Justices H.R. Khanna, M. Hameedullah Beg, Y.V. Chandrachud and P.N.

Bhagwati. Five judgments were delivered by all the five judges separately, but the majority opinion, of Chief Justice A.N. Ray, Justice M.H. Beg, Justice Y.V. Chandrachud and Justice P.N. Bhagwati, upheld the preliminary objection of the government, and held that in view of the Presidential Order dated 27 June 1975, no person had the right to move a writ petition under Article 226 before a High Court for habeas corpus or any other writ, to challenge the legality of the detention order on the ground that the order is not under or in accordance with the act, or is illegal, or is vitiated by malafides, factual and legal, or is based on extraneous consideration.

Justice Khanna, in his dissenting opinion held, inter alia, that Article 226, empowering the High Court to issue writ of habeas corpus, was an integral part of the Constitution, and no power had been conferred by the Constitution on any authority for suspending the power of the High Court to issue a writ in the nature of habeas corpus during Emergency. His Lordship further held that a Presidential Order under Article 359(1) could suspend, during Emergency, the right to move any court for the enforcement of fundamental rights mentioned in the order. But rights under statute, being not fundamental rights, could be enforced during the Emergency, despite the Presidential Order. His Lordship also held that Article 21 could not be considered to be the sole repository of the right to life and personal liberty. Even without Article 21, the state does not have the power to deprive a person of his life and liberty without the authority of law, as the same is a basic postulate and assumption of the rule of law in every civilized society. His Lordship further explained that even before the Constitution came, no one could be deprived of his life or liberty without the authority of law. Such a legal position continued in force after the commencement of the Constitution in view of Article 372.

We find these thoughts in an embryonic form in the opinion of Justice Khanna in *Kesavananda Bharti*[3] as well. Justice Khanna held in *Kesavananda*, 'It would, in my opinion, not be a correct approach to say that amendments of the Constitution relating to abridgment or taking away of fundamental rights would not have the effect of denuding human beings of basic dignity and would result in the extinguishment of essential values of life.' Therefore, His Lordship upheld the views taken by the nine high courts that the Presidential Order dated 27 June 1975 could not affect the maintainability of a habeas corpus petition. His Lordship, however, did not pronounce on the validity of Section 16A (9) of MISA since the habeas corpus petitions were pending a decision on merits before the High Courts.

About the majority judgment, Chief Justice M.N. Venkatachaliah, in his H.R. Khanna Memorial Lecture delivered in New Delhi on 25 February 2009, opined that it should be 'confined to the dustbin of history'. The learned chief justice equated the dissent of Justice Khanna with that of Lord Atkins in *Liversidge v. Sir John Anderson.*[4] Noted jurist Fali S. Nariman described the majority judgment of the Supreme Court as one of its 'most deplorable decisions'[5], and further said, '…it was judicial pusillanimity at its worst.'[6] The Supreme Court also noted that the dissenting judgment of Justice Khanna became the law of the land[7] in view of the 44th Constitution Amendment Act by which Article 359 of the Constitution was amended and clauses (1) and (1A) of Article 359 made it very clear that the right to move any court for the enforcement of the rights under articles 20 and 21 could not be suspended. Previously, the bar under Article 359 operated against moving the courts for enforcement of any of the rights under Part III of the Constitution.

Another matter of some importance is that, apart from Chief Justice A.N. Ray, all the other three judges who shared the majority opinion with the chief justice became chief justices of India later. Even though chief justiceship was due to Justice Khanna, on the retirement of Chief Justice Ray, Justice Khanna knew the consequence of his dissent and he said to his younger sister, about his dissenting judgment, 'I have prepared a judgment which is going to cost me the Chief Justiceship of India.'[8] In fact, it did. F.S. Nariman noted:

> It was directly as a result of the dissent in this case that Justice Khanna was subsequently 'superseded' in January 1977 when it was his turn as the senior most judge, to be appointed Chief Justice of India. Contrary to long standing practice, he was not appointed Chief Justice of India. Khanna then promptly resigned.[9]

H.M. Seervai, in *The Emergency, Future Safeguards and the Habeas Corpus: A Criticsm*, wrote that the censor banned even publication of Justice Khanna's dissent in the newspaper.[10]

Justice Khanna's memorable dissent upheld the concept of rule of law being opposed to arbitrariness, and the learned judge was very poignant in his observations:

> Even in the absence of Article 21 of the Constitution, the State has got no power to deprive a person of his life or liberty without the authority of law. This is the essential postulate and basic assumption of the rule of law and not of men in all civilized nations. Without such sanctity of life and liberty, the distinction between a lawless society and one governed by laws would cease to have any meaning. The principle that no one shall be deprived of his life or liberty without the authority of law is rooted in the consideration that life and liberty are priceless possessions which cannot be made the plaything of individual whim and caprice and that any act which has

> the effect of tampering with life and liberty must receive sustenance from and sanction of the laws of the land.[11]

From the aforesaid proposition, Justice Khanna defined the contours of the rule of law and held that the rule of law was not a nebulous concept. According to the learned judge, the important facets of the rule of law are 'absence of arbitrariness and the need of the authority of law for official acts affecting prejudicially the rights of individuals'. Along with that, the learned judge held that the power of the court to grant relief against arbitrariness or in the absence of authority of law, in a matter relating to the liberty of the subject, is a normal feature of the rule of law and pointed out that government under law means the supremacy of law over the government. The learned judge also said that 'the powers of the executive should not only be derived from law, but should also be limited by law'.[12]

Therefore, in formulating the concept of rule of law, being antithetical to arbitrariness, Justice Khanna's dissenting opinion heralded the subsequent expansion of the doctrine of equality by the Supreme Court in *Maneka Gandhi* that arbitrariness is the reverse of rule of law.

In addition, Justice Khanna's dissenting opinion, by recognizing the locus of the detainee to approach the courts for redress, expanded the concept of access to justice, and thus strengthened the concept of procedural due process. But the majority opinion, by withholding access to court to an aggrieved person who was illegally denied of his liberty, took the most cramped view of liberty. This is an instance of a very constricted constitutional adjudication during Emergency. It has already been noted that the dissenting opinion of Justice Khanna has become the law of the land in view of the 44th Constitution Amendment Act. If we look at the Statement of Objects and Reasons of the 44th Constitution Amendment Act, it is clear that it was inspired by the historic dissent of Justice Khanna. Relevant excerpts from the Statement of Objects and Reasons are excerpted:

> As a further check against the misuse of the Emergency provisions and to put the right to life and liberty on a secure footing, it would be provided that the power to suspend the right to move the court for the enforcement of a fundamental right cannot be exercised in respect of the fundamental right to life and liberty.[13]

Towards the concluding portion of the dissenting opinion, the learned judge made it clear that the question of utmost importance and gravity, and a question which is not only important for interpreting the Constitution but which has an impact upon the basic values affecting life, liberty and the rule of law, was raised in the case, which, according to the learned judge, was 'whether the law speaking through the authority of the courts would be absolutely silenced and rendered mute'[14] because of the Emergency. In the penultimate paragraph of his opinion, the learned judge referred to the observation of Chief Justice Hughes, that dissent in a court of last resort is an appeal to the brooding spirit of law so that in future days a later decision may correct the error which has crept into the majority opinion. This has really happened in the case of the dissenting opinion of Justice Khanna. By a future amendment of the Constitution, his dissenting opinion has now become the law of the land, and the majority opinion has virtually lost its relevance in the context of the 44th Constitution Amendment Act.

About the role of the higher courts in dealing with preventive detention during the Emergency, Seervai observed that the High Courts rose to the occasion, but 'the Supreme Court sank'.[15] However, one dissenting opinion in the Supreme Court provoked the 44th Constitution Amendment Act to ensure access to justice of any person for enforcing his rights to life and liberty even during Emergency. Thus, the eternal values of civil liberty and freedom have been recognized in our Constitution as non-derogable standards and are to be regarded as principles of 'jus cogens' in international law.

F.S. Nariman rightly found some similarity between the decision of the ADM Jabalpur and that of Dred Scott, rendered more than a century ago in 1857 by a 6:2 majority of the American Supreme Court. The majority in *Dred Scott* held that a black person could never be a citizen of the US. A strong criticism of this view by Abraham Lincoln got national attention and ultimately helped him win the presidential election, which changed history. In both the cases, powerful dissenting opinions brought about far-reaching changes in these two democracies.

NOTES

1. (1976) 2 SCC 521.
2. (1978) 1 SCC 248.
3. (1973) 4 SCC 225, para 1496, pp. 786–87.
4. (1942) AC 206.
5. F.S. Nariman, *Before Memory Fades: An Autobiography*, (Hay House, 2010), p. 168.
6. Ibid., p. 170.
7. *Ramdeo Chauhan @ Rajnath Chauhan v. Bani Kant Das and Others*, (2010) 12 SC 516.
8. H.R. Khanna, *Neither Roses nor Thorns*, (Eastern Book Co., 2010), p. 83.
9. Nariman, *Before Memory Fades*, op. cit., p. 175.
10. H.M. Seervai, *The Emergency, Future Safeguards and the Habeas Corpus: A Criticism*, (N.M. Tripathi Ltd, 1978), p. viii.
11. (1973) 4 SCC 225, para 530.

12. Ibid., para 560.
13. Statement of Objects and Reasons of the 44th Constitution Amendment Act, para 8.
14. (1973) 4 SCC 225, para 573.
15. H.M. Seervai, *Constitutional Law of India*, Vol II, (Universal Law Pub. Co. P. Ltd., 2013), p. 2177.

3

FROM GOPALAN TO GANDHI

The Evolving Mosaic of Constitutional Interpretation

THE JOURNEY OF the Supreme Court, from its judgment in *A.K. Gopalan v. State of Madras*[1]—heard by the Constitution Bench of the Supreme Court in 1950—to the one heard by its Constitution Bench in the case of *Maneka Gandhi v. Union of India and Ors*[2]—in which the judgment was rendered in January 1978—is a very engrossing one, covering a span of about twenty-eight years. It shows the swing of the judicial pendulum from the tradition of black-letter law in *Gopalan* to the resurgence and firm assertion of the concept of 'due process' in *Maneka Gandhi*. This dynamic, generic and more expansive interpretation of fundamental rights by the Supreme Court in *Maneka Gandhi* in the post-Emergency period not only affected the lives of Indians, but also considerably influenced jurisprudential development in different countries.

The decisions in *Maneka Gandhi* and the allied group of cases are not concerned with constitutional amendments, but they would disclose a paradigm shift in the Supreme Court's interpretation of the basic guarantees given in the Constitution in its chapter on fundamental rights. Fundamental rights have already been discussed in an earlier chapter as higher laws, to the extent that all laws made by the state, after the commencement of the Constitution, would have to conform to its mandate, failing which the laws would be declared void (Article 13[2] of the Constitution). Even laws prior to the Constitution can continue only if they are consistent with fundamental rights and to the extent of their inconsistencies, they are to be declared void (Article 13[1]).

Therefore, the changing pattern of interpretation of fundamental rights is integral to our jurisprudence, affecting both the enactment of statutory law and the practice of administrative law.

In *Gopalan*, the validity of the Preventive Detention Act, 1950, was challenged, mainly on two grounds:

(1) Whether the act violated the guarantee under Article 21
(2) Whether the act fell foul of the freedom guaranteed under Article 19

One of the questions raised by *Gopalan* was that the procedure provided by the act does not stand the test of 'procedure established by law' under Article 21, and it was argued that the procedure under Article 21 must comply with the principles of natural justice. Chief Justice Kania dismissed the said argument, saying:

> The Courts are not at liberty to declare an Act void because in their opinion it is opposed to a spirit supposed to pervade the constitution but not expressed in words. Where the fundamental law has not limited, either in terms or by necessary implication, the general powers conferred upon the Legislature we cannot declare a limitation under the notion of having discovered something in the spirit of the constitution which is not even mentioned in the instrument.[3]

The court, by laying down the aforesaid proposition, refused to examine whether the procedure was fair, as the word 'due' is absent in Article 21, and the learned chief justice held that 'the justiciable aspect of the law, i.e. to consider whether it is reasonable or not by the Court, does not form part of the Indian Constitution'.[4] Therefore, the learned Chief Justice opined that 'the Constitution gave the Legislature the final word to determine the law'.[5]

On the second question, namely, on the interrelationship between articles 19 and 21, all the judges, excepting Justice Fazl Ali, held that articles 19 and 21 had to be read as mutually exclusive. It was held by the majority that articles 19 and 21 are not complementary to each other, as there is no mention of right to life in Article 19.[6] However, the dissenting view, expressed by Justice Fazl Ali, demonstrates judicial thinking which is much ahead of his time. The learned judge, in his dissent, held:

> To my mind, the scheme of the chapter dealing with the fundamental rights does not contemplate what is attributed to it, namely, that each article is a code by itself and is independent of the others. In my opinion, it cannot be said that Articles 19, 20, 21 and 22 do not to some extent overlap each other.[7]

As in other cases, discussed in the previous chapter, in this case also the dissenting opinion was subsequently accepted by the Supreme Court. This was done in *Rustom Cavasjee Cooper v. Union of India* (hereinafter Cooper's case)[8] which is referred to later.

On 11 January 1952, which is within a year and a half of the decision rendered in *Gopalan*, the Constitution Bench of the Supreme Court, this time consisting of seven judges, in *State of West Bengal v. Anwar Ali Sarkar*,[9] examined the vires of the West Bengal Special Courts Act, 1950, and the Constitution Bench held that the provision of Section 5 (1) is ultra vires the Constitution, insofar as it allows the state government to direct any case to be tried by a special court.

While agreeing with the majority opinion, and defining what is meant by 'classification', Justice Vivian Bose virtually leaned in favour of an interpretation which amounted to introducing the 'due process' principle. While determining whether a classification was valid or not, the learned judge held:

> However much the real ground of decision may be hidden behind a screen of words like 'reasonable', 'substantial', 'rational' and 'arbitrary' the fact would remain that judges are substituting their own judgment of what is right and proper and reasonable and just for that of the legislature [sic]; and up to a point that, I think, is inevitable when a judge is called to crystallise a vague generality like Article 14 into a concrete concept.[10]

This is in stark contrast to the interpretation of Chief Justice Kania in *Gopalan* about a year and a half ago, and it may be mentioned that three learned judges—M.C. Mahajan, B.K. Mukherjee and S.R. Das—who shared the views of Chief Justice Kania in *Gopalan*, were also members of the bench in Anwar Ali. Justice Bose gave the aforesaid interpretation as His Lordship thought, if I may say so, rightly, that the words in the Constitution are not dull, lifeless and static words 'as in some mummified manuscript'. According to Justice Bose, they are 'living flames' and 'tongues of dynamic fire potent enough to mould the future as well as guide the present'. The learned judge rightly understood the basic tenets of constitutional interpretation by holding: 'The Constitution must, in my judgment, be left elastic enough to meet from time to time the altering conditions of a changing world with its shifting emphasis and differing needs'.[11]

It is thus clear that the germs of future jurisprudential interpretations of fundamental rights were there in the judgment of Justice Bose as early as in January 1952. However, the *Gopalan* doctrine was not overruled in *Anwar Ali*. The majority ratio in *Gopalan* held the field till it was examined and overruled by the majority judgment of the Supreme Court in the eleven-judge decision in Cooper's case.[12]

Cooper held shares in several banks and also had bank accounts. He was also a director of the Central Bank of India. Before the Supreme Court he challenged the Banking Companies (Acquisition and Transfer of Undertakings) Ordinance, 1969, and the Banking Companies (Acquisition and Transfer of Undertakings) Act, 1969, which replaced the ordinance. Cooper also challenged the promulgation of another ordinance, on the same day, that is, 19 July 1969, whereby the undertaking of fourteen named commercial banks were transferred and vested, under the ordinance, in the government. Apart from the other questions, the challenge on which the constitutional interpretation of fundamental rights by the Supreme Court changed from where it rested in *Gopalan* was in examining the petitioner's challenge that the impugned enactments violated his fundamental rights under Article 14, 19(1)(f) and (g) and 31(2) of the Constitution. A challenge was also made to the invasion of his right under Article 301.

In upholding the said challenge, Justice Shah, delivering the majority judgment, held that Articles 19(1)(f) and 31(2) were not mutually exclusive. Before reaching the said conclusion, the learned judge dealt in detail with *Gopalan* and various other cases, namely the case of *Ram Singh and Others v. State of Delhi*,[13] and the ratio in *Gopalan* was expressly departed from. In paragraph 49, the learned judge summed up the ratio in Cooper's case, saying:

> In determining the impact of State action upon constitutional guarantees which are fundamental, it follows that the extent of protection against impairment of a fundament right is determined not by the object of

> the Legislature nor by the form of the action, but by its direct operation upon the individual's rights.[14]

Thus, the object test in *Gopalan* was replaced in Cooper's case by the 'effects test'. In fact, referring to various articles in Part III of the Constitution, the learned judge said that they do not follow 'a uniform pattern'. But according to the learned judge there was one common thread running through them, namely the protection of the rights of the individuals, or groups of individuals, against infringement by state action. That is why the learned judge held that 'Part III of the Constitution weaves a pattern of guarantees on the texture of basic human rights. The guarantees delimit the protection of those rights in their allotted fields: they do not attempt to enunciate distinct rights'.[15]

Subsequently, two Constitution Bench decisions of the Supreme Court delivered within a gap of about four and a half years expanded the ambit and reach of the court's interpretation of fundamental rights, and were in favour of protecting those rights which were facing invasion by the state authority. The first was delivered before the Emergency in the case of *E.P. Royappa v. State of Tamil Nadu*[16] while the second was delivered after the Emergency in the case of *Maneka Gandhi*.[17]

E.P. Royappa, who held the post of chief secretary in the Government of Tamil Nadu, was transferred to a newly created post of a temporary nature, and challenged the said transfer in an Article 32 petition on the ground that he had been denigrated to a relatively unimportant post as he had incurred the displeasure of the chief minister of the state. The Supreme Court, while dismissing the petition, gave a new interpretation to Article 14, which was further developed in the subsequent decision in *Maneka Gandhi*. Justice Bhagwati, delivering a concurring opinion with Chief Justice Ray, relied on the concept of reasonableness, hitherto unknown in the arena of Article 14.

Justice Bhagwati raised a question on the content and reach of Article 14 and then answered it in very glowing terms:

> It is a founding faith, to use the words of Bose, J., a 'way of life', and it must not be subjected to a narrow pedantic or lexicographic approach. We cannot countenance any attempt to truncate its all-embracing scope and meaning, for to do so would be to violate its activist magnitude. Equality is a dynamic concept with many aspects and dimensions and it cannot be 'cribbed, cabined and confined' within traditional and doctrinaire limits. From a positivistic point of view, equality is antithetic to arbitrariness. In fact, equality and arbitrariness are sworn enemies; one belongs to the rule of law in a republic while the other, to the whim and caprice of an absolute monarch. Where an act is arbitrary, it is implicit in it that it is unequal both according to political logic and constitutional law and is therefore violative of Article 14.[18]

The expression 'a way of life' was used by Justice Bose in his concurring opinion in the case of *Bidi Supply Co. v. Union of India and Others*[19] while interpreting Article 14. Justice Bose referred to certain other important ideas and opined:

> Article 14 sets out, to my mind, an attitude of mind, a way of life, rather than precise rule of law. It embodies a general awareness in the consciousness of people at large of something that exists and which is very well and which cannot be pinned down to any precise analysis of facts.[20]

Justice Bhagwati virtually enlarged the embryo of the said concept in extremely elegant prose, and in the process was inspired by the Shakespearean turn of phrase in Macbeth.[21] In doing so, Justice Bhagwati, in his opinion, broadened the sweep of Article

14 by taking it beyond the doctrine of classification based on an intelligible differentia with the nexus between the basis of classification and the object of the law under consideration as laid down by Chief Justice S.R. Das in *Shri Ram Krishna Dalmia v. Shri Justice S.R. Tendolkar and Ors.*[22]

However, one thing of some interest is that in a matter of less importance, like the transfer of a chief secretary, which is not a punishment in service law, Justice Bhagwati propounded the aforesaid doctrine of Article 14 by holding that equality is antithetic to arbitrariness and they are sworn enemies. But when questions of a far greater import relating to deprivation of personal liberty and a citizen's access to a court of justice came up before him later in *ADM Jabalpur v. S.S. Shukla*, Justice Bhagwati did not take the aforesaid view, which was actually put forward by Justice Khanna in his lone dissenting voice (as noted in previous chapters). However, it has already been noted that several decades before, Justice Vivian Bose, in his opinion in *Anwar Ali*, rejected the narrow doctrinaire approach to Article 14, as pointed out (supra). However, this doctrine of reasonableness and non-arbitrariness emerged with much greater force in *Maneka Gandhi v. Union of India and Ors.*

(1) Maneka Gandhi (presently union minister for women and child development) was noticed by the Regional Passport Authority to the effect that her passport had been impounded and she was asked to surrender the same within seven days. Challenging the same in an Article 32 petition, several contentions were raised by her before the Supreme Court, the chief among them being that the right to go abroad is a component of the Right to Life and Personal Liberty under Article 21 of the Constitution.
(2) She was denied the said right without a hearing and without any reason for the denial of the said right.

(3) Section 10(3)(c) of the Passport Act, 1967, empowering the Passport Authority to impound a passport, in the interest of the general public, was vague and unreasonable.

The Supreme Court held that Section 10(3)(c) is not violative of Article 14, but the order of impounding was in violation of the principles of natural justice. Since the attorney general assured the court of expeditious consideration of any representation that may be made by Mrs Gandhi, the court felt that the vice could be removed and the order could not be assailed on the ground that it violated principles of natural justice. In doing so, the court relied on the concept of post-decisional hearing, curing the defects in an earlier order, which had been passed without a hearing.

In the opinion of Chief Justice M. Hameedullah Beg, in *Maneka Gandhi*, there was tacit approval of the dissenting opinion of Justice Khanna in *ADM Jabalpur*, even though Chief Justice Beg had not agreed with Justice Khanna in *ADM Jabalpur*. But in *Maneka Gandhi*, Chief Justice Beg clearly stated: 'I think that both the rights of personal security and of personal liberty recognized by what Blackstone termed "natural law" are embodied within Article 21 of the Constitution.'[23] Thus, the learned chief justice also relied on the majority doctrine in the case of *I.C. Golaknath v. State of Punjab*[24], that fundamental rights are natural rights embodied in the Constitution itself.[25] Chief Justice Beg, after quoting the dissenting view of Justice Fazl Ali in *Gopalan*, seems to have agreed with the said dissenting view, saying:

> Articles dealing with different fundamental rights contained in Part III of the Constitution do not represent entirely separate streams of rights which do not mingle at many points. They are all parts of an integrated scheme in the Constitution. Their waters must mix to constitute that grand flow of unimpeded and impartial Justice.[26]

Expanding his doctrine in *Royappa*, Justice Bhagwati in *Maneka Gandhi* held that the attempt of the court should be to expand the reach and ambit of fundamental rights, rather than attenuate their meaning and content by a process of judicial construction.[27] His Lordship also held that Article 14 pervades, like a brooding omnipresence, and the procedure contemplated by Article 21 must answer the test of reasonableness and must be in conformity with Article 14. His Lordship further held that it should be 'right, just and fair and not arbitrary, fanciful or oppressive'.[28]

This refreshingly right-oriented approach of Justice Bhagwati was quite contrary to his view in *ADM Jabalpur*. However, the matter which is of greater importance is that for the first time in the constitutional history of India, a majority judgment of the Supreme Court acknowledged that the Right to Life and Personal Liberty must stand the test of fairness and reasonableness, even though the principle of 'due process' was expressly deleted from our Constitution by the founding fathers. However, there is a substantial difference between the doctrine of reasonableness articulated in Khanna's dissent in *ADM Jabalpur* and the one formulated by the majority opinion of Justice Bhagwati in *Maneka Gandhi*. In *ADM Jabalpur*, Justice Khanna rested his doctrine on the concept of natural law, but in *Maneka Gandhi*, Justice Bhagwati rested his doctrine on the text of the Constitution itself—Article 14—by employing a protean and flexible interpretation of fundamental rights under our Constitution, and in doing so Justice Bhagwati endorsed the interpretation of fundamental rights in Cooper's case.

NOTES

1. AIR 1950 SC 27.
2. (1978) 1 SCC 248.

3. AIR 1950 SC 27, para 26, p. 42.
4. Ibid., para 19, p. 39.
5. Ibid.
6. Ibid., para 172, p. 91.
7. Ibid., para 58, p. 52.
8. (1970) 1 SCC 248.
9. AIR 1952 SC 75.
10. Ibid., para 82, p. 102.
11. Ibid., para 85, p. 108.
12. (1970) 1 SCC 248.
13. (1951) SCR 451.
14. (1970) 1 SCC 248, para 49, p. 288.
15. Ibid., para 52, p. 289.
16. (1974) 4 SCC 3.
17. Ibid., para 85, p. 38.
18. (1951) SCR 451, para 85, p. 38.
19. AIR 1956 SC 479.
20. Ibid., para 16, p. 485.
21. Shakespeare used the expression in a slightly different order, as 'cabin'd, cribb'd, confin'd', spoken by Macbeth in Act 3 Scene IV of *Macbeth*.
22. AIR 1958 SC 538, para 11, p. 547.
23. Ibid., para 208, p. 397.
24. AIR 1967 SC 1643.
25. Ibid., para 212.
26. (1974) 4 SCC 3, para 202, p. 394.
27. (1978) 1 SCC 248, p. 280.
28. Ibid., para 7, p. 284.

4

STRENGTHENING THE ROOTS OF DEMOCRACY IN INDIA AND ENSURING A FREE AND TRANSPARENT ELECTION PROCESS

S.R. Bommai and Subsequent Decisions

THE NEXT MAJOR decision which rejuvenated the roots of democracy in India was rendered by a nine-judge Constitution Bench of the Supreme Court in the case of *S.R. Bommai and Others v. Union of India and Others.*[1]

The provision of Article 356 of the Constitution that came up for interpretation in *Bommai* is in Part XVIII of the Constitution, which deals with Emergency Provisions. Article 356 empowers the president, in the case of failure of the constitutional machinery in the state, to impose President's Rule by overthrowing the elected government of the state. This provision had its counterpart in Section 93 of the Government of India Act, 1935. Even though the framers of our Constitution had had an unhappy experience of the application of Article 93 in the colonial days, a similar provision was retained in the form of Article 356 in the Constitution. This is because the founding fathers, with regard to the prevalent situation in India in or about 1947–48, thought that as the country was going through grave and difficult times the 'danger of grave emergency in India is very real'.[2] However, the said provision was incorporated by the founding fathers with the pious hope that the same 'would remain a dead letter', and would be used very sparingly.[3]

Contrary to their expectations independent India saw repetitive use, and at times flagrant misuse, of Article 356. Article 356 provisions were invoked on more than a hundred occasions prior to the decision in *Bommai*. In the background of the flagrant abuse of Article 356, which topples a democratically elected government, the Supreme Court's decision in *Bommai* provides certain salutary safeguards. It is heartening to note that the decision in *Bommai* has proved to be a deterrent to the misuse of the powers of Article 356. This explains the importance of this decision.

Prior to the decision in *Bommai*, the question of whether a presidential proclamation dissolving a state assembly could be challenged before the High Courts came up for consideration before different High Courts. Most of the High Courts, including those of Kerala, Calcutta, Punjab and Haryana, Andhra Pradesh, and Orissa, pronounced that a presidential proclamation is not justiciable before a court.

The question, in a slightly different form, came up for consideration before the Supreme Court in *State of Rajasthan v. Union of India*.[4] The bare facts of the case are that in April 1977, the union home minister addressed a letter to the chief ministers of several states where the Congress party had suffered reverses in the electoral poll, asking the respective governors of such states to dissolve the state assemblies and seek a fresh mandate. This was followed by a broadcast by the union law minister that the governments in those states have lost the confidence of the electorate, and their continuance in power is undemocratic.

Six out of those nine states petitioned the Supreme Court

under Article 32, urging that the home minister's letter and the broadcast by the law minister posed a threat to the continuance of the state assemblies on grounds which are dehors Article 356 of the Constitution. In that context, the Supreme Court rejected the contention that a judicial review of the presidential proclamation was barred. The leading judgments of Justice Bhagwati (as His Lordship then was) and of Justice Gupta expressly held that merely because a question of political complexion had been raised, that by itself could not be a ground precluding the court from discharging its duty if the questions had raised issues of constitutional import.[5] The Supreme Court made it very clear that the area of judicial review in respect of an exercise of power under Article 356 may be narrow, but if the crucial satisfaction for the exercise of that power was founded only on malafide, extraneous or irrelevant grounds, the court had the jurisdiction to examine it.[6]

However, subsequently, in *A.K. Roy v. Union of India*,[7] the Constitution Bench of the Supreme Court held that after deletion of clause (5) of Article 356 by the 44th Constitution Amendment Act, which was in existence when the Rajasthan case was decided, the statement of law in the Rajasthan case on the basis of clause (5) was no longer good law.

Before *Bommai* was decided by the Supreme Court, Article 356(5), which banned judicial review of an order under Article 356, was repealed by the 44th Constitution Amendment Act.

In *Bommai,* as many as six judgments were delivered by nine judges and the judgments revealed some areas of divergence on key issues. The majority judgment was by Justices Sawant, Kuldip Singh, Jeevan Reddy, Aggarwal and Pandyan, while the minority comprised Justices Ahmadi, Verma, Dayal and K. Ramaswamy.

In *Bommai*, the Supreme Court enriched our constitutional jurisprudence by upholding many constitutional values, like the parliamentary system, federalism, secularism and judicial control over executive function.

One of the most significant aspects of the judgment is that the majority held that the emergent situation which called for the invocation of Article 356 contemplated a situation of an impasse. Justice Sawant held, relying on the word *cannot* occurring in Article 356, that this would only mean a situation of physical impossibility which could not be remedied. Short of such a situation Article 356 cannot be invoked.[8] This interpretation strengthened the roots of democracy in our country. The power conferred under Article 356 is virtually similar to the powers under Article 58(2)(b) of the Pakistan Constitution and is an extreme power. Therefore, the Supreme Court held that this power can only be exercised when there is an actual or imminent breakdown of constitutional machinery.

This concept for reviewability of presidential power, which has been affirmed in *Bommai*, is virtually a facet of human rights jurisprudence. This concept was developed by the European Commission and the European Court of Human Rights under the European Convention of Human Rights (ECHR). It has been established at Strasbourg that the existence of Public Emergency is a justiciable issue.[9] Following the same, the Supreme Court, in *Bommai*, held that the satisfaction of the president in issuing a proclamation under Article 356 was open to judicial review. However, on the extent of judicial review, there was some divergence. Justice Sawant opined that the use of the power under Article 356 would be improper if in some situations set out by the learned judge the president gave no prior notice or opportunity to the state government to correct itself.[10] It is, therefore, clear that the learned judge read in the requirement of observing principles of natural justice before exercise of power under Article 356.

But Justices Jeevan Reddy and Aggarwal, even though sharing

the majority view with Justice Sawant, adopted a lesser test of scrutiny of presidential power under Article 356 by holding that the satisfaction of the president in issuing a proclamation under Article 356 is subjective in nature. The learned judges formulated the proposition as follows: 'Since it is a case of subjective satisfaction, question of observing the principle of natural justice does not and cannot arise.'

The learned judges clearly opined that natural justice principles cannot be imported into the situation.[11] From the discussion it appears that Justices Sawant and Kuldeep Singh actually relied on the principle of reasonableness in examining the justiciability of a presidential proclamation under Article 356. However, the judgment rendered by Justice Jeevan Reddy on behalf of himself and Justice Aggarwal adopted a slightly different test.

The importance of this judgment is that in answering the question that the satisfaction of the president is judicially reviewable, the judges relied on the basic structure doctrine and founded the principles as such:

> The federal principle, social pluralism and pluralist democracy which formed the basic structure of our constitution demand that the judicial review of the proclamation issued under Article 356(1) is not only an imperative necessity but is a stringent duty.[12]

The one remarkable thing about applying the basic structure test in *Bommai* is that prior to *Bommai*, the basic structure test was applied by the Supreme Court in judging the validity of constitutional amendments. In *Bommai*, however, the satisfaction of the president in passing a presidential order, which is an executive order, was tested through the prism of the basic structure doctrine.

The other important question laid down in *Bommai* was

that the court used the preamble of the Constitution as a basis for formulating the basic structure test. The court upheld the presidential action of the dismissal of three state governments as it found that those state governments were incapable of complying with the principle of secularism, which is one of the preambular values in the Constitution. Initially, secularism did not figure in the Preamble of the original Constitution but was added by the 42nd Constitution Amendment Act. However, the court held in *Bommai* that the principle of secularism was implicit in the constitutional principles and was made explicit by the 42nd Constitution Amendment Act.

The view in the *State of Rajasthan* case was that a proclamation under Article 356 is valid and the state legislature can be dissolved by the centre without waiting for the approval of the houses of Parliament.[13] This view was departed from in *Bommai*, and it was held that even if the proclamation is not approved by both houses of Parliament within two months, it would lapse automatically after that. Thus the dissolution of the legislative assembly in the state does not automatically happen with the presidential proclamation under Article 356.

It is therefore clear that the judgment in *Bommai* has really fortified the democratic fabric in the country. After *Bommai*, instances of invoking the provision of Article 356 have been substantially curtailed.

In the case of the dissolution of the Bihar Assembly in 2005, the Supreme Court, being moved under Article 32 in *Rameshwar Prasad (VI) v. Union of* India,[14] quashed the dissolution notification by holding that the use of Article 356 cannot be justified on 'mere ipse dixit, suspicion, whims and fancies of the Governor'. The principles in the *Bommai* decision were followed.

After the decision in *Bommai*, two more decisions, each by a three-judge bench of the Honourable Supreme Court, have further toughened the democratic fabric of our country. Both these decisions—*Union of India v. Association for Democratic Reforms & Another*[15] and *People's Union for Civil Liberties & Another (PUCL) v. Union of India & Another*[16]—are very important and brought about a fundamental paradigm shift in our election laws. It is axiomatic that holding of a fair election is of the essence in any democracy.

In the first case, the Union of India challenged the decision of the Delhi High Court, which had directed the Election Commission to secure to the voters certain information relating to each candidate seeking election. Thereafter, the Supreme Court was petitioned by those who went before the Delhi High Court and prayed for similar directions, which were issued by the Delhi High Court. They further prayed that the Supreme Court may frame guidelines under Article 141 of the Constitution by taking into consideration the 170th Report of the Law Commission of India.

While deciding the controversy, the Supreme Court held that in any election the choice of the voter is of utmost importance, and in making an effective choice, the voters must know the background of the candidate they are choosing in the election. The Supreme Court traced this right to vote as a natural right flowing from the concept of open democracy in Article 19(1) and 19(2) of the International Covenant of Civil and Political Rights. The Supreme Court also held that the right to know is a facet of the fundamental right of freedom of speech and expression of a voter under Article 19(1)(a) of the Constitution. The Supreme Court categorically held that the voter's expression in an election is articulated by the casting of a vote and that is how the voter speaks in an election. This was the first time that the Supreme Court equated the right to vote with the fundamental right of speech and expression under Article 19(1)(a) of the Constitution and further held that for a fair election in an open participatory democracy, proper information is a must for voters to make a meaningful choice.

Proceeding on the aforesaid principles, the Supreme Court endorsed the directions of the Election Commission by arguing that the reservoir of power in Article 324 of the Constitution empowers the Election Commission to issue necessary direction when the Representation of People Act is silent in that regard. Thus the Supreme Court upheld the directions issued by the High Court and directed that the Election Commission could call for an affidavit by issuing an order in exercise of its power under Article 324 of the Constitution from each candidate seeking election to Parliament or a state legislature to furnish the following items of information:

(1) Whether the candidate is convicted/acquitted/discharged of any criminal offence in the past—if any, or whether he is punished with imprisonment or fine.
(2) Prior to six months of filing of nomination, whether the candidate is accused in any pending case of any offence punishable with imprisonment for two years or more, and in which charge is framed or cognizance is taken by the court of law. If so, provide the details thereof.
(3) The assets (immovable, movable, bank balance, etc.) of a candidate and of his/her spouse and that of dependants.
(4) Liabilities, if any, particularly whether there are any overdues of any public financial institution or government dues.
(5) The educational qualifications of the candidate.

This is a path-breaking judgment of the Supreme Court in seeking to streamline the election process, which is crucial in a democracy.

In view of the judgment of the Supreme Court in *Union of India v. Association for Democratic Reforms & Another*, the Representation of People Act was amended. By way of amendment,

Section 33A was added under the caption 'Right to Information'. Section 33A, which came by way of amendment, did not give full effect to the judgment of the Supreme Court in *Union of India*. Rather, the amendment gave effect to the same in a truncated manner by providing that the candidate in an election has to furnish information on (1) whether he is accused of any offence punishable with imprisonment for two years or more in a pending case in which charge has been framed by a competent court and (2) whether the candidate has been convicted of any offence other than the offence in sub-sections (1) and (2) of Section 8 of the Representation of People Act and sentenced to imprisonment for one year or more.

Section 33B, which also came by way of the same amendment, on the other hand, imposed a ban on disclosure of any other information despite anything to the contrary in any judgment, decree or order of any court. Challenging Section 33B, as amended, People's Union for Civil Liberties filed a second case on several grounds in *People's Union for Civil Liberties v. Union of India*.[17]

Dealing with the said challenge, the Supreme Court held that the amendment of Section 33 is ultra vires as it stifles free and fair elections. The three learned judges delivered three separate opinions.

Justice Shah held that the amended Section 33B was beyond the legislative competence of Parliament as in the case of *Union of India*, the Supreme Court had held that the voter has the fundamental right under Article 19(1)(a) of the Constitution to know the antecedents of a candidate and the said judgment had attained finality. The learned judge held that the voter's fundamental right to know the antecedents of a candidate was independent of his statutory rights under election laws. The learned judge further held that there is no fixed content on fundamental rights and they are empty vessels, which generations of judges have filled up with their thoughts in the light of their experience and by way of constitutional interpretation. Thus the contents of these rights have been expanded and enriched. Such a right cannot be ignored as a derivative fundamental right but is part of the named fundamental right. Justice P. Venkatrama Reddy, in His Lordship's judgment, also concurred with the formulation of Justice Shah and held that the right to vote in an election is not merely a statutory right but is a facet of a fundamental right under Article 19(1)(a) and therefore held that the amended Section 33B was not valid, as it was imposing a blanket ban on the right to information of a voter.

Justice Dharmadhikari also substantially agreed with the judgment of the other two learned judges, with minor differences from the conclusion of Justice Reddy.

These two judgments have sought to transform the election process in the largest democracy of the world by making it more transparent and participatory.

NOTES

1. (1994) 3 SCC 1.
2. Constituent Assembly Debates Vol. IX, p. 170 (http://164.100.47.132/LssNew/constituent/vol9pm.html, last accessed on 15 September 2014).
3. Ibid., p. 177.
4. (1977) 3 SCC 592.
5. Ibid., p. 661.
6. Ibid., p. 663.
7. (1982) 1 SCC 271.
8. (1994) 3 SCC 1, para 75, p. 103.
9. (1961) 1 EHRR 15.

10. Ibid., para 82, p. 106–7.
11. Ibid., p. 280.
12. Ibid., p. 304.
13. (1977) 3 SCC 592, pp. 1398, 1410.
14. (2006) 2 SCC 1.
15. (2002) 5 SCC 294.
16. (2003) 4 SCC 399.
17. Ibid.

5

ACCESS TO EDUCATION AND ITS DENIAL BY THE FALLACIOUS DICTUM

T.M.A. Pai and Two Subsequent Judgments; Part Restoration of Access by Article 15(1) (5), RTE and Society's Judgment

THE CONSTITUTION BENCH judgment of the Supreme Court in *T.M.A. Pai Foundation v. State of Kerala*[1] has been decided on such principles as to put severe constraints on the right to education of ordinary citizens. The judgment has substantially affected the right to education, especially the higher education of Indian citizens, by taking it beyond the means of most of us through a process of reasoning that, with utmost respect, is unconstitutional. *T.M.A. Pai* held that the right to establish an educational institution, whether for charity or for profit, being an occupation, is a fundamental right and is protected by Article 19(1)(g) of the Constitution. The said judgment has also held that the imposition of quota of state seats in unaided professional institutions constitutes a serious encroachment on the rights and autonomy of the private professional colleges and they are not saved under reasonable restrictions under Article 19(6) of the Constitution. However, fortunately, this position has been neutralized by the Constitution (93rd Amendment) Act, 2005, (henceforth the 93rd Constitution Amendment Act) which introduced clause (5) in Article 15.

This finding in *T.M.A. Pai*, that the right to establish and administer an educational institution is available to all citizens under 19(1)(g), subject to the restriction under Article 19(6), was reiterated by the Supreme Court in *Islamic Academy of Education and Another v. State of Karnataka*[2] and later on in *P.A. Inamdar and Others v. State of Maharashtra and Others.*[3]

In *T.M.A. Pai*, it has been held that both religious and linguistic minority status will be decided on the basis of the population of each state and not on the basis of the whole of India. The Supreme Court also held that transfer of the item 'education' from the state list to the concurrent list of the 7th Schedule in our Constitution does not bring about any difference. The same position has been reiterated in both *Inamdar* and *Islamic Academy* (supra).

The aforesaid interpretation by the Supreme Court seems to run counter to the object and scope of Article 30 of the Constitution. The rights under Article 30 are not given to citizens but have been given to minorities. Article 30 does not seem to protect an educational entrepreneur who is a majority in his own state, but if he crosses over to a neighbouring state, he becomes a minority and enjoys the protection under the said article. In my humble understanding, for coming under the protection of minorities under Article 30, the vulnerability of a religion or a language is an essential element. The article is meant to protect insulated sections of society. Therefore, minorities under Article 30 must necessarily mean those who form a distinct and identifiable group of citizens in India.

A concomitant right of the right under Article 30 is recognized under Article 30(1A) of the Constitution. The said article runs as under:

> In making any law providing for the compulsory acquisition of any property of an educational institution

established and administered by a minority, referred to in clause (1), the State shall ensure that the amount fixed by or determined under such law for the acquisition of such property as would not restrict or abrogate the right guaranteed under that clause.[4]

A perusal of the Article 30(1A) makes it clear that the minorities establishing and administering an educational institution have a fundamental right to the property of the educational institution, to such an extent that the state cannot acquire the said property in a manner which restricts or abrogates the fundamental right granted under Article 30(1). In the event of an acquisition, the Constitution's mandate on the state is to fix such an amount of compensation which will not restrict or abrogate the right of minorities under Article 30(1). In other words, the property in which the minorities establish and run an educational institution gets protection by way of Article 30(1A) from the ordinary mode of acquisition. It is made clear that in the event of an acquisition, the right to establish and administer the educational institution cannot be diluted; rather, it will have be protected by the amount of compensation.

Therefore, by holding that the right to establish an educational institution is a fundamental right of every citizen under Article 19(1)(g) of the Constitution, *T.M.A. Pai* has conferred on every citizen the right which has been conferred only on minorities under Articles 30(1) and 30(1A). By the same logic, as discussed earlier, the property in which an educational institution is established by anyone qualifies for the same protection which is given under Article 30(1A). An educational institution can only be established on some immovable property. So the fundamental right of a person to establish and run an educational institution is inextricably connected to the fundamental right to hold and own the said property on which the educational institution is established and run. Thus a citizen who has no fundamental right to property, in view of the express deletion of Article 19(1)(f) by the 44th Constitution Amendment Act, is conferred with the said fundamental right over property if he chooses to establish an educational institution on his property. This is also true on the principle of emanation as developed in *Maneka Gandhi v. Union of India and Others.*[5] It is axiomatic that no one can enjoy the fundamental right of founding and running an educational institution if the property on which the institution is run is acquired.

While deleting the fundamental right to property from Article 19(1)(f) of the Constitution, the following relevant recitals have been made in the Statement of Objects and Reasons of the 44th Constitution Amendment Act:

> In view of the special position sought to be given to fundamental rights, the right to property, which has been the occasion for more than one amendment of the Constitution, would cease to be a fundamental right and become only a legal right. Necessary amendments for this purpose are being made to Article 19 and Article 31 is being deleted. It would however, be ensured that the removal of property from the list of fundamental rights would not affect the rights of minorities to establish and administer educational institutions of their choice.[6]

It is thus clear that by recognizing the fundamental right to establish an educational institution of every citizen under Article 19(1)(g), *T.M.A. Pai* has virtually revived the already deleted fundamental right to property of a citizen if he is an educational entrepreneur. In addition, the distinction between an educational institution established by minorities and non-minorities in matters relating to acquisition of properties, as mentioned in Article 30

(1-A) and the clear intentions expressed in the 44th Constitution Amendment Act while deleting Article 19(f), stand obliterated.

This interpretation that the right to establish educational institutions is a fundamental right under Article 19(1)(g), in my humble understanding, is therefore not constitutionally sustainable as it seeks to revive a deleted fundamental right in respect of educational entrepreneurs and equates their property rights with those of the educational institutions set up by minorities. This is opposed to the tenets of the equality clause under Article 14, as a citizen setting up a cultural society, a dancing school or a sports complex—all extensions of educational activity—does not have the right to bring the property on which these institutions are set up and run under the protection of fundamental rights.

Apart from the aforesaid clear constitutional anomalies, the Supreme Court, in *T.M.A. Pai*, has, with respect, given an erroneous interpretation to the concept of education by equating it with a commercial venture and made it clear that an entrepreneur setting up an educational institution can earn profit; however, profiteering is not permissible. In these times of commercialization, it has become difficult to distinguish between earning legitimate profit and profiteering. But by giving the private entrepreneur a fundamental right to establish an educational institution, which necessarily recognizes his fundamental right over the property on which such an educational institution is administered, *T.M.A. Pai* encourages profiteering and property motives in the field of education, which has the effect of denying access to education to the vast majority of Indians who are priced out of these educational institutions that are established to earn profit. The logic which has been employed by *T.M.A. Pai* is that since an educational institution has been held to be an industry by the Supreme Court in *Bangalore Water Supply and Sewerage Board v. R. Rajappa*,[7] by the same parity of logic an educational institution is to be equated with an industrial establishment. This is per se unsustainable. In my humble understanding, the right to establish an educational institution must not be extended in such a way as to circumscribe the common man's access to education, as the constitutional thrust is towards extending the ambit of such access which is clear from Article 21A of the Constitution. There may be some common features between an industry and an educational institution; at the same time, there are also some basic fundamental differences. To equate the two is like equating a tiger with an elephant, as both have tails. Such logic is vitiated by the fallacy of undistributed middle.

Normally, setting up of an educational institution is a charitable venture in view of Article 26A of the Constitution, wherein such rights have been conferred on a religious denomination or any other section thereof. Relying on this, even *T.M.A. Pai* recognized that education is an identified head of charity.[8] Thereinafter, pronouncing that it is an entrepreneurial activity with profit motive is inconsistent with the core constitutional values in the Preamble, which have been articulated in the fundamental rights and directive principles.

After the judgment of the Supreme Court in *T.M.A. Pai* several questions arose, mostly concerning the fixation of fees structure in different minority and non-minority educational establishments, most of which were professional institutions. To clarify the various directions in *T.M.A. Pai*, the Supreme Court again constituted another Constitution Bench of five judges in *Islamic Academy.*[9]

In that case, the court, after reiterating the judgment in *T.M.A. Pai*, directed the setting up of a committee headed by a retired High Court judge to be nominated by the chief justice of the concerned state for fixing the proposed fee structure of the concerned institution. That direction was passed by the Supreme Court in *Islamic Academy* in exercise of its power under Article 142 of the Constitution, as the educational institutions were collecting exorbitant fees in a manner which did not meet the approval of the Supreme Court. The judgment in *Islamic Academy* also sought to explain the judgment in *T.M.A. Pai* on various other aspects.

In *P.A. Inamdar*[10] again, another Constitution Bench of the Supreme Court, consisting of Chief Justice Lahoti and six other learned judges, examined the reasons in *T.M.A. Pai* to find out whether the clarification given in *Islamic Academy* ran counter to the decision in *T.M.A. Pai*. By doing so the court was aware of the situation that even if the bench in *Inamdar* disagreed with the findings in *T.M.A. Pai*, it could not make any declaration to that effect since *T.M.A. Pai* was the decision of an eleven-judge bench.

I am of the opinion that as the *T.M.A. Pai* reasoning is unfortunately based, with respect, on unsound principles, as pointed out above, the Supreme Court was required to do the job of repairing the damage caused by the *T.M.A. Pai* decision through two subsequent Constitution Bench judgments—in *Islamic Academy* and in *Inamdar*.

About the decision in *T.M.A. Pai*, the Supreme Court, in *Inamdar*, expressed its unhappiness by quoting its observation in the *Annual Survey of Indian Law* on *T. M.A. Pai,* that 'the judgment raises more questions than it has answered'.[11] However, *Inamdar* was primarily concerned with settling the procedure of admission in institutions offering professional education, the aim being to evolve some methods to ensure that meritorious students are given access to education on 'non-exploitative norms'. The decision aimed at structuring the admission procedure to make it 'fair, transparent and non-exploitative' so that it may promote merit and excellence, and curb malpractices. The court therefore held that in matters of education, no capitation fee should be charged directly or indirectly and a committee was to be set up for regulating admission, apart from the committee which had been set up in *Islamic Academy* for regulating the fee structure. All these had to be safeguarded by the Supreme Court by these two successive Constitution Bench decisions in *Islamic Academy* and *Inamdar*, as the educational scenario after *T.M.A. Pai* became, so to say, very elitist and, if I may add, claustrophobic.

An attempt has been made to salvage the situation by inserting Sub-article (5) to Article 15 by the 93rd Constitution Amendment Act and then by enacting the Right of Children to Free and Compulsory Education Act, 2009 (hereinafter RTE Act 2009) whereby the provisions of Article 15(5) read with Article 21A of the Constitution were implemented. Article 21A of the Constitution recognized the fundamental right to free and compulsory education of children between the ages of six and fourteen, and mandated the state to make a provision for the same. Article 15(5) enabled the state to make a special provision for admission to educational institutions, including private educational institution, other than minority institutions, despite anything to the contrary in 19(1)(g) of the Constitution.

In fact, the 93rd Constitution Amendment Act, which inserted clause (5) to Article 15, watered down the interpretation of Article 19(1)(g) as given in *T.M.A. Pai*.

The constitutional validity of RTE was challenged in *Society for Unaided Private Schools of Rajasthan v. Union of India*,[12] and was upheld by a majority verdict of 2:1.

This is a landmark judgment. In this judgment, the Supreme Court, speaking through Chief Justice S.H. Kapadia, declared that Article 15(5) of the Constitution is valid and virtually nullified the decision in *P.A. Inamdar* in vital areas. *P.A. Inamdar* held that (1) there will be no reservation in private unaided colleges and (2) there will be no difference between unaided minority and non-minority institutions.[13]

These findings were reached in *Inamdar* in view of the decision in *T.M.A. Pai.*[14] It is thus clear that Article 15(5) of the Constitution, read with RTE, as upheld in *Society for Unaided Private Schools*, widened the access to education for common people. The Supreme Court held in *Society for Unaided Private Schools* that an educational institution is charitable and that the crucial role of universal elementary education is to strengthen the social fabric of democracy through equal opportunities to all. The court also maintained that the duty of the court is to interpret fundamental rights in light of the directive principles. These principles convey the message of social justice in the Constitution.

The Supreme Court, in *Society for Unaided Private Schools*, held that the right to live, recognized in Article 21, covers access to education, but that the high costs of education which make it unaffordable 'defeats access'. The court also decided to give such access to education, and Article 21A was introduced to give effect to Article 45 of the directive principles.

Thus access to education, which was virtually impeded in *T.M.A. Pai*, was somewhat restored in view of three factors: (1) Article 15(5) of the Constitution, which was inserted by the 93rd Constitution Amendment Act; and (2) the RTE Act 2009 and (3) the Supreme Court judgment in *Society for Unaided Private Schools*, which upheld the RTE Act 2009.

When access to education is shackled, it definitely retards human development and stifles social harmony. Tyrants and despots have always attempted to cramp opportunities of education. In this connection, Adolf Hitler's speech against universal education, quoted by the Supreme Court in *Unnikrishnan, J.P. and Others v. State of Andhra Pradesh and Others,*[15] is very pertinent.

NOTES

1. (2002) 8 SCC 481.
2. (2003) 6 SCC 697.
3. (2005) 6 SCC 537.
4. *Ins.* by the Constitution (44th Amendment) Act, 1978, S. 4 (w.e.f. 20 June 1979).
5. (1978) 1 SCC 248.
6. Source: indiacode.nic.in/coiweb/amend/amend44.htm
7. (1978) 2 SCC 213.
8. (2002) 8 SCC 481, para 26, p. 534.
9. (2003) 6 SCC 697.
10. (2005) 6 SCC 537.
11. *Annual Survey of Indian Law*, (Indian Law Institute, 2002).
12. (2012) 6 SCC 102, p. 1.
13. Ibid., para 60, p. 43.
14. Para 125, p. 601.
15. (1993) 1 SCC 645, p. 733.

6

AFFIRMATIVE STATE ACTION AND PROTECTION OF REVERSE DISCRIMINATION BY COURTS

Protection of the Scheduled Castes, Scheduled Tribes and Other Backward Classes

AN APT PERCEPTION of the constitutional mandate of reverse discrimination in favour of Scheduled Castes (SCs), Scheduled Tribes (STs) and Other Backward Classes (OBCs), for bringing them within the sweep of equal opportunity, would require appreciating this constitutional imperative in the backdrop of our national freedom movement, which gives legitimacy to these concepts.

The seeds of constitutionalism, which blossomed in our National Charter, were sowed through our national independence movement which began in 1885 and culminated in 1947.

The chapters on fundamental rights and directive principles in our Constitution demonstrate a picture of India of the future, in which common men and women are to be empowered. In our country, for a long time the Hindu caste system divided people and determined the status of persons according to the caste in which he/she was born. Dr B.R. Ambedkar, the chief of the drafting committee of our Constitution, experienced both caste-based discrimination and colonial rule in the time of the

British Raj. This era had two prominent vices—one was British dominance and the other, more widespread and threatening, was the Brahminical order suppressing social equality. The two, more often than not, combined and crushed common Indians. Our Constitution tried to eradicate both, by asserting India's sovereignty and resolving to establish a new social order based on justice of the widest dimension, encompassing the social, economic and political aspects.

Under our Constitution, India is a welfare state with an activist agenda. Articles 16(4), 16(4A), 17, 23, 24, 38 and 46 enjoin upon the state to promote, with special care, the educational and economic interests of the weaker sections and of SCs and STs. This is in order to protect them from social injustice and all forms of exploitation and to provide for their social advancement by reserving posts for them in civil service if they are not adequately represented. Thus our Constitution endorses the state's affirmative stance for ensuring social equality. That is why our fundamental rights are diverse enough to include both civil and political rights, as also social and economic rights, such as abolition of untouchability, prohibition of trafficking in human beings, prohibition of forced labour, non-employment of children in hazardous jobs and now, compulsory free education for children between the ages of six and fourteen. These articles embody social rights of the widest variety and call upon the state to pass suitable laws for making these rights enforceable. Our Constitution thus underscores the interventionist character of the state.

The provision of caste reservation in our Constitution comes in for comparison with the racial preferences in the American Constitution. In the US, caste is a matter of policy and not of right. Ronald Dworkin argued that it is a good policy to have social preferences in universities, in the interest of securing greater diversity in the social perspective. In the US, social preferences never figure in the text of the Constitution but are adopted as measures of policy long after the adoption of the Constitution and without any amendment in its text.

In India, provision for reservation by way of reverse discrimination was made from the very inception and the Constitution was further amended to widen its scope. Such provisions are of two types: mandatory provisions and enabling provisions. Article 330 of the Constitution, which provides for reservation of seats in the Lok Sabha, is a mandatory provision, but the ones under Article 16(4) are enabling provisions. However, in the course of time, the distinction between mandatory and enabling provisions became blurred in view of emphasis on social justice.

The Supreme Court of the United States dealt with this question of reservation as an affirmative action of the state in various celebrated decisions, notable among them being *Oliver Brown v. Board of Education of Topeka,*[1] *Spottswood Thomas Bolling v. C. Melvin Sharpe,*[2] *Marco DeFunis v. Charles Odegaard,*[3] *Regents of the University of California v. Allan Bakke,*[4] *H. Earl Fullilove v. Philip M. Klutznick*[5] and *Metro Broadcasting Inc. v. Federal Communications Commission.*[6]

As such, the affirmative actions of the state have been endorsed by the Supreme Court of the United States as they seek to eradicate the continuing effects of past discrimination and make equal opportunities accessible to all members of society. The court states that such availability of access results in fuller participation in governance by the disadvantaged and discriminated social groups and balances the chronic under-representation of such groups. The Supreme Court of the United States has held an adequate representation as an important governmental objective.

India's Supreme Court, in *Indra Sawhney v. Union of India,*[7] held that these principles of the Supreme Court of the United

States apply '*ex proprio vigore*' to Indian society and opined that discrimination in our society is more chronic.

However, our Supreme Court, in *Ashoka Kumar Thakur v. Union of India and Others*,[8] felt that in view of the structural difference between the Indian and American Constitutions, the principles of affirmative action in the US would not automatically hold good in our Constitution. For instance, in our Constitution there are no principles of 'suspect legislation' or 'strict scrutiny' or 'compelling state necessity' as there are in the US Constitution.

Under our Constitution, every legislation passed by a competent legislature is presumed to be valid unless the contrary is proved. Further, in our Constitution, the main goal is to achieve unity in our country through the integration of different social groups, which cannot be achieved without giving equal status to all. Neither democracy nor social integration can become real unless all sections of society have an equal voice in the affairs and governance of society.

This emphasis on social justice has been explained by the Supreme Court in its Constitution Bench judgment in *State of Kerala and Anr v. N.M. Thomas and Ors*[9] by His Lordship Justice K.K. Mathew. His Lordship pointed out that the directive principles in Article 46 are binding not only on the lawmakers. According to the learned judge, these principles should inform and guide the approach of the court when the court decides any controversy involving these questions as the court, being a state within the meaning of Article 12, 'makes law, even though interstitially, from the molar to the molecular'. The learned judge explained that the egalitarian principles enshrined in the Constitution impose an affirmative duty on the government to eliminate discrimination. That is made clear by the language used in Article 16, which, contrary to the negative phraseology of Article 14, is couched in a positive mandate.[10]

The learned judge observed very succinctly:

> Today the sense that Government has affirmative responsibility for elimination of inequalities, social, economic or otherwise, is one of the dominant forces in Constitutional law.[11]

The learned judge referred to Daniel P. Moynihan, an American scholar, to elaborate the concept of equality of opportunity for diverse social groups. He quoted excerpts, which are strikingly relevant:

> The point of semantics is that equality of opportunity now has a different meaning for Negroes than it has for Whites. It is not (or at least no longer) a demand for liberty alone but also for equality in terms of group results. In Bayard Rustin's terms, 'it is now concerned not merely with removing the barriers to full opportunity but with achieving the fact of equality.' By equality Rustin means a distribution of achievements among Negroes roughly comparable with Whites.[12]

The controversy over reservation came up before the Supreme Court in many cases and the divergence of opinion was recorded therein. The most landmark judgment on these issues was rendered in the case of *Indra Sawhney*,[13] wherein a nine-judge Constitution Bench of the Supreme Court decided the question by a 6:3 majority.

Article 16(4) of the Constitution does not define the backward class of citizen as is elaborated in Article 15(4) by the expression 'socially and educationally'. The SCs and STs are defined in Article 366(24) and 366(25) of the Constitution respectively as under:

> Article 366 (24): 'Scheduled Castes' means such castes, races or tribes or parts of or groups within such castes,

races or tribes as are deemed under Article 341 to be Scheduled Castes for the purposes of this Constitution;

Article 366 (25): 'Scheduled Tribes' means such tribes or tribal communities or parts of or tribal communities as are deemed under Article 342 to be Scheduled Tribes for the purposes of this Constitution.

The Constitution also does not define backward classes. Article 340 provides the appointment of a commission by the president of India to investigate the conditions of socially and educationally backward classes (SEBCs).

The factual background that led to the caste controversy commenced with the appointment of the First Backward Classes Committee (the Kaka Welfare Commission) by the president, which submitted its report in 1955, identifying 2,399 castes as socially and educationally backward. However, the report was not accepted, as no objective criteria for identifying the OBCs were ever stated.

Then, in 1979, by an order issued under Article 340 of the Constitution, the president appointed a Second Backward Classes Committee to investigate matters relating to the socially and economically backward classes in India. This commission came to be known as the Mandal Commission. The recommendations were given in December 1980. The commission recommended 27 per cent reservation in favour of OBCs in addition to 22.5 per cent in favour of SCs and STs. The government did not take any step to implement the report till 1990, when an office memorandum dated 13 August 1990 was issued.

The first memorandum sought to implement the Mandal Commission report by reserving 27 per cent vacancies in civil posts, to be filled in by direct recruitment from SEBCs.

The issue of this memorandum led to widespread protests, leading to damage of public properties and self-immolation by various young persons. Proceedings were filed in the Supreme

Court challenging the memorandum. By an order dated 1 October 1990, the operation of the office memorandum was stayed by the Supreme Court.

With the change of government in the first half of 1991, it was decided to implement the office memorandum in a modified form and another office memorandum dated 25 September 1991 was issued.

The second memorandum referred to the poorer sections of SEBCS in respect of 27 per cent reservation by the first memorandum and made an additional reservation of 10 per cent vacancies for other economically backward sections of people.

The controversy over the whole issue was then decided by the Constitution Bench of nine judges in *Indra Sawhney*.[14]

It may be noted that the controversy in *Indra Sawhney* was not about rights under Article 15(4) but the ones under Article 16(4). Article 15(4) enables the state to make laws for the advancement of any SEBCs or for SCs or STs. Article 16(4) enables the state to provide for reservation of posts in favour of backward classes of citizens, which are inadequately represented in the employment under the state. By 6:3 majority, in *Indra Sawhney*, the Supreme Court upheld the first memorandum but invalidated the addition of the 10 per cent by the second.

In *Indra Sawhney*, the court had to deal with all the available groups, sections and classes in society since caste represented an existing, identifiable social group/class encompassing an overwhelming majority of the country's population. One could, according to the court, well begin with caste and then go to other groups, sections and classes. Caste, however, was not an essential factor for determining social and educational backwardness. It was also not necessary that the SEBCs should be similarly situated as the SCs and STs. Within SEBCs the classification between the backward and the more backward was permissible. To maintain the cohesiveness and character of a class, the 'creamy layer' could and must be excluded from SEBCs. The court also clarified that 'backward class of citizens' in Article 16(4) was a wider category than SEBCs in articles 15(4) and 340. In the former, the accent is on social backwardness while in the latter it is on both social and educational backwardness.

After a very elaborate discussion, the majority judgment of Justice B.P. Jeevan Reddy answered these questions by holding:[15]

(1) (a) It is not necessary that the '*provision*' under Article 16(4) should necessarily be made by the Parliament/Legislature. Such a provision can be made by the Executive also. Local bodies, Statutory Corporations and other instrumentalities of the State falling under Article 12 of the Constitution are themselves competent to make such a provision, if so advised.[16]

(b) An executive order making a provision under Article 16(4) is enforceable the moment it is made and issued.[17]

(2) (a) Clause (4) of Article 16 is not an exception to clause (1). It is an instance and an illustration of the classification inherent in clause (1).[18]

(b) Article 16(4) is exhaustive of the subject of reservation in favour of backward class of citizens, as explained in this judgment.[19]

(c) Reservations can also be provided under clause (1) of Article 16. It is not confined to extending of preferences, concessions or exemptions alone. These reservations, if any, made under clause (1) have to be so adjusted and implemented as not to exceed the level of representation prescribed for '*backward class of citizens*'—as explained in this judgment.[20]

(3) (a) A caste can be and quite often is a social class in India. If it is backward socially, it would be a backward class for the purposes of Article 16(4). Among non-Hindus, there are several occupational groups, sects and denominations, which for historical reasons are socially backward. They too represent backward social collectivities for the purposes of Article 16(4).[21]

(b) Neither the Constitution nor the law prescribes the procedure or method of identification of backward classes. Nor is it possible or advisable for the court to lay down any such procedures or method. It must be left to the authority appointed to identify. It can adopt such method/procedure as it thinks convenient and so long as its survey covers the entire populace, no objection can be taken to it. Identification of the backward classes can certainly be done with reference to castes among, and along with, other occupational groups, classes and sections of people. One can start the process either with occupational groups or with castes or with some other groups. Thus one can start the process with the castes and when they are found, apply the criteria (evolved for determining backwardness) and find out whether it satisfies the criteria. If it does—what emerges is a *'backward class of citizen'* within the meaning of and for the purposes of Article 16(4).

Similar process can be adopted in the case of other occupational groups, communities and classes, so as to cover the entire populace. The central idea and overall objective should be to consider all available groups, sections and classes in society and since caste represents an existing, identifiable social group/class encompassing an overwhelming minorities [sic] of the country's population one can well begin with it and then go to other groups, sections and classes.[22]

(c) It is not correct to say that the backward class of citizen contemplated in Articles 16(4) is the same as the socially and educationally backward classes referred to in Article 15(4). It is much wider. The accent in Article 16(4) is on social backwardness. Of course, social, educational and economic backwardness are closely intertwined in the Indian context.[23]

(d) '*Creamy layer*' can be, and must be excluded.[24]

(e) It is not necessary for a class to be designated as a backward class that it is situated similarly to the Scheduled Caste/Schedule Tribes.[25]

(f) The adequacy of representation of a particular class in the services under the State is a matter within the subjective satisfactions of the appropriate Government. The judicial scrutiny in that behalf is the same as with other matters within the subjective satisfaction of an authority.[26]

(4) (a) A backward class of citizens cannot be identified only and exclusively with reference to economic criteria.[27]

(b) It is, of course, permissible for the Government or other authority to indentify the backward class of citizens on the basis of occupation-cum-

Income, without reference to caste, if it is so advised.[28]

(5) There is no constitutional bar to classify the backward classes of the citizens into backward and more backward categories.[29]

(6) (a) and (b) The reservation contemplated in clause (4) of Article 16 should not exceed 50%. While 50% shall be the rule, it is necessary not to put out of consideration certain extraordinary situations inherent in the great diversity of this country and the people. It might happen that in far-flung and remote areas the population inhabiting those areas might, on account of their being out of the mainstream of national life and in view of the conditions peculiar to and characteristic of them need to be treated in a different way, some relaxation in this strict rule may become imperative [sic]. In doing so, extreme caution is to be exercised and a special case made out.[30]

(c) The rule of 50% should be applied to each year. It cannot be related to the total strength of class, category, service or cadre, as the case may be.[31]

(d) *Devadasan* was wrongly decided and is accordingly overruled to the extent it is inconsistent with this judgment.[32]

(7) Article 16(4) does not permit provision for reservations in the matter of promotion. This rule shall, however, have only prospective operation and shall not affect the promotions already made, whether made on regular basis or on any other basis. We direct that our decision on this question shall operate only prospectively and shall not affect

promotions already made, whether on temporary, officiating or regular/permanent basis. It is further directed that wherever reservations are already provided in the matter of promotion—be it Central Services, or for that matter services under any Corporation, authority or body falling under the definition of '*State*' in Article 12—such reservations may continue in operation for a period of five years from this day. Within this period, it would be open to the appropriate authorities to revise, modify or reissue the relevant rules to ensure the achievement or the objective of Article 16(4). If any authority thinks that for ensuring adequate representation of '*backward class of citizens*' in any service, class or category, it is necessary to do so. (Ahmadi, J expressed no opinion on this question upholding the preliminary objection of Union of India). It would not be impermissible for the State to extend concessions and relaxations to members of reserved categories in the matter of promotion without compromising the efficiency of the administration.[33]

(8) While the rule of reservation cannot be called anti-meritarian, there are certain services and posts to which it may not be advisable to apply the rule of reservation.[34]

(9) There is no particular or special standard of judicial scrutiny applicable to matters arising under Article 16(4).[35]

(10) The distinction made in the impugned Office Memorandum dated September 25, 1991 between '*poorer sections*' and others among the backward classes is not invalid; if the classification is

understood and operated as based upon relative backwardness among the several classes identified as Other Backward Classes.[36]

(11) The reservation of 10% of the posts in favour of '*other economically backward sections*' of the people who are not covered by any of the existing schemes of the reservation made in the impugned Office Memorandum dated September 25, 1991 is constitutionally invalid and is accordingly struck down.[37]

(12) The Government of India and the State Governments have the power to and ought to create a permanent mechanism, in the nature of a Commission, for examining requests of inclusion and complaints of over-inclusion or non-inclusion in the list of OBCs and to advise the Government, which shall ordinarily be binding upon the Government. Where, however, the Government does not accept the advice, it must record its reasons thereunder.[38]

(13) In view of the answers given by us herein and the directions issued herewith, it is not necessary to express any opinion on the correctness and adequacy of the exercise done by the Mandal Commission. It is equally unnecessary to send the matters back to the Constitution Bench of five Judges.[39]

In *Indra Sawhney*, the Supreme Court held by a majority that reservation cannot be applied in matters of promotion. To circumvent this finding, the Constitution (77th Amendment) Act, 1995 (henceforth the 77th Constitution Amendment Act) was introduced whereby Article 16(4A) was brought in, providing that reservation could be applied in promotion in favour of SCs and STs. Again, in 2001, by the Constitution (85th Amendment)

Act, 2001 (henceforth the 85th Constitution Amendment Act) the benefit of consequential seniority was also inserted in Article 16(4A) with effect from 17 June 1995. This was done in order to give effect to the constitutional amendment before the expiry of the time limit given in *Indra Sawhney*, viz. five years from the date of the judgment for the rule permitting reservations in promotion to end. Prior to that, in 2000, Article 16(4B) was introduced by the Constitution (81st Amendment) Act, 2000 (henceforth the 81st Constitution Amendment Act) to ensure that with respect to carry-forward vacancies too, the consequential benefits would be given in promotion in favour of the SC and ST candidates with retrospective effect. With the Constitution (82nd Amendment) Act, 1992, (henceforth the 82nd Constitution Amendment Act) Article 335 was amended to introduce provisions for relaxation of qualifying marks or standard of evaluation in relation to SC and ST candidates.

In the case of *M. Nagaraj and Others v. Union of India and Others*,[40] the validity of the 77th Constitution Amendment Act, the 81st Constitution Amendment Act and the 82nd Constitution Amendment Act was challenged on the ground that these amendments sought to alter the basic structure of the Constitution.

Repelling the said contention, the Constitution Bench of the Supreme Court, in its landmark decision in *M. Nagaraj*, held that a constitutional provision must not be construed in a narrow, pedantic and constricted sense but in a wide and liberal manner so as to anticipate and take account of changing conditions and purposes, so that the constitutional provision does not get fossilized but remains flexible enough to meet newly emerging problems and challenges.

While exercising the power of judicial review, the court felt that it should ascertain whether a constitutional principle qualifies as an essential feature. In order to be an essential feature it must be established that the said principle is a part of the constitutional law binding on the legislature. Only thereafter is the second step to be considered, namely, whether the principle is so fundamental as to bind even the amending power of Parliament to form a part of the basic structure. This is the standard of judicial review of constitutional amendments in the context of the doctrine of basic structure.

The theory of basic structure, therefore, is based on the concept of constitutional identity. As has been noted in the case of *Kesavananda Bharati v. State of Kerala*,[41] the word 'amendment' postulates that the old Constitution survives without loss of its identity despite the change and it continues even though it has been subjected to alteration. To destroy its identity is to abrogate the basic structure of the Constitution. The main purpose behind the theory of constitutional identity is continuity, and within that continuity of identity changes are admissible, depending upon the situation and circumstances of the day.

Therefore, the court held that in the matter of application of the principle of basic structure, twin tests have to be satisfied, namely the 'width test' and the test of 'identity'.

The court, in *M. Nagaraj*, further went on to pronounce that basic structure is based on the principle that a change in a thing does not involve its destruction, and destruction of a thing is a matter of substance and not of form. Therefore, one has to apply the test of overarching principle to be gathered from the scheme and the placement and the structure of an article in the whole scheme of the Constitution.

The court held that in the background of social justice, a constitutional creed, reservation is necessary for transcending caste and not for perpetuating it. Reservation has to be used in a limited sense, otherwise it will perpetuate casteism in the country. Equality in Article 16(1) is individual-specific, whereas provisions for reservation in Article 16(4) and Article 16(4A) are enabling. The discretion of the state is, however, subject to the existence of 'backwardness' and 'inadequacy of representation' in public employment. Backwardness has to be based on objective factors, whereas inadequacy has to factually exist. This is where judicial review comes in. However, whether reservation in a given case is desirable or not, is not for the court to decide as long as the parameters mentioned in Articles 16(4) and 16(4A) are maintained. The court has to uphold the exercise of the enabling power that provides for reservation.

As stated above, equity, justice, merit and efficiency contemplated in Article 335 are variables which can only be identified and measured by the state. Therefore, in each case a contextual case has to be made out, depending upon different circumstances, which may exist state-wise.

The court, in upholding the validity of the impugned amendments, held that they did not alter the structure of articles 14, 15 and 16. The parameters mentioned in Article 16(4) have been retained and clause (4A) is derived from clause (4) of Article 16. Clause (4A) is confined to SCs and STs alone. Therefore, the amendments do not change the identity of the Constitution. Applying the 'width test', and the test of 'identity', the court did not find any alteration in the existing structure of the equality code. Apart from that, none of the axioms like secularism, federalism etc., which are overarching principles, had been violated by the impugned constitutional amendments.

The court concluded that Article 16(4A) and Article 16(4B) fell in the pattern of Article 16(4) and as long as the parameters mentioned in those articles were complied with by the states, the provision of reservation could not be faulted. Articles 16(4A) and 16(4B) are classifications within the principle of equality under Article 16(4).

The court also found that the object in enacting enabling provisions like articles 16(4), 16(4A) and 16(4B) was that the state was empowered to identify and recognize the compelling interests. If the state had quantifiable data to show backwardness and inadequacy then the state could make reservations in promotions keeping in mind the maintenance of efficiency, which is held to be a constitutional limitation on the discretion of the state in making reservation as indicated by Article 335. As stated above, the concepts of efficiency, backwardness and inadequacy of representation are required to be identified and measured. That exercise was to be done by the state, depending on the availability of data.

After applying the above tests to the proviso to Article 335 inserted by the 82nd Constitution Amendment Act, the court found that the said proviso had a nexus with articles 16(4A) and 16(4B). Efficiency in administration is held to be a constitutional limitation on the discretion vested in the state to provide for reservation in public employment. Under the proviso to Article 335, it is stated that nothing in Article 335 shall prevent the state from relaxing qualifying marks or standards of evaluation for reservation in promotion. In the court's view, even after insertion of this proviso, the limitation of overall efficiency in Article 335 was not diluted.

This is a landmark decision, as it laid down the test for judging the validity of all future laws that may provide for reservation under Article 16. As a result, no government can implement the amendments and provide reservation in promotion, with consequential seniority, without ensuring that the creamy layer among the backward classes is kept out of the reservation scheme and the efficiency of administration under Article 335 is maintained.

Also, all existing and future laws made under Article 16(4), that do not identify the creamy layer, stand the risk of being declared unconstitutional. This comes as a welcome step as governments now will have to produce concrete data showing these required conditions before implementing any such reservation policy.

In *Indra Sawhney* and in *M. Nagaraj* the concept of creamy layer came in for a lot of controversy. This concept is not in our Constitution, but evolved out of the experience in the implementation of the constitutional principle of reverse discrimination by way of reservations. The ground reality is that, in some cases, the benefits of reservation have been cornered by the elite among the backward, giving rise to a new class within the backward class. Therefore, in both *Indra Sawhney* and *M. Nagaraj* the apex court opined that exclusion of those in the creamy layer from the benefits of reservation would really serve the constitutional mandate of Article 16(4) of the Constitution.

The next landmark judgment rendered by the Supreme Court is in *Ashoka Kumar Thakur v. Union of India*[42] in the following background.

To give adequate educational opportunities to SEBCs and to SCs and STs by way of admission to unaided educational institutions other than minority institutions, Parliament amended Article 15 of the Constitution by introducing Article 15(5) by the 93rd Constitution Amendment Act. That being an enabling provision, Parliament passed the Central Educational Institution (Reservation on Admission) Act 2006 (Act 5 of 2007) to provide for greater access to higher education and professional education to SCs, STs and OBCs.

The aforesaid 93rd Constitution Amendment Act and the vires of Act 5 of 2007 were challenged inter alia on the ground that the 93rd Constitution Amendment Act was violative of the basic structure of the Constitution and Act 5 of 2007 was ultra vires the Constitution.

Repelling those contentions, the Constitution Bench of the Supreme Court in *Ashoka Kumar Thakur*, by a majority of 4:1, upheld the constitutional amendment and the act.

Delivering the majority verdict, Chief Justice K.G. Balakrishnan held that the basic structure of the Constitution is to be taken as a larger principle on which the Constitution itself is framed. If any constitutional amendment moderately abridges or alters the equality principle or the principles under Article 19(1)(g), it cannot be said that it violates the basic structure of the Constitution. The majority judgment held that if such a principle were accepted, the Constitution would not be able to adapt itself to the changing conditions of a dynamic human society.

The court further held that when a constitutional provision is interpreted, the cardinal rule is to look to the Preamble to the Constitution as the guiding star and the directive principles of state policy as the 'Book of Interpretation'. Hence, the 93rd Constitution Amendment Act does not violate the basic structure of the Constitution insofar as it relates to aided educational institutions.

The learned chief justice very clearly opined that reservation is one of the many tools used to preserve the essence of equality so that the disadvantaged groups can be brought to the forefront of civil life. It is the duty of the state of promote positive measures to remove barriers of inequality. Justices Pasayat and Thakkar, sharing the majority view and affirming the verdict in what is commonly known as Cooper's case[43], held that all fundamental rights are to be read together and classification on the basis of mere caste in the long run has the tendency of inherently becoming pernicious. Therefore, affirmative action is nothing but a crucial component of social justice in the constitutional dispensation.

The Supreme Court further said that minority institutions are a separate class and their rights are protected by other constitutional provisions. Therefore, exemption of minority educational institutions from the application of Article 15(5) is consistent with the mandate of Article 30 of the Constitution.

The court also upheld the constitutional validity of Act 5 of 2007 in view of the definition of 'backward class' and held that the identification of backward class cannot be done solely based on caste. Other parameters are followed in identifying the backward class.

The court held that a social class is a homogeneous unit, from the point of view of status and mutual recognition, whereas a caste is a homogeneous unit from the point of view of common ancestry, religious rites and strict organizational control. Thus, the manner in which caste is structured, both in the organizational and biological sense, makes it different from social class.

The chief justice, speaking for the majority, further held that both the concept of social justice echoed in the Preamble and the object of directive principles had been secured by including Article 15(5) as a fundamental right in Part III of the Constitution. The chief justice further clarified that the distinction between fundamental rights and directive principles had virtually reached a vanishing point. The fundamental rights, the learned chief justice held, represented civil and political rights and the directive principles embodied social and economic rights. Merely because the directive principles are non-justiciable does not mean that they are subordinate.[44]

The Supreme Court further opined that the creamy layer was to be excluded from SEBCs. Identification of SEBCs would not be complete without the exclusion of the creamy layer and such identification might not be valid under Article 15(1) of the Constitution. Determination of backward classes could not be exclusively based on caste and the principle of creamy layer had been introduced merely to exclude a section of a particular caste on the ground that they were economically advanced or educationally forward. They were excluded because unless this segment of caste was excluded from that caste group, there could not be proper identification of the backward class. The principle of creamy layer is applied not as a general principle of reservation but for the purpose of identifying the socially and educationally backward classes.[45]

The Supreme Court held that the creamy layer principle was not applicable to SCs and STs.

NOTES

1. 347 US 483:481 Ed 2d 873 (1954).
2. 347 US 497.
3. 40L Ed 2d 164: 416 US 312 (1974).
4. 57L Ed 2d 750 : 438 US 265 (1978).
5. 448 US 448:65 Led 2d 902 (1980).
6. 58IW 5053 (decided on 27 June 1990).
7. (1992) Supp 3 SCC 217.
8. (2008) 6 SCC 1.
9. (1976) 2 SCC 310.
10. Ibid., para 64, p. 343.
11. Ibid., para 67, p. 344.
12. The Moynihan Reports and the Politics of Controversy, quoted in Ibid., para 76.
13. (1992) Supp 3 SCC 217.
14. Ibid.
15. Ibid., para 859, pp. 766–69.
16. Ibid., pp. 735–737.
17. Ibid., pp. 738–40.
18. Ibid., pp. 741–42.
19. Ibid., p. 743.
20. Ibid., p. 745.

21. Ibid., pp. 746–79.
22. Ibid., 780–85.
23. Ibid., 786–89.
24. Ibid., pp. 790–93.
25. Ibid., pp. 794–97.
26. Ibid., p. 798.
27. Ibid., p. 799.
28. Ibid., p. 800.
29. Ibid., pp. 801–03.
30. Ibid., pp. 804–13.
31. Ibid., p. 814.
32. Ibid., pp. 815–18.
33. Ibid., pp. 819–31.
34. Ibid., pp. 832–41.
35. Ibid., p. 842.
36. Ibid., pp. 843–44.
37. Ibid., p. 845.
38. Ibid., p. 847.
39. Ibid., pp. 848–50.
40. (2006) 8 SCC 212.
41. (1973) 4 SCC 225.
42. (2008) 6 SCC 1.
43. (1970) 1 SCC 248.
44. Ibid., p. 152.
45. Ibid., p. 163.

7

THE RAREST OF RARE DOCTRINE

Death Penalty and the Evolving Mosaic of Fairness in Penology

DESPITE CONTINUING INTERNATIONAL efforts to initiate and implement policies aimed at complete abolition, or at least to impose a partial moratorium on the death penalty, it is still very much enforced in various countries.

The death penalty has always been an issue around which basic values and human rights are continuously discussed, since the age of Enlightenment till today. However, the current status of the death penalty worldwide indicates that there is still a great need to continue the debate on abolishing or retaining the death penalty, from international, normative, empirical and comparative angles in order to promote the international discourse on human rights.

The Law Commission of India, in an intensive study on the subject of death penalty, submitted its 35th Report in 1967[1] to the central government, stating that

> ...having regard, however, to the conditions in India, to the variety of the social upbringing of its inhabitants, to the disparity in the level of morality and education in the country, to the vastness of its area, to [the] diversity of its population and to the paramount need for maintaining

law and order of the country *in the present juncture*, India cannot risk the experiment of abolition of capital punishment.

It is clear from the opinion of the Law Commission that its report is not valid for all time to come.

The statutory provisions for the death penalty under Indian laws are found in several Indian statutes. Several sections of the Indian Penal Code (IPC) make provision for the death penalty.[2] There are other statutes as well that provide for the death penalty.[3] The most frequently used section in awarding the death penalty is, of course, Section 302 of the IPC, a pre-constitutional colonial piece of legislation.

Section 302 falls under Chapter XVI of the IPC, which deals with offences affecting the human body. The human body is treated as an impersonal entity and offences against it are treated separately. The law is totally silent on the person against whom the crime is committed and the person committing the crime.

The concept of personhood, which is the basic postulate and a value consideration under Article 21 of the Constitution, has apparently no relevance under Section 302 of the IPC.

However, the validity of the death penalty provision was challenged before the Hon'ble Supreme Court in the case of *Jagmohan Singh v. State of Uttar Pradesh*[4] inter alia on the ground that the provision of Section 302 of the IPC conferring absolute discretion on the judge to award the death penalty is violative of Article 14 of the Constitution and the same interferes with the right to life of an accused awarded the death penalty. The Constitution Bench in *Jagmohan* rejected those contentions. In doing so the court considered and relied on the recommendations of the Law Commission's 35th Report.

The next landmark judgment on the death penalty relating to female criminals came up for consideration in *Ediga Anamma v.*

State of Andhra Pradesh[5] wherein Justice Krishna Iyer, speaking for a two-judge bench, noticed the changes in the Criminal Procedure Code 1973 (hereinafter, the Code) with the insertion of Section 354(3), which mandates recording of the special reasons for giving the death penalty.

According to the learned judge, that provision made life imprisonment the rule and death sentence an exception, in stark contrast to the provision of Section 367(5) of the Code of 1898, which required reasons to be recorded as to why the death penalty is not given in a case where the offence is punishable by death. Section 367(5) of the old Code was deleted by the Amendment Act 26 of 1955.

In paragraph 21 of *Ediga Anamma*, Justice Iyer summed up the progressive humanization of penology in India by observing: 'It is obvious that the disturbed conscience of the State on the vexed question of legal threat to life by way of death sentence has sought to express itself legislatively, the stream of tendency being towards cautions, partial abolition and a retreat from total retention.'[6]

Although the majority of countries in the world have abolished the death penalty—about 121 countries, to be precise—the legitimacy of the death penalty against the background of constitutional values continues to be agitated in India.

Despite the various decisions of the Supreme Court of India to uphold the constitutional validity of capital punishment, the debate must continue and cannot be foreclosed on the abstract doctrine of stare decisis (determining points in litigation according to precedent). The very nature of the problem is such that it must be the subject of review from time to time in order to be in tune with the evolving standards of decency in a maturing democracy.

The constitutionality of the death penalty was challenged again in the case of *Bachan Singh v. State of Punjab*[7] wherein it was upheld by a majority of 4:1. The challenge was the result of some legal and jurisprudential developments. The insertion of Section 354(3) in the Code by way of amendment made death penalty an exception. The doctrine of 'due process' propounded in *Maneka Gandhi v. Union of India and Ors*[8] completely changed the connotation of our fundamental rights recognized under articles 14, 19 and 21. The 'substantive due process' and the 'procedural due process' principles introduced in *Maneka Gandhi* demanded that unless a law is just, reasonable and fair in procedure, it would fall foul of the above articles. In *Bachan Singh*, the majority held that after the interpretation of Article 21 in *Maneka Gandhi*, it acquired a new dimension. Article 21 of the Constitution is couched as follows: 'No person shall be deprived of his life or personal liberty except according to procedure established by law'.

If this article is expanded in accordance with the interpretative principle indicated in *Maneka Gandhi*, it will read as follows: 'No person shall be deprived of his life or personal liberty except according to fair, just and reasonable procedure established by valid law.'

In the converse positive form, the expanded article will read thus: 'A person can only be deprived of his life or personal liberty in accordance with fair, just and reasonable procedure established by valid law.'[9]

In this changed jurisprudential context, the legality of the death penalty was examined in the landmark judgment in *Bachan Singh* and Justice P. Bhagwati, in a glowing dissent,[10] held that the death penalty is unconstitutional.

We find that apart from the decision in *Maneka Gandhi*, which introduced the concept of due process in our laws, the Indian government also ratified the International Covenant on Civil and Political Rights (ICCPR) and thereby supported the move for progressive abolition of the death penalty. Also, the

Supreme Court in *Sunil Batra v. Delhi Administration*[11], relying on the dictum in *Rustom Cavasjee Cooper v. Union of India*[12] and *Maneka Gandhi*, held that pre-Constitution laws have to be read so as to conform with the constitutional principles. The court also said that on such an interpretation, Section 302 of the IPC and Section 354(3) of the Code must be read in the humane light of Parts III & IV of the Constitution as illuminated by the preambular values. Relying on these principles, the court in *Bachan Singh* explained the requirement of Section 235(2) of the Code[13] for pre-sentence hearing of the accused, read with Section 354(3) of the Code,[14] which mandates recording of special reasons for imposing the death sentence. The court explained that pre-sentence hearing would mean a full-fledged bifurcated hearing, in which further evidence could be adduced by the accused, which might not be related to the crime but might be relevant to his socio-economic background. It was held that this would provide a safeguard against the arbitrary imposition of the death penalty and would allow the court to exercise discretion, being informed with reasons based on the evidence on the socio-economic background of the accused collected in the bifurcated hearing.

The rationale of introducing Section 354(3) of the Code was considered by a Joint Committee of Parliament, after which the committee stated: 'A sentence of death is the extreme penalty of law and it is but fair that when a court awards that sentence in a case where the alternative sentence of imprisonment for life is also available, it should give special reasons in support of the sentence.'

The Law Commission of India, in its 48th Report, pointed out the deficiency of the sentencing procedure which led to the enactment of Section 354(3). In para 45 of the report, the Law Commission insisted on having sufficient information on, and background of, the offenders in the following words: 'It is now being increasingly recognized that a rational and consistent sentencing policy requires the removal of several deficiencies in the present system. One such deficiency is the lack of comprehensive information as to characteristics and background of the offender.'[15]

While enacting Section 235(2) of the Code, the aforesaid recommendations of the Law Commission were taken into consideration by Parliament. About the nature of the hearing under Section 235(2) of the Code, the Supreme Court, in a number of judgments, emphasized its importance and relevance in the sentencing procedure.

Explaining the importance of pre-sentence hearing, the Supreme Court in *Santa Singh v. State of Punjab*[16] held that Section 235(2) is in accordance with the modern trends in penology and the same is an effective stage in the process of administration of justice. The court held that in most countries of the world, intensive study of sociology of crime has shifted the focus from the crime to the criminal, thus widening the objectives of sentencing. It was pointed out that a proper sentencing discretion calls for consideration of both extenuating and aggravating circumstances, prior criminal record of the criminal, his age, social adjustment, emotional and mental condition, his background, his education, his personal life and prospects for his rehabilitation. The court also held that non-compliance with a proper hearing under Section 235(2) is not curable under Section 465 of the Code. The apex court opined that the new dimension in constitutional values must be reflected in penology and sentencing procedure.

Chief Justice Chandrachud in *Muniappan v. State of Tamil Nadu*[17] held that the obligation to hear the accused under Section 235(2) cannot be discharged by just putting a few questions to the accused. There must be a genuine effort to gain a clue to the genesis of the crime by casting aside the formalities of the court scene and approaching the question from a broad sociological point of view.

In *Allauddin Mian and Ors, Sharif Mian and Anr v. State of Bihar*,[18] the Supreme Court expressed the same view and held that Section 235(2) conforms to the principles of natural justice and has a significant bearing on the sentencing procedure. It is a salutary provision and not a matter of mere formality. In *Rajesh Kumar v. State*,[19] the Supreme Court held that the object of recording special reasons being intrinsically connected with the sentencing procedure, both Sections 235(2) and 354(3) of the Code must be read together. For effective recording of special reasons, a proper hearing has to be accorded under Section 235(2) of the Code.

Immediately after the decision in *Maneka Gandhi*, another Constitution Bench of the Supreme Court rendered its decision in *Sunil Batra*. The Constitution Bench in *Sunil Batra*, speaking through Justice Krishna Iyer, held: 'True, our Constitution has no "due process" clause or the Eighth Amendment; but, in this branch of law, after Cooper and Maneka Gandhi, the consequence is the same.'[20]

The Eighth Amendment (1791) to the Constitution of the United States virtually emanated from the English Bill of Rights (1689). The text of the Eighth Amendment reads: 'Excessive bail shall not be required, nor excessive fines imposed, nor cruel and unusual punishments inflicted.'[21]

In *Bachan Singh*, the Supreme Court also held that apart from the aforesaid two procedural safeguards engrafted in Sections 235(2) of and 354(3) of the Code, there are other statutory safeguards which are provided against arbitrary imposition of the death penalty. Section 366(1) of the Code provides that no sentence of death shall be executed unless the same is confirmed by the High Court. Sections 367 of the Code further provides that in such confirmation proceedings, the High Court has the power to direct further enquiry and take additional evidence. Section 368 empowers the High Court to confirm the death sentence or pass any sentence warranted by law, or to annul or alter the conviction or order a new trial or acquit the accused. Such confirmational proceeding has to be done under Section 369 by two judges of the High Court and, in case of difference, the matter has to be referred to a third judge under Section 370 of the Code.

In *Bachan Singh*, the Supreme Court catalogued the aggravating and mitigating circumstances vide paragraphs 202 and 206 of the report and held that life imprisonment is the rule and death penalty is an exception. It further made it clear that a real and abiding concern for the dignity of human life postulates resistance in taking a life through the law's instrumentality and ruled that it could only be done in the 'rarest of rare' cases when the alternative option was unquestionably foreclosed.

Actually, the Supreme Court, by those observations, was showing the importance of the principle of lenity—'a common law principle that penal statutes should be strictly construed against the government or parties seeking to enforce statutory penalties and in favour of the persons on whom penalties are sought to be imposed'.[22] This principle of lenity encompasses the widely held jurisprudential values developed in seventeenth-century England to thwart the will of legislature bent on seeing the statutory violators hanged and was also developed by the Supreme Court of the United States of America.[23]

But in the actual application of the said 'rarest of rare' doctrine, subsequent smaller benches of the Supreme Court did not follow it uniformly. In *Machhi Singh and Others v. The State of Punjab*,[24] the 'rarest of rare' doctrine was diluted inasmuch as the bench suggested two further questions to be considered before awarding the death sentence. They are:

(1) Is there something uncommon about the crime which renders sentence of imprisonment for life inadequate and calls for a death sentence?

(2) Are the circumstances of the crime such that there is no alternative but to impose death sentence, even after according maximum weightage of the mitigating circumstances which speak in favour of the offender?

The reference to the balancing of aggravating and mitigating circumstances, and the questions posted by the judge, appear to show a dilution of the *Bachan Singh* guidelines. This is not permissible as the *Bachan Singh* decision was rendered by a five-judge Constitution Bench and the *Machhi Singh* one by a regular three-judge bench.

From the subsequent judgments of the Supreme Court, it became clear that the court was trying to articulate a doctrine of 'cry for justice' and of social necessity, which led to the fading impact of *Bachan Singh*'s ratio. In *Lok Pal Singh v. The State of Madhya Pradesh*,[25] a two-judge bench held that once cruel, heinous murder was proved, the death sentence would follow and thus turned the clock back without discussing the rarest of rare doctrine. It held that there was no reason to show leniency. A similar attitude of the Supreme Court is discernible in *Mahto s/o Ram Narain v. State of Madhya Pradesh*[26], *Darshan Singh* v. *State of Punjab*[27] and in several other decisions of smaller benches. In *Amrik Singh v. The State of Punjab*,[28] the Supreme Court opined that *Machhi Singh* was retrieving the virtually abolitionist situation created in *Bachan Singh*.

In *Amrik Singh*, a smaller bench of the Supreme Court adversely commented on the decision in *Bachan Singh* by saying that the unfortunate result of the decision in *Bachan Singh* is that capital punishment is seldom employed, even though it may be a crime against society and the brutality of the crime 'shocks the judicial conscience'. Thus, the *Bachan Singh* ratio was being slowly diluted by the Supreme Court till it reached its peak when the Supreme Court rendered its decision in *Ravji alias Ram Chandra v. The State of Rajasthan.*[29] In *Ravji*, a two-judge bench concluded that the court would be failing in its duty if it did not respond to society's 'cry for justice' against the criminal by giving the death sentence.

It is interesting to note that on 12 December 2006, a two-judge bench of the Supreme Court, in *Aloke Nath Dutta and Others v. State of West Bengal*[30], admitted the failure of the court to evolve a uniform sentencing policy in capital cases. The court was critical of the fact that different criteria had been adopted by different benches in awarding the death sentence even though the offences were similar in nature. But on the same day, in a startling contrast, another two-judge bench of the Supreme Court in *Bablu alias Mubarak Hussain* v. *State of Rajasthan*[31] upheld the death sentence without discussing the *Bachan Singh* principle. This shows the disparity in sentencing standards even at the level of the Supreme Court, which is very frustrating and virtually makes the awarding of the death penalty a 'lethal lottery'.

In a rather recent judgment, the Supreme Court, in the case of *Santosh Kumar Satishbhushan Bariyar v. State of Maharashtra*,[32] pointed out that the *Ravji* case and six other subsequent judgments which followed it were decided per incuriam, that is, in the exercise of sentencing discretion, it followed principles that are contrary to the law laid down by the Constitution Bench of the Supreme Court in *Bachan Singh*.

The Supreme Court made it very clear in *Bariyar* that in those six cases[33] it did not consider any mitigating circumstances or a circumstance relating to criminals at the sentencing phase and thus, by judgments rendered contrary to law, the death sentence was imposed.

In a way, the two-judge bench judgment in *Bariyar* is a landmark decision on sentencing in our laws. In *Bariyar*, the rarest of rare doctrine was further restricted by an added criterion that it has to be proved by the state that the accused is beyond reform. It has also laid down that post-*Bachan*, capital sentencing has come within the fold of constitutional adjudication by virtue of the safeguards entrenched in articles 14 and 21 of the Constitution. In *Bariyar*, the Supreme Court interpreted the rarest of rare doctrine to say that it has breathed fresh life into 'special reasons' in Section 354(3) of the Code by imposing a wide-ranging embargo on the death penalty.

The court also emphasized that justice must be the first virtue in sentencing and the sentencing court must consider itself a 'forum of principle'. The sentencing court has to follow 'principled reasoning' flowing from judicial precedent or from legislation and draw power from them.

The court in *Bariyar* bemoaned the state of uncertainty in the capital sentencing law and held that it thus falls foul of 'constitutional due process and equality'. The court wanted, and rightly so, that judicial discretion only be exercised within defined principles and on the basis of clarity.

A similar view has been expressed in *Swamy Shraddananda @ Murali Manohar Mishra v. The State of Karnataka*[34], wherein the court lamented that 'no standards' can be culled out from the judge-made law which governs selection of death penalty, apart from the broad guidelines of rarest of rare case in *Bachan Singh*. This has created a total uncertainty in the manner of giving death sentences following the concept of 'rarest of rare' doctrine. Even though the decision in *Bachan Singh* has received approval from the international legal community and has been favourably referred to by David Pannick[35] and by Roger Hood and Carolyn Hoyle[36] in their treatise on the death penalty, this has not been uniformly applied by the Supreme Court.

Reference in this connection may also be made to the right-based approach in exercising discretion in the death penalty, as suggested by Edward Fitzgerald,[37] the British barrister. It has been suggested by him that the right approach towards exercising discretion in capital cases is to start from a strong presumption against death penalty. It is argued that 'the presence of any significant mitigating factor justifies exemption from the death penalty even in the most gruesome cases' and Fitzgerald further says:

> Such a restrictive approach can be summarized as follows: The normal sentence should be life imprisonment. The death sentence should only be imposed instead of the life sentence in the 'rarest of rare' cases where the crime or crimes are of exceptional heinousness and the individual has no significant mitigation and is considered beyond reformation.[38]

Justice Bhagwati anticipated that the doctrine of rarest of rare cases formulated in *Bachan Singh*[39] would vary from judge to judge depending upon the 'value system, responses and social philosophy of the judges' constituting the benches in the Supreme Court and feared that there would be 'chaotic arbitrariness in imposition of death sentence'. The learned judge agreed with the observation of Justice Krishna Iyer in *Rajendra Prasad Etc. Etc. v. State of Uttar Pradesh*[40], where it was held that various factors 'play a part in swinging the pendulum of sentencing justice erratically'. The apprehensions of both these great judges have come true.

A penalty which is irrevocable and a damage which is beyond repair on the most precious right of a human being—the right to life—cannot be left at the present state of uncertainty in which freakish and arbitrary modes of death sentencing is currently exercised. This has been repeatedly acknowledged by the last court in the largest democracy of the world.

The matter should be examined by the Law Commission of India fully and from all angles. In a recent exercise, the Law Commission focused on peripheral issues by discussing whether hanging was the most humane way of carrying out the death sentence.[41] But the matter needs to be addressed in much greater depth.

Therefore, Parliament cannot ignore such a vital aspect of constitutional values involving the death penalty. It is urgently required that Parliament address the issue adequately and put the matter on a statutory basis, thereby structuring the sentencing process in the imposition of the death penalty in accordance with the constitutional values of human dignity and the right to life. The sooner it is done, the better.

NOTES

1. Indian Law Commission, *Capital Punishment: 35th Report*, (Government of India Press, 1967).
2. See Sections 121, 132, second para of Section 194 and sections, 302, 303, 305, 307, 396. Based on the principal of vicarious liability, the IPC also provides for death penalty for acts done in pursuance of common intention—Section 34 (common object); Section 149 (by way of abatement); Sections 109 and 119 (criminal conspiracy); Section 120B, and in cases of dacoity with murder (if any one of the persons, while committing dacoity, murders someone).
3. Air Force Act (Section 34), Army Act (Section 34), Arms Act (Section 27[3]), Commission of Sati (Prevention Act) (Section 4), Narcotic Drugs and Psychotrophic Substances Act, 1985.
4. (1973) 1 SCC 20.
5. (1974) 4 SCC 443.
6. Ibid., para 21, p. 452.

7. AIR 1980 (2) 684.
8. (1978) 1 SCC 248.
9. AIR 1980 (2) 684, para 136, p. 730.
10. (1978) 4 SCC 494.
11. (1978) 4 SCC 409.
12. (1970) 1 SCC 248.
13. Section 235(2): 'If the accused is convicted, the Judge shall, unless he proceeds in accordance with the provisions of Section 360, hear the accused on the question of sentence, and then pass sentence on him according to law'.
14. Section 354(3): 'When the conviction is for an offence punishable with death or, in the alternative, with imprisonment for life or imprisonment for a term of years, the judgment shall state the reasons for the sentence awarded, and, in the case of sentence of death, the special reasons for such sentence.'
15. Law Commission of India, *Some Questions under the Code of Criminal Procedure*, (Government of India, Ministry of Law and Justice, 1972).
16. (1976) 4 SCC 190.
17. (1981) 3 SCC 11.
18. (1989) 3 SCC 5.
19. (2011) 13 SCC 706.
20. Ibid., para 52, p. 518.
21. Source: legal-dictionary.thefreedictionary.com/Eighth+Amendment
22. Norman J. Singer and J.D. Shambie Singer, *Statutes and Statutory Construction*, 5th edition, 1992, para 59.03.
23. *Moskal* v. *United States*, 498 US 103 (1990).
24. 1983 AIR 957.
25. AIR 1985 SC 891.
26. (1970) 1 SCC 25.
27. 1988 AIR 747.
28. (1988) Supp. SCC 685.

29. AIR 1996 SC 787.
30. (2007) 12 SCC 230.
31. AIR 2007 SC 597.
32. (2007) 12 SCC 288.
33. *Shivaji v. State of Maharashtra* (2008) 15 SCC 269; *Mohan Anna Chavan v. State of Maharashtra* (2008) 7 SCC 561; *Bank v. State of UP* (2008) 11 SCC 113; *Surja Ram v. The State of Rajasthan* (1996) 6 SCC 271; *Dayanidhi Bisoi* v. *State of Orissa* (2003) 9 SCC 310; *State of UP v. Sultan* (2009) 4 SCC 736.
34. (2008) 13 SCC 767.
35. David Pannick, *Judicial Review of the Death Penalty*, (Duckworth, 1982), para 83–84, pp. 104–05.
36. Roger Hood and Carolyn Hoyle, *The Death Penalty: A Worldwide Perspect*, 4th Edition (Oxford University Press, 2008), p. 285.
37. Edward Fitzgerald, 'The Mitigation Exercise in Capital Cases', in *Death Penalty Conference, 3–5 June 2005, Barbados Conference Papers and Recommendations,* quoted in *Rajesh Kumar v. State* (2011) 13 SCC 706, p. 732.
38. Hood and Hoyle, *The Death Penalty*, op. cit., p. 285.
39. (1982) 3 SCC 24, para 75, p. 116.
40. (1979) 3 SCC 646, para 18, p. 659.
41. *187th Report on Mode of Execution of Death Sentence and Incidental Matters*, (Law Commission of India, 2003).

8

POWERS OF THE PRESIDENT AND THE GOVERNOR TO GRANT PARDON AND REMISSION

The Doctrine in Maru Ram and the Conflicting Trend in Swamy Shraddananda and Subsequent Judgments

THE PROVISION OF the Constitution under Article 72 empowers the president to grant pardons, reprieves, respites or remission of punishment, or to suspend or commute the sentence of any person convicted of any offence in all cases where punishment or sentence is by a court martial. It is also applicable in all cases where the punishment or sentence is for an offence against any law to which the executive power of the Union of India extends; and in all cases where the sentence is one of death. Similar provisions have been made to enable the governor of a state under Article 161 to grant pardon, reprieve, etc., but that power is confined only to a matter to which the executive power of a state extends, which obviously includes the power to remit or grant pardon in respect of a death sentence.

The law relating to the exercise of this power by the president of India or the governor of a state, which is known as clemency power, and its impact on the sentencing procedure, has given rise to some recent debate in view of the conflict of decisions in the Supreme Court. This concerns public interest in very vital areas of crime and punishment.

One of the leading decisions on the exercise of clemency power was rendered by the Constitution Bench of the Supreme Court in *Maru Ram Etc. Etc. v. Union of India and Another*[1]. Here, the Constitution Bench of the Supreme Court construed the provision of the Code of Criminal Procedure (Amendment Act, 1978) whereby Parliament inserted Section 433A in the code, which makes a full fourteen-year term of imprisonment on a prisoner mandatory for two classes of prisoners—those prisoners who are to be punished by death and those who are sentenced to death but whose sentence was commuted to life imprisonment under Section 433. As a result of this amendment, a convict must undergo fourteen years' imprisonment till his release is sanctioned under Article 72/161 of the Constitution.

The Constitution Bench in *Maru Ram* made it clear that Section 433A does not affect the pardon power under articles 72 and 161 of the Constitution. The Supreme Court opined that in the exercise of its constitutional power under articles 72 and 161, neither the president nor the governor is to act on his own judgement but should act in accordance with the aid and advice of the council of ministers. Such power cannot be exercised arbitrarily since it is an exercise of constitutional power. In the exercise of such power, Section 433A itself is to be treated as a guideline. Justice Krishna Iyer, in the concluding part of his judgment, speaking for the bench in *Maru Ram*, made this position very clear by saying:

> Considerations for exercise of power under Articles 72/161 may be myriad and their occasions protean, and are left to the appropriate Government, but no consideration nor occasion can be wholly irrelevant, irrational, discriminatory or mala fide. Only in these rare cases will the court examine the exercise.[2]

The Supreme Court, in *Maru Ram*, also felt that for proper exercise of the pardon power, till rules are framed, Section 433A can be treated as a guideline. In most countries where the death penalty is retained, clemency can be sought even when appeal and confirmation proceedings are pending and even after a final judgment is pronounced. In the opinion of the Privy Council in the case of *Neville Lewis v. The Attorney General of Jamaica and Others*[3] it was held that the exercise of prerogative mercy should, in light of Jamaica's international obligation, be exercised by procedures that were fair and proper, such as disclosure to the applicant of all materials to go before the review committee and making them amenable to judicial review. The same principles have been virtually accepted in *Maru Ram*.

About the clemency procedure, the US Supreme Court in *Herrera v. Collins* held that 'clemency is the historic remedy for preventing miscarriages of justice where judicial process has been exhausted—the fail safe in our criminal justice system'[4]. Across the United States as a whole, clemency authorities have stopped some executions and commuted sentences on the grounds of lingering doubt.

In a rather recent judgment, a three-judge bench of the Supreme Court, in the case of *Swamy Shraddananda@Murali Manohar Mishra v. State of Karnataka*[5], dwelt elaborately on the question of remission of sentences. Before doing so, the Supreme Court referred to its judgment in the case of *Subash Chander v. Krishan Lal and Ors.*[6] In *Krishan Lal*, the Supreme Court, on the invitation of the counsel for the accused, sentenced Krishan Lal, the accused, to imprisonment for the rest of his life and made it clear that Krishan Lal shall not be entitled to any commutation or premature release under Section 401 of the Code of Criminal Procedure or the Prisoner's Act, Jail Manual, or any other standard or rules made for the purpose of granting commutation and remission. Recording this stand, the court in *Shraddananda* came to the conclusion that in some cases imprisonment for a term of twenty years with further direction that the convict must not be released from the prison for the rest of his life, or before actually serving out the term fixed by the court means imprisonment for the rest of the life of the prisoner and a convict undergoing such extended term of imprisonment has no right to claim remission.

It was argued before the Supreme Court in *Shraddananda* that it is not open to the court to direct the appropriate government not to consider a case for the grant of remission of sentence. It was also contended that giving the punishment for an offence is a judicial function, but the execution of the punishment passes into the hands of the executive and the court cannot control the execution of sentences.

However, the court, repelling those contentions, came to a very innovative conclusion after considering the unsound way in which remission is allowed in cases of life sentence. The court opined that a strong case should be made out for creating a special *category* for the punishment for life in excess of a period of fourteen years and put that category beyond the application of remission.[7] The court found that in cases when an appellant comes before the Supreme Court challenging the death sentence awarded by the High Court, and the Supreme Court finds that the case falls short of the 'rarest of rare' category and feels reluctant to endorse the death sentence, then the death sentence should be substituted with such a 'special category of punishment'.

With great respect to the learned judges, this proposition appears legally unsustainable.

Section 302 of the IPC runs as follows: Punishment for murder—'Whoever commits murder shall be punished with death or imprisonment for life, and shall also be liable to fine.' It is clear that the word 'or' placed between these two punishments has to be treated disjunctively, meaning thereby that these two punishments fall under two totally different categories, both quantitatively and qualitatively. The concept of substitution can only apply in a situation when there is some degree of equivalence or resemblance between the two options.

According to the *Oxford Advanced Learner's Dictionary*, the word 'substitute' means 'a person or thing that you use or have instead of the one you normally use or have'. The word 'substitution' is very close to the word 'similar', but under Section 302 of the IPC, the two punishments have been referred to as two substantively different punishments, both qualitatively and quantitatively, and one cannot be a substitute for the other.

Both in *Bachan Singh*[8] and *Maru Ram*, the Constitution Benches treated these two sentences as qualitatively different. One can never be a substitute for the other by way of judicial interpretation. Apart from Section 302 of the IPC, the Code of Criminal Procedure also treats them differently by mandating in Section 354(3) of the Code that for giving death sentence in a judgment special reasons are to be recorded.

Section 53 of the IPC also treats death penalty differently from life imprisonment while grouping punishments. Death penalty and imprisonment for life are placed in different classifications:

> *Punishments.—The punishments to which offenders are liable under the provisions of this Code are—*
> First—Death;
> Secondly—Imprisonment for life;[9]

It is therefore clear that the death penalty stands at the forefront in the category of punishment. It is of a different genus and cannot be a substitute for imprisonment for life. They are in two completely separate leagues.

Therefore, the jurisprudential strategy in *Shraddananda*

to earmark a 'special category' of punishment on the premise of substituting death penalty with life imprisonment beyond remission militates against deeply entrenched values in constitutionalism and penology.

Looked at from another point of view, if death penalty and life imprisonment are considered as substituting one another, this seriously affects the integrity and clarity in the sentencing structure and will unfortunately introduce an element of uncertainty and arbitrariness in choosing over the other without the objective considerations evolved in *Bachan Singh*.

The trend in *Shraddananda* has been followed subsequently in some judgments of the Supreme Court. In *Haru Ghosh*,[10] the Supreme Court directed that the life imprisonment of Haru Ghosh shall not be less than thirty-five years of actual jail sentence. Subsequently, in another judgment in *Sandeep v. State of Uttar Pradesh*,[11] the Bench, relying on the *Shraddananda* principle, directed that Sandeep should serve a minimum of thirty years in jail without remission.

However, in a subsequent decision in *Sangeet and Anr v. State of Haryana*[12] a two-judge bench of the Supreme Court, after considering *Shraddananda*, struck a different note, saying: 'The appropriate government cannot be told that it is prohibited from granting remission of a sentence. Similarly a convict cannot be told that he cannot apply for a remission in his sentence, whatever the reason'[13].

In paragraph 59 of *Sangeet*, the bench made it clear that a convict does not have the right to get a remission of sentence, although he certainly has the right to have his case considered for the grant of remission. In saying so, the bench rightly relied on the principle laid down in *State of Haryana v. Mahinder Singh*[14] and *State of Haryana v. Jagdish*.[15]

In the concluding portion of the judgment, the bench in

Sangeet summed up its finding on the question of remission as follows: 'The grant of remissions is statutory. However, to prevent its arbitrary exercise, the legislature has built in some procedural and substantive checks in the statute. These need to be faithfully enforced'.[16]

This seems to be a legally sustainable opinion formulated by the Supreme Court on the structure of sentencing.

If we examine the principle in *Shraddananda* and other cases that followed it from a more fundamental standpoint, it also appears seriously flawed.

One of the non-derogable fundamental rights given to any person under our Constitution is protection against ex post facto laws. This common law principle of great antiquity has been assimilated and summed up in Article 20(1) in the following words:

> *Protection in respect of conviction for offences*: 1) No person shall be convicted of any offense except for violation of the law in force at the time of the commission of the act charged as an offence, nor be subjected to a penalty greater than that which might have been inflicted under the law in force at the time of commission of the offence.

It has been held by the Constitution Bench of the Supreme Court in *Kerdar Nath Bajoria and Anr v. State of West Bengal*[17] that the prohibition under Article 20(1) will operate not only against the passing of any retroactive law but also against punishment under such law.

In cases relating to murder, the relevant law of punishment, Section 302 of the IPC, has remained the same. It provides for two different kinds of punishment—death penalty or imprisonment for life with fine. They are not substitutes.

In all these cases, namely in *Shraddananda*, *Haru Ghosh* and

Sandeep, the Supreme Court dealt with appeals filed by appellants against the orders of the High Court imposing the death penalty. In each of these cases, the learned judges of the Supreme Court found that the death penalty could not be awarded as the facts and circumstances did not bring the cases of the appellants within the category of 'rarest of rare' case. The Hon'ble Supreme Court did not approve of the death penalty. Instead, the court did not merely award imprisonment for life; rather, it awarded a 'special category' of punishment evolved in *Shraddananda* and fixed a specified period of life imprisonment, either for the rest of life of the appellant, or for thirty years or thirty-five years, with a mandate that there would be no remission of the sentence. The obvious question is this: can the sentencing court, ignoring the statutory provision and the fundamental guarantee in the Bill of Rights (Articles 20[1] and 21 of the Constitution) which corresponds with the statute, evolve a new sentencing structure in the name of a special category of sentence? The answer seems to be decidedly in the negative.

The guarantee of fundamental rights, a non-derogable right, recognized under Article 20(1) of the Constitution of these appellants, is thus violated. It is clear that life imprisonment includes the prospect of remission, as is evident from the wordings of Section 55 of the IPC and also sections 432, 433 and 433-A of the Code of Criminal Procedure.

Therefore, a prayer for grant of remission of life sentence by a convict is certainly provided in the procedure established under law. In view of Article 21 of the Constitution, the appellants in those cases are entitled to avail of the same.

Therefore, the guarantee of Article 20(1), read with Article 21 of the Constitution, stands violated by this exercise of judicial discretion. The procedure of remission is one established under law and the penalty of life imprisonment of a convict would include all the procedural safeguards in the awarding of such a penalty. A court, in the exercise of its discretion, cannot denude a convict of the benefits of statutory safeguards, which are covered within the sweep of 'procedure established under law' and are protected under Article 21 of the Constitution, by awarding a special category of sentence. In view of the decision in *Maneka Gandhi* v. *Union of India and Others*,[18] the procedure established under law has been equated to due process in our jurisprudence. Therefore, such 'special category of sentence' violates the due process guarantee of the convicts.

The guarantees contemplated under articles 20(1) and 21 of the Constitution are included within the basic structure of the Constitution and cannot be curtailed by law in view of the injunction against it under Article 13(2) of the Constitution. Such a guarantee cannot be abridged even by a constitutional amendment under Article 368 of the Constitution in view of the majority decision in *Kesavananda Bharati*, which is now part of our jurisprudence. The decision in *Shraddananda*, and the judgments which followed it, with respect, seem to have bypassed these principles.

It may be noted that the rights under articles 20(1) and 21 are so basic that they cannot be suspended even during a period of Emergency in view of the Constitution (44th Amendment) Act, 1978, whereby it has been specifically stated that during the period when a proclamation of an Emergency is in operation, the rights conferred by Part III, except articles 20 and 21, may cease to operate. These rights are non-derogable rights and given to every person, whether he or she is a citizen or not, and enjoy the status of 'jus cogens' in international law.

However, these rights of the appellants in the aforementioned cases have been apparently breached and taken away by an exercise of judicial discretion. If the convicts in those cases apply before the president/governor under Articles 72 and 161 of the Constitution, a fair consideration of their case for clemency also stands stultified and impeded in view of the mandate given by the Supreme Court while giving them life imprisonment. With due respect, this is clearly against the rule of law.

Therefore, this confusion and divergence in the sentencing policy created by the Supreme Court in *Shraddananda* and subsequent cases should be re-examined by a larger bench of the Supreme Court. This is a matter of immense public importance from both the constitutional point of view and in view of the larger public interest involved in maintaining a uniform sentencing structure that is not judge-centric, but is based on constitutional values and rule of law.

In this connection, it is appropriate to keep in mind what was said by Justice Black in *Williams v. People of State of New York.*[19]

> A sentencing judge, however, is not confined to the narrow issue of guilt. *His task, within fixed statutory or constitutional limits, is to determine the type and extent of punishment* after the issue of guilt has been determined. Highly relevant—if not essential—to his selection of an appropriate sentence is the possession of the fullest information possible concerning the defendant's life and characteristics. And modern concepts individualizing punishment have made it all the more necessary that a sentencing judge not be denied an opportunity to obtain pertinent information by a requirement of rigid adherence to restrictive rules of evidence properly applicable to the trial.

However, some recent judgments of the Supreme Court have considerably enlarged the scope of clemency jurisdiction, based on broad principles of constitutionalism.

First came the two-judge bench decision of the Supreme Court in *Devendra Pal Singh Bhullar v. State of NCT, Delhi*,[20] which was a setback to the developing trends of penology. In that decision the court held that even though the mercy petition of Bhullar for commutation of death penalty to life was kept pending before the president of India for eight years (it should have been disposed of in 2005 but instead it was decided upon in 2011), that is not a ground of commutation in view of the nature of crime committed by Bhullar.

The court held that even though there was no undue delay on Bhullar's part, he was, inter alia, an accused under the Terrorist and Disruptive Activities (Prevention) Act, 1987. Therefore the court would not judicially review the exercise of mercy by the president, even if there was undue and unexplained delay in the disposal of the petition. This was decided on 12 April 2013.

Within a year, precisely on 21 January 2014, came a three-judge bench judgment of the Supreme Court in *Shatrughan Chauhan and Another v. Union of India and Others*,[21] overruling the ratio in Bhullar. In Shatrughan Chauhan, a landmark decision, the court held that the power to pardon is neither a matter of grace nor a matter of privilege, but it is a constitutional responsibility reposed by the people on the highest authority[22] and a limited judicial review is permitted over exercise of such power.

The court held that the right enshrined in Article 21 of the Constitution inheres in every prisoner and is available to him 'till his last breath', even when 'the noose is being tied on the condemned prisoner's neck'. The court also held that international covenants on human rights, to which India is a party, are parts of our domestic law unless they are contrary to any specific law in force.[23]

On these premises, the court held that where there is undue and unexplained delay in the execution of death sentence for the pendency of mercy petition before the authority, it is within its right to commute death sentence to life.[24] The unanimous court, speaking through Chief Justice Sathasivam, held that this jurisprudence is based on our constitutionalism, meshed with various international covenants of the United Nations. The court thus held that the ratio in Bhullar (supra) was rendered per incuriam.[25]

Following the Shatrughan ratio, the court, on a curative petition filed by Navneet Kaur,[26] wife of Bhullar, commuted Bhullar's death penalty to life imprisonment in a judgment rendered on 31 March 2014.

Another judgment of far-reaching significance was delivered by the Constitution Bench of the Supreme Court in *Md Arif@ Ashfaq v. Registrar, Supreme Court of India and Ors.*[27] Delivering the majority opinion, Justice R.F. Nariman traced, possibly for the first time, the genesis of the principles in Article 21 from the precepts of Magna Carta of thirteenth-century England. The learned judge admirably compared the halting odyssey of the great liberating principles enshrined in both till they reached their bloom.

Discussing the developing jurisprudence of Article 21, the learned judge found that the 'wheel has turned full circle' and 'substantive due process must be applied to fundamental rights to life and liberty'. He also opined that 'death sentence cases are a distinct category of cases altogether' primarily for two reasons: (1) irreversibility of death penalty and (2) different judicially trained minds arriving at diametrically opposite conclusions on the same facts.

The learned judge noted, and rightly so, that unlike in many countries there is no statutory sentencing policy in India.

Considering all these factors, Justice Nariman ruled that when a convict, who has been given death sentence, files a review petition, granting an oral hearing to him is an integral part of reasonable procedure under Article 21 of the Constitution.

It is clear that the irreversible nature of the death sentence weighed so heavily on the conscience of the learned judge that His Lordship held that denial of 'limited oral hearing' in a review petition to a convict on death row amounts to denial of fairness and falls short of the fair procedure contemplated under Article 21. This is a judgment of great moment, which makes our sentencing procedure compatible with the evolving human rights norms against the death penalty. In formulating his propositions, the learned judge took refuge to the profound relevance of Justice Holmes's pronouncement that the life of law is not logic, but experience.

Consistent with this judicial thinking, there has been a modification of Supreme Court rules in 2013, which mandate that every cause, appeal or proceeding, arising out of a death sentence awarded by a High Court, shall be heard by a bench of not less than three judges.

These are post-*Bachan Singh* judicially evolved safeguards by the Supreme Court to prevent gross miscarriage of justice by freakish infliction of death sentence.

NOTES

1. (1981) 1 SCC 107.
2. Ibid., pp. 107–154.
3. 2001 Vol. 2, Appeal Cases, p. 50.
4. (1993) 506 US 390.
5. (2008) 13 SCC 767.
6. (2001) 4 SCC 458.
7. (2008) 13 SCC 767, para 91.
8. (1980) 2 SCC 684.

9. Source: indiankanoon.org/doc/543586
10. (2009) 15 SCC 551.
11. (2012) 6 SCC 107.
12. (2012) 11 SCALE 140.
13. Ibid., para 58, p. 156.
14. (2007) 13 SCC 605.
15. (2010) 4 SCC 216.
16. (2012) 11 SCALE 140, para 80, p. 162.
17. AIR 1953 SC 404.
18. (1978) 1 SCC 248.
19. (1949) 337 US 241, p. 288.
20. (2013) 6 SCC 195.
21. (2014) 3 SCC 1.
22. Paragraph 19 of the report.
23. Paragraph 46.
24. Paragraph 48.
25. Paragraph 72.
26. *Navneet Kaur v. State*, (2014) 7 SCC 264.
27. (2014) 10 SCC 84.

9

FAST-CHANGING SOCIAL PERSPECTIVE

Creative Jurisprudence by the Supreme Court to Promote Equal Justice and Gender Equality

THE JUDGMENT OF the Supreme Court in *Vishaka* v. *The State of Rajasthan*[1] by Chief Justice J.S. Verma is a landmark decision and is a benchmark in constitutionalism in more ways than one. First, it very adequately addressed an age-old social evil, of harassment of women and female workers in the workplace, against which there was no specific legal protection. Apart from strategizing such protection, this decision also enlivened our jurisprudence with human rights values and highlighted the doctrine that our laws, in the absence of a contrary municipal law, should absorb and assimilate the concerns of the international community expressed through covenants and treaties to march towards a global jurisprudence of shared values.

Reading the decision in *Vishaka*, a discerning reader may remember what was said by Justice Benjamin Cardozo.[2]

'The judge,' Cardozo wrote, 'interprets the social conscience, and gives effect to it in law, but in so doing he helps to form and modify the conscience he interprets. Discovery and creation react upon each other'[3].

The interpretation of social conscience was very meaningfully done in *Vishaka* by ensuring the women workers and employees a safe space in their workplace and by holding that they are, in view of the fundamental rights in our Constitution, entitled to it.

A writ petition under Article 32 of the Constitution was filed by social activists and a non-governmental organization (NGO) as a class action before the Supreme Court, for the enforcement of the rights of working women under articles 14, 19 and 21, in view of the prevailing conditions in workplaces, where violation of these rights was very common. The petition was filed for the realization of gender equality and to prevent sexual harassment of working women in workplaces through the 'judicial process', in the absence of any suitable legislation to prevent such harassment. The incident which triggered the filing of the petition was the brutal gang rape of a social worker in a village in Rajasthan.

The Supreme Court found that the violation of working women's rights, apart from giving rise to a criminal trial, also violates the provisions of articles 14, 15, 19(1)(g) and 21 of the Constitution, and the filing of a petition under Article 32, being a fundamental right itself, is a potent redressal mechanism.

The *Vishaka* judgment made it clear that gender equality and the right to a safe and secure working place is part of the fundamental rights guaranteed by the Constitution and it is the duty of the judiciary to ensure that the state enforces these rights. This the judiciary has to ensure as it is a part of the constitutional machinery. It will also to make our jurisprudence compatible with the global jurisprudence on human rights by reading the nation's obligation to comply with international treatises and covenants into our laws.

In paragraph 14 of the judgment in *Vishaka* the following principles have been enunciated:

> The meaning and content of the fundamental rights guaranteed in the Constitution of India are of sufficient amplitude to encompass all the facets of gender

> equality including prevention of sexual harassment or abuse. Independence of judiciary forms a part of our constitutional scheme. The international conventions and norms are to be read into them in the absence of enacted domestic law occupying the field when there is no inconsistency between them. It is now an accepted rule of judicial construction that regard must be had to international conventions and norms for construing domestic law when there is no inconsistency between them and there is a void in the domestic law.

The Supreme Court found that there was an absence of a domestic law protecting the rights of women in working places and therefore the court, in the exercise of its power under Article 32, gave some guidelines and norms. In so doing it considered the definition of 'human rights' under Section 2(d) of the Protection of Human Rights Act, 1993.

In this process, the court took into consideration the objectives of the judiciary, which were accepted in the Conference of the Chief Justices of Asia and the Pacific at Beijing in 1995. Those objectives are mentioned below:

(1) To ensure that all persons are able to live securely under the rule of law.
(2) To promote, within the proper limits of the judicial function, the observance and the attainment of human rights.
(3) To administer the law impartially among persons and between persons and the state.

The court also took into consideration the provisions of the Convention on the Elimination of all Forms of Discrimination against Women (CEDAW). The court also noted that the government ratified those conventions.

Against the background of all these facts and the position held in the international covenants, the court fixed certain guidelines for protecting women from sexual harassment in the workplace, and directed that those guidelines should hold the field till a law was made.

In terms of the *Vishaka* judgment, guidelines were formed to protect women workers from harassment in working places and in various universities and other places.

A legislation under the name of Sexual Harassment of Women at Workplace (Prevention, Prohibition and Redressal) Bill, 2012, was introduced in Parliament. There was no debate in Parliament when the bill was introduced on 3 September 2012 and the matter was sent before the Rajya Sabha for approval. Ultimately, it was assented to by the president on 22 April 2013 and gazetted on 23 April 2013. This is a social welfare legislation of far-reaching consequence, giving protection and the right to work with dignity to women, and is the result of the judicial intervention in *Vishaka*.

Again, in *Apparel Export Promotion Council v. A.K. Chopra*[4] the principles laid down in *Vishaka* were followed in a case of sexual harassment of a female employee in her workplace.

A female employee, who was working as a clerk-cum-typist, spurned some repeated sexual overtures by her superior in the office. Ultimately, the lady lodged a formal complaint with the management and a regular departmental proceeding was initiated against the offending male officer. This led to the dismissal of the officer and thereupon several proceedings were taken by the officer to challenge his order of dismissal. On a writ petition filed by that officer, a learned judge of the Delhi High Court opined that the officer tried to molest the female employee but had not, in fact, actually done so and as such, the dismissal order of that officer was quashed. The Division Bench of the Delhi High Court also maintained the same judgment and thereupon a special leave petition (SLP) was filed by the employer. After admitting the said

SLP, and overturning the judgment of the Delhi High Court, the Supreme Court gave a landmark decision following the principles of *Vishaka*.

Chief Justice Dr Anand, delivering the judgment, held that each incident of sexual harassment at the workplace results in violation of the fundamental right of gender equality for female employees and is also an invasion of their right to life and liberty. The learned chief justice referred to an International Labour Organization (ILO) seminar held in Manila and opined that the sexual harassment of female workers at the workplace is incompatible with their dignity and honour. He also referred to international covenants of CEDAW and also to the International Covenant on Economic, Social and Cultural Rights. A special reference was made to Article 7 of the said convention, in para 27 of the judgment. It was made clear that in cases involving the violation of human rights, the court must be alive to international instrumentation and covenants and apply the same to a given case where there is no inconsistency between the international norms and the domestic law.

In a subsequent judgment, in the case of *Chairman Railway Board and Ors.* v. *Chandrima Das and Ors*,[5] a very proactive court gave a very expansive definition of 'life' by bringing it at par with the interpretation of 'life' in the Universal Declaration of Human Rights, 1948.

In brief, the facts of the case are as follows: one Bangladeshi national came to Howrah station to catch a train for Ajmer. Being new to the busy railway station, she was misled by some employees of the railways and was ultimately taken to a room in the Railway Yatri Niwas which had been booked by some railway employees previously. She was raped there by the railway employees. Later on she was taken to a rented house by another railway employee and was raped again. In view of the hue and cry raised by her, she was rescued by the police. Ms Chandrima Das, a practicing advocate of Calcutta High Court, filed a public interest litigation (PIL), asking for compensation for the victim. A Division Bench of Calcutta High Court, after hearing the parties, granted compensation of ₹10 lakh to be paid to the victim by the Union of India, of which the railways is a wing.

Challenging the said judgment, the chairman of the Railway Board approached the Supreme Court. Upholding the High Court judgment, the Supreme Court laid down that in view of the expanding horizon of Article 14 read with other articles, every executive action of the government is now amenable to the scrutiny of the writ jurisdiction of the High Court and the Supreme Court in appropriate cases. The Supreme Court held that the writ jurisdiction of the High Court is wide enough to be extended in the realm of tort in the matters of granting compensation to a victim who had suffered personal injuries at the hands of the officers of the government.

The court held that where public functionaries are involved in matters of invasion of fundamental rights or of enforcement of public duties, the remedy of compensation by writ is available. A case of rape does not merely violate an ordinary right of a victim but it violates a fundamental right to life of the victim and such a right is protected under Article 21 of the Constitution.

In coming to the said conclusion, the court relied on the judgment of the Supreme Court in *Bodhisattwa Gautam v. Subhra Chakraborty*.[6] The learned judges held that international covenants and declarations adopted by the United Nations are to be respected by all signatory states and the meaning given to the provisions of those declarations and covenants have to be such that would help in effective implementation of those rights. The Supreme Court made a very significant ruling by holding that the Universal Declaration of Human Rights and the principles thereof, if need be, ought to be read into our domestic jurisprudence.[7]

In arriving at the said conclusion, the Supreme Court drew support from the dictum of Lord Diplock in *Salomon v. Commissioner of Customs and Excise*[8] and the opinion of Lord Bridge in the decision of the House of Lords in *Brind v. Secretary of State for the Home Department.*[9] Referring to these decisions, the Supreme Court held that where there is a domestic legal provision which admits of some ambiguity and does not conflict with an international convention, the court should presume that Parliament intends to legislate in conformity with the convention and not in conflict with it.[10]

Proceeding on this basis, in Paragraph 32, the Supreme Court held that the word 'life' has been prominently used in the Universal Declaration of Human Rights, 1948 and that the fundamental rights in our Constitution are in consonance with the rights in the said declaration and also the rights recognized in the Covenant of Civil and Political Rights and Covenant of Economic, Social and Cultural Rights. In that view of the matter, right to life is considered a basic human right in the Universal Declaration of Human Rights, 1948, and must have the same meaning and interpretation as has been placed by the Supreme Court on 'life' in various decisions. The meaning of the word 'life' cannot be narrowed down. Thus the Supreme Court, for the first time, interpreted an international covenant through the prism of our constitutional jurisprudence. This is a landmark step in internationalizing our laws by fostering the trend of a globalized human rights regime of shared values.

This judgment has great significance as it brings about a fusion between our constitutional law and the Universal Declaration of Human Rights, which is considered the Magna Carta of mankind. In a way, this judgment has taken forward the jurisprudential strategy in *Vishaka* of reading into our constitutional law the global concepts of human rights, which are inseparable and inalienable from the evolving standards of decency in a ripening democracy.

NOTES

1. (1997) 6 SCC 241.
2. Benjamin Cardozo, *The Growth of the Law,* (Yale University Press, 1924), pp. 96–97.
3. Ibid.
4. (1999) 1 SCC 759.
5. 2000 (2) SCC 465.
6. (1996) 1 SCC 490.
7. (1997) 6 SCC 241, para 24.
8. (1967) 2 QB 116.
9. (1991) 1 All ER 720.
10. (1997) 6 SCC 241.

AFTERWORD

'The Constitution,' said Justice Alby Sachs, 'is the autobiography of a nation.' My perception of the Constitution is that it articulates the conscience of the nation in particular and of mankind in general. This voice is most eloquent in the judgments of the constitutional courts.

Therefore, the Constitution of a country is never completed in one go. Its development is a continuous process. Sidney Low put it very pithily when he perceived, 'We are not concerned with a solid building, to which a room may be added here, or a wing there, but with a living organism, in a condition of perpetual growth and change, of development and decay.'[1]

The same awareness about constitutional growth and development was shown by Sir Ivor Jennings when he said, 'The building has been constantly added to, patched, and partially re-constructed, so that it has been renewed from century to century, but it has never been razed to the ground and rebuilt on new foundations.'[2]

This is very true of our Constitution. Our Constitution today is vastly different from what it was in 1950. This is not only because over the years it has had more than 100 amendments but because it has also undergone varied interpretation, as is clear from the judgments discussed here, to unfold new ranges and vistas of meaning. After all, a Constitution is what the judges say it is. This is bound to be so when a nation adopts a Constitution, setting out a list of human rights, which are given the constitutional status of a 'higher law' as fundamental rights or a Bill of Right. The impact of such a constitutional design on judicial reasoning is bound to boost an expansive right regime with a human right-leaning.

Therefore the judicial acquiescence, if not supineness, of the constitutional interpretation of the 1950s, with the glorious exception of Justice Vivian Bose, was replaced by the most sensitized and forthright generation of judges towards the mid-1970s.

Those bold spirits of judges went about making the Constitution and the laws relevant for the common man and in the process, they actually made laws. The situations which these judges faced have been best expressed by Lord Denning, with his characteristic lucidity and boldness:

> The truth is that the law is uncertain. It does not cover all the situations, where the decision may go either way. No one can tell what the law is until the Courts decide it. The judges do every day make laws, though it is almost heresy to say so. If the truth is recognized then we may hope to escape from the dead hand of the past and consciously mould new principles to meet the needs of the present.[3]

This is the essence of constitutionalism, very simply and unerringly put. In the preceding chapters I have tried to show the meandering way in which constitutionalism was developed by the Supreme Court and its indelible impact on our nation and the society.

Looking at this fascinating development of our constitutional jurisprudence for more than the last six decades, I am tempted to quote the profound statement of Herman Hesse,

> And once again when the rivers swelled during the rainy season and roared loudly, Siddhartha said: 'Is it not true, my friend that the river has many voices? Has it not the voice of a King, of a warrior, of a bull, of a night bird,

> of a pregnant woman, and sighting man, and a thousand other voices?'
>
> 'It is so,' nodded Vasudeva, 'the voices of all living creatures are in its voice.'[4]

This is also true of our national charter in the largest democracy in the world.

NOTES

1. Sidney Low, *The Governance of England*, (T. Fisher Unwin, 1914), p. 2.
2. Ivor Jennings, *The Law and the Constitution*, 5th edition, (University of London Press, 1959), p. 8.
3. Quoted by Stevens in *Law and Politics* 490.
4. Herman Hesse, *Siddhartha*, (Rupa Publications, 1960).

APPENDIX 1: LIST OF CASES

ADM Jabalpur v Shrikant Shukla, etc. etc. [(1976) 2 SCC 521]
AK Gopalan v. State of Madras [AIR 1950 SC 27]
AK Roy, Etc vs Union Of India And Anr [(1982) 1 SCC 271]
Allaudin Mian and Others Sharif Mian and Another v. The State of Bihar [(1989) 3 SCC 5]
Aloke Nath Dutta and Others v. State of West Bengal [(2007) 12 SCC 230]
Amrik Singh v. The State of Punjab [(1988) Supp SCC 685]
Apparel Export Promotion Council v. A.K. Chopra [(1999) 1 SCC 759]
Ashoka Kumar Thakur v. Union of India and Others [(2008) 6 SCC 1]

Bablu alias Mubarak Hussain v. State of Rajasthan [AIR 2007 SC 697]
Bachan Singh v. State of Punjab [AIR 1980 (2) 684]
Bank v. State of UP [(2008) 11 SCC 113]
Bangalore Water-Supply & Sewerage Board, Etc. v. R. Rajappa and Othrs [(1978) 2 SCC 213]
Bidi Supply Co. v. Union of India [AIR 1956 SC 479]
Biede v. General Accident Fire and Life Insurance Corporation [(1968) 2 AER 995]
Bodhisattwa Gautam v. Subhra Chakraborty [(1996) 1 SCC 490]
Brind v. Secretary of State for the Home Department [(1991) 1

All ER 720]

Chairman Railway Board & ors. v. Chandrima Das and Ors [2000 (2) SCC 465]

Darshan Singh v. State of Punjab [1988 AIR 747]

Devendra Pal Singh Bhullar v. State of NCT, Delhi [(2013) 6 SCC 195]

Dayanidhi Bisoi v. State of Orissa [(2003) 9 SCC 310]

E.P. Royappa v. State of Tamil Nadu [(1974) 4 SCC 3]

Ediga Anamma v. State of Andhra Pradesh [(1974) 4 SCC 443]

H. Earl Fullilove v. Philip M. Klutznick [448 US 448]

Herrera v. Collins [(1993) 506 US 390]

Haru Ghosh v. State of West Bengal [(2009) 15 SCC 551]

I.C. Golaknath and Ors v. State of Punjab and Anr [AIR 1967 SC 1643]

Indira Nehru Gandhi v. Shri Raj Narain and Anr [1975 Supp SCC 1]

Indra Sawhney v. Union of India [(1992) Supp 3 SCC 217]

Islamic Academy of Education and Another v. State of Karnataka [(2003) 6 SCC 697]

Jagmohan Singh v. The State of UP [(1973) 1 SCC 20]

Kedar Nath Bajoria v. State of West Bengal [AIR 1953 SC 404]

Kesavananda Bharati Sripadagalvaru and Ors v. State of Kerala and Anr. [(1973) 4 SCC 225]

L. Chandra Kumar v. Union of India [AIR 1997 SC 1125]

Lawless v. Ireland [(1961) 1 EHRR 15]
Liversidge v. Sir John Anderson [(1942) AC 206]
Lok Pal Singh v. The State of Madhya Pradesh [AIR 1985 SC 891]

M. Nagaraj and Others v. Union of India and Others [(2006) 8 SCC 212]
Machhi Singh and Others v. The State of Punjab [1983 AIR 957]
Mahto s/o Ram Narain v. State of Madhya Pradesh [(1970) 1 SCC 25]
Maneka Gandhi v. Union of India and Ors [(1978) 1 SCC 248]
Marco DeFunis v. Charles Odegaard [416 US 312]
Maru Ram Etc. Etc vs Union Of India & Anr [(1981) 3 SCC 11]
Md Arif @ Ashfaq v. Registrar, Supreme Court of India and Ors [(2014) 10 SCC 84]
Metro Broadcasting Inc. v. Federal Communications Commission [58IW 5053]
Minerva Mills Ltd and Ors v. Union of India and Ors [(1980) 3 SCC 225]
Mohan Anna Chavan v. State of Maharashtra [(2008) 7 SCC 561]
Moskal v. United States [498 US 103]
Muniappan v. State of Tamil Nadu [(1981) 3 SCC 11]

Navneet Kaur v. State [(2014) 7 SCC 264]
Neville Lewis v. The Attorney General of Jamaica and Others [(2001) 2 AC 50]

Oliver Brown v. Board of Education of Topeka [347 US 483]

P.A. Inamdar and Others v. State of Maharashtra and Others [(2005) 6 SCC 537]
Palko v. Connecticut [302 US 319 (1937)]
People's Union for Civil Liberties & Another (PUCL) v. Union

of India & Another [(2003) 4 SCC 399]

Rajendra Prasad Etc. Etc. v. State of Uttar Pradesh [(1979) 3 SCC 646]

Rajesh Kumar v. State [(2011) 13 SCC 706]

Ram Singh and Others v. State of Delhi [(1951) SCR 451]

Rameshwar Prasad And Ors vs Union Of India And Anr [(2006) 2 SCC 1]

Ramdeo Chauhan @ Rajnath Chauhan v. Bani Kant Das and others [(2010) 12 SC 516]

Ravji alias Ram Chandra v. The State of Rajasthan [AIR 1996 SC 787]

Regents of the University of California v. Allan Bakke [438 US 265]

Regina v. Director of Public Prosecutions Ex Parte Kebeline and Ors [(2000) 2 AC 326]

Rustom Cavasjee Cooper v. Union of India [(1970) 1 SCC 248]

S.R. Bommai and Others v. Union of India and Others [(1994) 3 SCC 1]

Salomon v. Commissioner of Customs and Excise [(1967) 2 QB 116]

Sandeep v. State of UP [(2012) 6 SCC 107]

Sangeet and Anr v. State of Haryana [(2012) 11 SCALE 140]

Sajjan Singh v. State of Rajasthan [AIR 1965 SC 845]

Santa Singh v. State of Punjab [(1976) 4 SCC 190]

Santosh Kumar Satishbhushan Bariyar v. The State of Maharashtra [(2007) 12 SCC 288]

Shatrughan Chauhan and Another v. Union of India and Others [(2014) 3 SCC 1]

Shivaji v. State of Maharashtra [(2008) 15 SCC 269]

Shri Ram Krishna Dalmia v. Shri Justice S.R. Tendolkar and Ors [AIR 1958 SC 538]

Society for Unaided Private Schools of Rajasthan v. Union of India and Anr [(2012) 6 SCC 102]
Spottswood Thomas Bolling v. C. Melvin Sharpe [347 US 497]
Sri Shankari Prasad Singh Deo v. Union of India and State of Bihar [AIR 1951 SC 458]
State of Haryana and Ors v. Jagdish [(2010) 4 SCC 216]
State of Haryana v. Mahinder Singh [(2007) 13 SCC 605]
State of Kerala and Anr v. N.M. Thomas [(1976) 2 SCC 310]
State of Rajasthan and Ors. Etc. Etc v. Union of India Etc. Etc [(1977) 3 SCC 592]
State of UP v. Sultan [(2009) 4 SCC 736]
State of West Bengal v. Anwar Ali Sarkarhabib Mohamed, State of Hyderabad, and I [AIR 1952 SC 75]
Subash Chander v. Krishan Lal and Ors [(2001) 4 SCC 458]
Sunil Batra Etc vs Delhi Administration And Ors. Etc [(1978) 4 SCC 494]
Surja Ram v. The State of Rajasthan [(1996) 6 SCC 271]
Swamy Shraddananda @ Murali Manohar Mishra v. The State of Karnataka [(2008) 13 SCC 767]

T.M.A. Pai Foundation v. State of Kerala [(2002) 8 SCC 481]
Thoburn v. Sunderland City Council [(2003) QB 151]
Towne v. Eisner [245 US 418]

Union of India v. Association for Democratic Reforms & Another [(2002) 5 SCC 294]
Union of India v. Tulsiram Patel [AIR 1985 SC 1416–1454]
Unnikrishnan, J.P. and Others v. State of Andhra Pradesh and Others [(1993) 1 SCC 645]

Vishaka v. The State of Rajasthan [(1997) 6 SCC 241]

West Virginia State Board of Education v. Barnette [(1943) 319 US 624]

Williams v. People of State of New York [(1949) 337 US 241]

Youngstown Sheet & Tube Co. v. Sawyer [343 US 579]

ACKNOWLEDGEMENTS

The idea of collecting my amorphous thoughts on the Constitution and presenting them in the form of a book was in my mind for quite sometime. However, there were various impediments. The most important of them was that our Constitution, in its pluralistic dimension, is so vast and oceanic that to encapsulate it in the form of a book requires a skill clearly beyond me. Thus, how to go about it was a major concern.

Suddenly it came to my mind that to trace the varying trends of constitutionalism through some of the vital judgments of the Supreme Court of India may be a way out. In this book, I have made that humble attempt.

In writing this book, I received invaluable assistance from various interns. I would especially like to mention the names of Aditya Aloke, Bhabna Jha and Stella James. Later on, Anchal Basu also helped me a lot. All of them were bright students of the West Bengal University of Juridical Sciences, Kolkata. It is futile for me to express my gratitude to these students as they are virtually like my children. I wish and pray that all of them have a bright future.

My son, Abhijit Ganguly, an advocate of the Calcutta High Court, gladly helped me a lot in typing out the manuscript, despite his professional work. It is very odd for me to express my gratitude to him.

I am grateful to Saswati Nandi, Prabir Mitra and Sasti Bhattacharya, all employees of the West Bengal Human Rights

Commission. They helped me substantially by typing out the manuscript and incorporating the many changes I made. This book would not have seen the light of the day without their sincere and able assistance. I am also grateful to Indrani Chowdhury, librarian, Calcutta High Court Judges' Library, as she, on my request, ungrudgingly made available to me various books and judgments.

I must also thank the team at Rupa Publications India, especially Amrita Mukerji, for chasing me all these months to complete the work.

I would be amply rewarded if this book succeeds in sustaining the fledgling interest of common readers in the fascinating developments in constitutional law.

BIBLIOGRAPHY

Annual Survey of Indian Law, (Indian Law Institute, 2002)

Alexander M. Bickel, *The Least Dangerous Branch: The Supreme Court at the Bar of Politics*, (Bobbs-Merrill, 1962)

Capital Punishment: 35th Report, Indian Law Commission, Government of India Press, 1967

Benjamin Cardozo, *The Growth of the Law*, (Yale University Press,1924)

Constituent Assembly Debates Vol. I, p. 99–100

Constituent Assembly Debates Vol. II

Constituent Assembly Debates Vol. VII

Constituent Assembly Debates Vol. IX

Ronald Dworkin, *Law's Empire*, (Harvard University Press, 1986)

_______________, *Taking Rights Seriously*, (Harvard University Press, 1978)

Michael Folly, *The Silence of Constitutions*, (Routledge, 1989)

H.L.A. Hart, *The Concept of Law*, (Oxford University Press, 2012)

Herman Hesse, *Siddhartha*, (Rupa Publications, 1960)

Roger Hood and Carolyn Hoyle, *The Death Penalty: A Worldwide Perspect*, 4th Edition, Oxford University Press, Oxford, 2008

Lord Irvine, 'The Human Rights Act Two Years On: An Analysis'

(*Public Law* 308, 2003)

Ivor Jennings, *Some Characteristics of the Indian Constitution*, (Oxford University Press, 1953)

________, *The Law and the Constitution*, 5th edition, (University of London Press, 1959)

Jowitt's Dictionary of English Law, 2nd Edition, (Sweet & Maxwell Ltd, 1977)

H.R. Khanna, *Neither Roses nor Thorns*, (Eastern Book Co., 2010)

Anthony King, *The British Constitution* (Oxford University Press, 2009)

Sidney Low, *The Governance of England* (T. Fisher Unwin, 1914)

Richard B. Morris (ed.), *The Basic Ideas of Alexander Hamilton*, (Pocket Library, 1957)

Fali S. Nariman, *Before Memory Fades: An autobiography*, (Hay House, 2010)

______________, *India's Legal System: Can it be saved?*(Penguin, 2006)

_______________, *The State of the Nation*, (Penguin Books, 2014)

Richard O'Sullivan, 'The Inheritance of the Common Law', *The Hamlyn Lectures*, Second Series, (Stevens and Sons Limited, 1950)

Thomas Paine, *Rights of Man (1791–92)*, (Penguin, 1984)

David Pannick, *Judicial Review of the Death Penalty*, (Duckworth, 1982)

The Federalist Papers ed. Clinton Rossiter, (Penguin Books, 1961)

H.M. Seervai, *Constitutional Law of India*, Vol II, (Universal Law Pub. Co. P. Ltd., 2013)

H.M. Seervai, *The Emergency, Future Safeguards and the Habeas Corpus: A Criticism*, (N.M. Tripathi Ltd, 1978)

Lawrence H. Tribe, *The Invisible Constitution,* (Oxford University Press, 2008)

William Wade and Christopher Forsyth, *Administrative Law* (Ninth Edition), (Oxford University Press, 2004)